MENSCHES IN THE TRENCHES

MENSCHES IN THE TRENCHES

Jewish foot soldiers in the anti-apartheid Struggle

JONATHAN ANCER

Batya Bricker

Published by Batya Bricker Book Projects
PO Box 28819, Sandringham, Johannesburg, South Africa, 2192.
Batya@batyabricker.co.za

Copyright © 2021 Jonathan Ancer

Cover design, typeset and layout by Patricia Crain

Printed by **novus print**, a division of Novus Holdings

ISBN: 978-0-620-94694-0 (paperback)

All rights reserved.
No part of this book may be reproduced or transmitted in any form or by any electronic or mechanical means, including photocopying and recording, or by any other information storage or retrieval system, without written permission from the publisher.

CONTENTS

Preface	v
Foreword	vii

Trailblazers and Torchbearers
Chapter 1	Two of a Kind	3
Chapter 2	Finding Jock	14
Chapter 3:	Brothers in ARM	21

A Well-Meaning Rebel
Chapter 4	The well read (and well red) Fanny Klenerman	31

Working-class heroes
Chapter 5	Sachs Appeal	41
Chapter 6	Swapping the universe for the union	50

The Art of Protest
Chapter 7	Jews, jazz and joy	63
Chapter 8	Barney Simon: creative thorn in the flesh of apartheid	71
Chapter 9	A Man of Letters and Integrity	76

Pursuit of Justice
Chapter 10	Denis Kuny: An Advocate for Human Rights	87
Chapter 11	Madiba's Lawyers	96
Chapter 12	Choosing to be part of the solution	104

Selma & Jules
Chapter 13	The Browde Brunch	113

Writing Wrongs
Chapter 14	'Facts, facts, facts, but with emotion'	125
Chapter 15	The Invisible Editor	134

The Heart of Business
Chapter 16   An officer and a gentle retail giant   147

Serving with Distinction
Chapter 17   The Human Being   159
Chapter 18   Schools of thought   170
Chapter 19   Testimonial: Marlene Silbert   178

Outspoken Rabbis
Chapter 20   Provocateur who was ordered to leave SA   186
Chapter 21   A Stand Against Injustice   191
Chapter 22   A Kippah of Hope   196

The Archaeologist & The Architect
Chapter 23   Mazel Tov   200
Chapter 24   Ivan the Terrific   212

Jews Who Said No
Chapter 25   Oy vey! We won't join the fray!   222

A degree of Activism
Chapter 26   'Comrade Rabbi Lael'   234

A Degree of Activism Testimonials
Chapter 27   Michael Bagraim   245
Chapter 28   David Shandler   248
Chapter 29   Carol Green   252
Chapter 30   Arona Dison   255
Chapter 31   Erica Elk   261

Acknowledgements   267

PREFACE

I remember from an early age the police coming in to our house in Soweto, kicking down the doors and looking for all manner of things – banned literature, firearms and anything else that might provide evidence of 'subversive activities'. My two elder brothers and uncle were arrested and harassed and as a result, first my uncle and then my brothers subsequently left the country and joined the ANC in exile. Thus, I became politically aware from a very early age. Why was all this happening, and what should I, a young black South African subjected on a daily basis to the injustices of a racially discriminatory regime, be doing about it?

Like other members of my family, my response once I was old enough was to become politically involved. I became part of the grassroots civic activities that began burgeoning in the townships from the late 1970s onwards and was very active in youth and student politics. For my troubles, I was in and out of prison for periods of varying length. After my last release in 1987, I was among those activists who were able through the South African Council of Churches and other supportive organisations to enrol at various universities, in my case at the University of the Witwatersrand (Wits). It was at Wits that I really began meeting and working with activists from other racial groups – Indian, coloured and white comrades who, like us, were committed to the overthrow of the Apartheid system and the creation in its place of a truly democratic and non-racial society.

At that time, black and white students were organised separately. Black students had their own organisations, such as the Black Students Society (BSS) as well as the Azanian Students Organisation (AZASO), later called the South African National Students Congress (SANSCO) while whites in the main were organised through the National Union of South African Students (NUSAS). Through our interaction with the ANC in exile, however, we realised the need to change this if the shared dream of a united, non-racial South Africa was to be realised. This was finally accomplished early in 1991, when the different representative bodies merged to become one student organisation, the South African Student Congress.

As resistance to the apartheid regime was stepped up during the second half of the 1980s, I worked very closely with many white comrades. What particularly stands out is how when on the run from the police many activists would be taken in by white families, who would hide and provide them with money and lawyers and the like. This provided a crucial support network for the anti-apartheid underground, enabling activists – myself included – to evade arrest and imprisonment (if not worse), and continue our work on the ground.

In all such instances, with rare exceptions, activists would be taken in by Jewish families. Such was my own experience and I remember well those Friday evenings when Shabbat was celebrated. From this, I came to realise how many white comrades, including in the banned SA Communist Party, the ANC itself, the independent trade unions and so on were in fact Jewish. I also learned about Jewish doctors who defied the law by refusing to report activists who came to them for medical assistance to the authorities. They would also treat comrades for free. How many other untold stories were there of Jewish South Africans who, despite being part of the privileged white population, chose to support the resistance movements, even when this put themselves at risk?

This question stayed with me, long after the fall of Apartheid and the ushering in of non-racial democracy in 1994.

My activism led to my working within the Jewish community through the social outreach organisation Tikkun (now Afrika Tikkun). I also spent some time in Israel as a participant in the Heatid training programme, as a result of which I got to know

Heatid's founder and director Wendy Kahn. Some years later, when Wendy was National Director of the SA Jewish Board of Deputies, I approached her with a proposal that had long been on my mind: Why not conduct a research project, with the view to writing a book on the role of the Jewish community in the anti-apartheid Struggle? Specifically, could this project not become a vehicle for relating the stories not of the well-known public figures in the Struggle but of the 'ordinary' foot soldiers, people who fought the system in practical ways outside of the public eye and whose names and deeds have largely gone unrecorded? Wendy was enthusiastic about my proposal, and thus was I able to go about laying the groundwork for what would subsequently become an outstanding new book by acclaimed author and journalist Jonathan Ancer. As the title Mensches in the Trenches indicates, the book tells the stories of those 'mensches' – that Yiddish-derived expression indicating someone who is decent, principled and strives to do the right thing – who were at the coalface of South Africa's successful transition from racist minority rule to multiracial democracy. I warmly congratulate all those involved in bringing to fruition this unique, revealing and inspiring new addition to the literature of the anti-apartheid saga.

It is my hope that through this book many other individuals, groups or communities will be inspired to document their own stories and the roles they played in the struggle to defeat apartheid and bring freedom to our nation.

Mohale Trevor Selebi
November 2021

FOREWORD

THABO MBEKI

The challenging struggle to liberate South Africa from apartheid rule produced many heroes and heroines. Even decades after our country's transition to democracy, we continue to celebrate many of them as our liberators.

However, that same struggle also gave us much larger numbers of unsung heroines and heroes whose own battles against the common enemy made an important contribution to the shared victory against apartheid tyranny.

Though regrettable, it is true that over time the memory dims, so younger and new generations forget what to the older were unforgettable moments of eminently good deeds and noble results.

It was to pay tribute to this important matter that one of our heroes, Lionel 'Rusty' Bernstein, titled his important political Memoir *Memory Against Forgetting*.

It is in this context that this small book has done all our people a special favour – lest we forget.

It has given us a roll call of some of our established heroes and heroines.

It has given us a roll call of some of our unsung heroes and heroines.

It has drawn important attention to the place of a component of the South African population in the national struggle for liberation – the Jewish section of our population.

Ever since it began forming in our country in significant numbers, from early last century, the Jewish community has always been a relatively small component part of even the white population and, therefore, the people as a whole.

It is also true that the larger part of that white population did not join the struggle to end apartheid white minority rule. As would have been expected, this held true for the Jewish element of that white population.

And yet this book of a roll call of some of those who contributed in various ways to the struggle to defeat apartheid tyranny is a roll call of Jewish heroes and heroines, both well-known and unsung.

Ilan Lax, a Jewish human rights lawyer, is one of the unsung heroes celebrated in this book.

Part of what he says on his pages is that 'What made me much more politicised was being subjected to lots of antisemitism as a kid at boarding school …

'I guess that part of the conundrum of the Jewish community is that we've been victims for so long in so many ways, and so we're afraid to stick our necks out, but that's exactly what we have to do. That's the conundrum: by putting up with injustice, you either become a victim or you become part of the problem, but you don't become part of the solution. At some point we've got to choose to be part of the solution.'

In the USA it is accepted that given its size as part of the white population, the Jewish community played a disproportionately significant part in support of the African Americans during the civil rights struggle.

In 1964 the outstanding African American leader and Nobel Peace Laureate, Martin Luther King Jnr, said, 'It would be impossible to record the contribution that the Jewish people have made toward the Negro's struggle for freedom – it has been so great.'

Earlier, in 1958, addressing a meeting of the American Jewish Congress, he had said:

'My people were brought to America in chains. Your people were driven here to escape the chains fashioned for them in Europe. Our unity is born of our common struggle for centuries, not only to rid ourselves of bondage, but to make oppression of any people by others an impossibility.'

But perhaps we should listen to another voice to explain the African American-Jewish cooperation which Martin Luther King Jnr celebrated.

Rabbi Joachim Prinz was expelled from Germany in 1937 because he would not keep quiet about the antisemitism by the Nazis. He settled in the US.

Many years later, as President of the American Jewish Congress, Rabbi Prinz helped to organise the famous 1963 US March on Washington at which Rev Martin Luther King Jnr delivered his outstanding 'I have a dream' speech.

The Rabbi also addressed the huge rally and one of the things he said:

'I speak to you as an American Jew …

'As Jews we bring to this great demonstration, in which thousands of us proudly participate, a two-fold experience – one of the spirit and one of our history.

'In the realm of the spirit, our fathers taught us thousands of years ago that when God created man, he created him as everybody's neighbour. Neighbour is not a geographic term. It is a moral concept. It means our collective responsibility for the preservation of man's dignity and integrity.

'From our Jewish historic experience of three and a half thousand years we say:

'Our ancient history began with slavery and the yearning for freedom. During the Middle Ages my people lived for a thousand years in the ghettos of Europe …

'(We share with our African American compatriots) a sense of complete identification and solidarity born of our own painful historic experience.

'When I was the rabbi of the Jewish community in Berlin under the Hitler regime, I learned many things. The most important thing that I learned under those tragic circumstances was that bigotry and hatred are not the most urgent problem. The most urgent, the most disgraceful, the most shameful and the most tragic problem is silence.

'A great (German) people which had created a great civilisation had become a nation of silent onlookers. They remained silent in the face of hate, in the face of brutality and in the face of mass murder.'

As was the case with the American Jews in the United States relative to the African American struggles, the Jewish community in South Africa played a disproportionately significant role in the struggle for the liberation of the black oppressed, given that it was but a small fraction of the white population.

It was and has been natural to ask the question – why?

Our own unsung hero, Ilan Lax, has said that because the Jewish community have been victims for so long in so many ways, it should not put up with injustice and thus become part of the problem, but must rather choose to be part of the solution.

Rabbi Prinz endorsed this view, attributing the extraordinary Jewish involvement we have mentioned both to religious or moral upbringing and the historical experience to which Ilan Lax referred.

Where Ilan Lax said it was imperative that the Jewish people should choose to be part of the solution, Rabbi Prinz said it would be disgraceful, shameful and tragic for the Jewish people to stay silent in the face of gross injustice, afraid to stick their necks out, as Ilan Lax put it.

The publication of this book does all of our people a great service because, apart from telling rivetting stories, it brings into sharp relief the critical importance for all of us of leading lives informed by a humanist value system.

Accordingly, it also makes the vitally important statement that the Jewish people did not act as they did, both here in South Africa and in the US, out of a condescending sense of pity. Rather, they were moved by an unshakable understanding that as human beings we must act together, regardless of colour, race or gender, to shape a common destiny.

Our years of liberation have taught us the strategic importance of both these lessons relating to national adherence to a healthy value system and relying on a shared patriotism to build a South Africa which truly belongs to all who live in it, united in their diversity.

It is important that this book has succeeded to place an honoured cohort of our Jewish compatriots firmly among the many in our country who practically share this vision.

This book might have set out to contribute to our national store of history – a noble past of struggle for justice.

Not only does it do this, but it must also serve to inspire those who read it to commit themselves never to betray the great vision about our country sustained by the inestimable numbers who remain, still, our heroes and heroines, sung and unsung.

TRAILBLAZERS AND TORCHBEARERS

CHAPTER 1

TWO OF A KIND

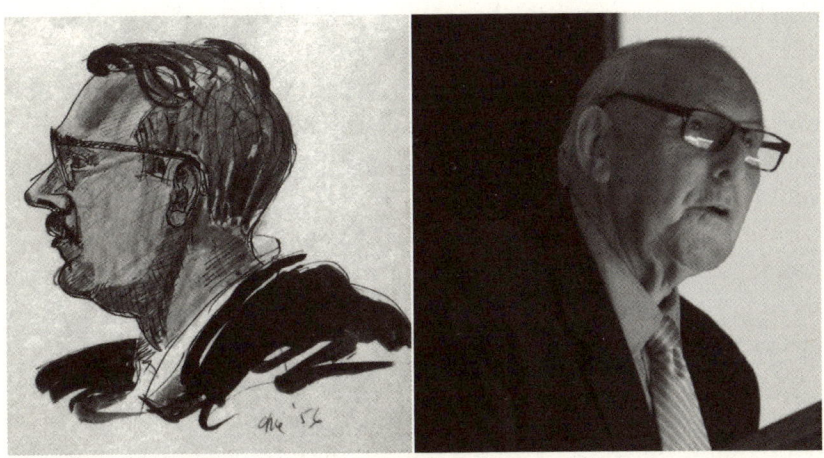

Identical twins Norman and Leon Levy began their political activities as schoolboys, and campaigned for freedom and equality all their lives. The brothers stood in the dock with Nelson Mandela, Walter Sisulu, Helen Joseph and 150 other leaders of the liberation movement in 'South Africa's trial of the 20th century' – the Treason Trial 1956-1961. For the Levy brothers it was a life of protest, picket lines, interrogation, torture, solitary confinement, jail, exile and, eventually, democracy.

There are thousands of unsung heroes of South Africa's struggle for liberation, and Norman and Leon Levy are definitely two of the giants. I stumbled upon the Levy twins while doing research for another book. I like to believe I'm knowledgeable about South Africa's struggle history and know the freedom movements who's who, but I was astonished that I hadn't heard of the Levys. Their massive contribution to the struggle has been largely unacknowledged.

I decided to write a profile on them for a local newspaper and arranged to interview the then 90-year-old brothers on Zoom in June 2020, just after the country had emerged from a hard lockdown.[1]

Norman was born on 7 August 1929. Four minutes later, his womb mate Leon saw the light of day. Their parents, Mary and Mark Levy, were immigrants from Lithuania who had settled in the Joburg suburb of Yeoville.

'We went to *cheder*, and went to synagogue only on the Jewish holidays,' said Norman. 'Our parents were Yiddishists and wanted us to get some of the Yiddish culture, but they saw themselves as atheists.'

'Our Jewishness was always there,' added Leon.

Mark ran a fish shop and died when the twins were six. Times were tough for Mary, a single mother with four children, and she took in lodgers to provide for the family. She spoke to the children about her experiences of antisemitism and pogroms, which made a big impression on them.

The brothers had been interested in politics ever since they could remember. Their older sister Goldie belonged to the multiracial Left Club and the boys tagged along to political talks and jazz sessions.

The twins had similar ideologies but took different paths to becoming radicals. Norman got involved in leftist politics by accident. When he was 14 he went on a bicycle ride around the streets of Hillbrow, turned a corner and came across a public meeting that was being addressed by Hilda Bernstein, the Communist Party candidate

---

1 Information for this chapter is from interviews with Leon and Norman Levy and Norman's children Simon and Jessica; and the articles Double Trouble (12 July 2020) and A Real Mensch of the Struggle (11 July 2021), both published in the *Sunday Times*.

for the Joburg council. He was enthralled by what he heard, and the next week he joined the Young Communist League.

Leon had become a member of the socialist-Zionist movement Hashomer Hatzair, which had groomed anti-apartheid radicals like Baruch Hirson.

In 1946, when they were 17, the twins became members of the Communist Party of SA. They later joined the SA Congress of Democrats, an ANC ally.

The twins experienced an intense period of politicisation. Leon's interest lay in the trade union movement while Norman, who became a teacher, focused on education.

The pair had been given nicknames by their comrades. Leon was known as Tsaba-Tsaba, a very energetic dance, which is a reference to how active he was in the various spheres of the liberation movement. Norman's nickname was Mahlalela, 'a loafer', which he explained he was called in contrast to Leon being 'here, there and everywhere'.

But Norman was hardly a loafer. He was involved in the Defiance Campaign of 1952 to protest against unjust laws and played a major role in challenging the National Party's iniquitous Bantu Education system. He went all over the country to set up 'cultural clubs' to provide alternative education for black pupils.

'The apartheid regime was oppressive and brutal and we were frustrated with all the terrible injustices, such as the pass laws, the Group Areas Act, and forced removals, where the police knocked down people's homes and did enormously terrible things. We were motivated to do whatever we could to end all of that,' said Leon.

It was a very rough period for activists, but it was also exciting.

'The world was changing,' said Leon. 'Colonial freedom was rolling across Africa and there was a lot of inspiration that the developments in these countries would spark freedom in South Africa.'

But not if the apartheid government could help it. The activists had to contend with a vicious security police who were given permission to act with impunity when the Suppression of Communism Act was passed in 1950.

'No sooner than the ink was dry than the government named and removed the trade union leaders – and they fell one by one,' recalled Leon.

Leon's generation stepped into the breach.

'On 5 March 1955 we formed the SA Congress of Trade Unions, and we developed trade unions throughout the country.'

Leon, who was in his 20s, served as Sactu president for nine years and helped organise the Congress of the People, where delegates of the ANC and its Congress allies gathered in Kliptown to discuss their political aspirations. The result was the Freedom Charter.

'It was two of the most spectacular days,' recalled Leon. 'I was on the platform and I saw hundreds of police on horses. They surrounded the entire site. Major Spengler [of the security police] mounted the platform and said he believed an act of treason had taken place. He ordered that no one was to leave until the police had interviewed them. People sat on low benches and sang freedom songs all through the day and well into the night.'

According to Norman, who was in charge of the statistics, 2,884 delegates had descended on Kliptown in spite of the police's efforts to prevent them from getting there.

'Rusty Bernstein gathered all the demands, grouped them into 10 clauses and framed them into the political and philosophical aspirations of the people. Each clause was discussed and adopted. The Freedom Charter was acceptable to all the congresses, from the ANC to the communists, even though it wasn't a communist document. This is why it is such a brilliant document,' Norman noted.

The Freedom Charter moved the anti-apartheid struggle from protests against single political issues (like the pass laws or the Group Areas Act) to one of a challenge; a challenge for power.

'We can crow about the fact that the Freedom Charter has become part of the values of our transformation – it's a real triumph of our struggle,' said Leon.

The charter's six signatories were ANC president Albert Luthuli; Jimmy La Guma of the SA Coloured People's Congress; Monty Naicker of the Natal Indian Congress; the Congress of Democrats' Pieter Beyleveld; and Leon, who signed on behalf of Sactu. Leon is the only surviving signatory.

At 5 am on 5 December 1956, a year-and-a-half after the Freedom Charter was adopted, there was a knock on the door of the Levys' flat. Mary opened it to find security policemen outside.

'Which twin do you want?' she asked.

'Both,' was the response, to her horror.

'We left her weeping,' Leon recalled.

The government was rounding up the leadership of the liberation movement and taking them to the Old Fort prison in Joburg.

'It was a blunder to put all the people together,' chuckled Leon. 'The movement's leadership was able to discuss our campaigns and carry on the work we were banned from doing. It helped to inject into the struggle a leadership that was thoughtful, careful and militant. The result was that the liberation movement grew phenomenally.'

The 156 accused were charged with high treason. According to the twins, it was the Freedom Charter that was really on trial. The government believed it was a communist document that advocated the violent overthrow of the state.

The accused were given bail of £75 each. High treason was £75. It was also a capital offence.

'We never believed we would hang, although it was a possibility,' said Leon.

'It was evident that the prosecution were determined to convict us and tried everything to get us. We were young and enthusiastic, and although we thought we might be sentenced to a long term of imprisonment, we didn't have sleepless nights about being in jail,' he added.

At a 2008 reunion, fellow accused Bertha Gxowa recalled the twins' defence strategy: 'In the courtroom, Leon and Norman planned to deliberately confuse the witnesses,' she said. 'After giving evidence, the lawyers would say: "Which one of the Levy twins do you mean?" That evidence would be dismissed because the witnesses could never say which one of the two they meant.'

Towards the end of 1957, charges were dropped against 61 of the accused, including Norman. The following year the prosecution reworded the indictment and launched a separate trial against 30 of the remaining accused. One of them was Leon. He remembered travelling on the 'Treason Bus' from Sauer Street in the Joburg CBD to the Old Synagogue in Pretoria, which had been expropriated by the government in 1952 and transformed into a court to hear anti-government cases.

'Being on the bus was wonderful,' said Leon. 'We talked about music, discussed politics and analysed the trial. Duma [Nokwe], Mandela and Kathy [Ahmed Kathrada] and I would play a word game. It was a bit like noughts and crosses but with words, and we'd announce the winner to the others on the bus.'

The four-year-long trial ended with a not-guilty verdict on 29 March 1961.

'There was jubilation and singing in the court. Our advocate Isie Maisels was lifted onto people's shoulders,' recalled Leon.

'Is it possible that you're the last living Treason Trial defendants?' I asked them.

'Could be,' Norman said, and the twins rattled off the names of fellow activists who were on trial with them. All the people they named had died.

'I'm not sure about the last,' said Leon, 'but I think it's safe to say we are one of the few left.'

'I think you mean we are two of the few left,' corrected Norman.

The twins continued to get involved in campaigns, but much of the activity had quietened down as a result of bans and state repression.

Shortly after marrying Lorna in May 1962, Leon became the first person to be arrested under the 90-day detention law. When he was released five months later he decided there was no scope for further activity in South Africa for him, and decided to continue his activism in exile. He moved to Britain and became a specialist in labour relations.

Six months later, Norman, who was involved in the underground area committee of the SACP, was arrested in an anti-communist purge. He was put in solitary confinement.

'The first week, after the rush and tumble of the arrest, was okay, but gradually you feel the oppression of the environment – the small cell – and the heaviness grows as you feel extremely isolated and disoriented. You are already in a weakened state and they break you down for interrogation,' he told me.

One day he saw what looked like a sweet wrapped in silver paper in his bucket of water. It was a note from Costa Gazidis, a political prisoner in the next cell. The note had instructions on how to communicate by knocking out letters on the wall.

'It took a lot of time but it was quite comforting.'

However, one day, during one of their clandestine conversations, a captain stormed into Norman's cell and demanded to know what he was doing.

'I'm reading the Bible,' Norman told him.

'You *bleddie* liar,' the captain screamed.

After 55 days in solitary confinement Norman was taken to Special Branch HQ for interrogation, where he was subjected to 'standing torture'.

'I was ordered to stand inside a circle that had been drawn with chalk. They wanted to establish if a meeting I had attended was a communist meeting. I told them about my history in the Congress of Democrats, but they weren't interested in that. They eventually stopped the interrogation and sent me back to prison for a week, and then brought me out again. That went on for weeks.'

Norman knew the game was up when he was greeted one morning by the aggressive interrogator with a cheerful 'Good morning, Bentley.'

Bentley was Norman's *nomme de guerre*.

Norman and 13 others were charged under the Suppression of Communism Act.

Norman, who was married to activist Philippa Murrell and had two small children, Deborah and Simon, was found guilty and handed a three-year prison term.

'I can't say it was the happiest moment of my life when we were convicted, but I had been involved in the struggle for some time and I knew that something like that could happen, so I resigned myself to serve the sentence.'

Prison was dehumanising.

'Our hair was shorn, we could write only one letter every six months, we had no newspapers or magazines, and we were allowed very few visits.'

He used the time to study for an honours degree in history, which gave him the foundation to move from being a schoolteacher to lecturing at university.

On 11 April 1968, four years after he had been arrested, Norman was released. Deborah was nine and Simon five.

'Deborah, who was five when I went to prison, didn't really know me. I remember that Simon was in the garden and was very tense. He had found a dead bird, which he held in his hand. I looked at the bird and realised we were all rather frozen and that it would take us time to thaw.'

Simon also recalled that day.

'I remember the bird, and I remember my father coming into the house and sitting in the lounge, lighting up his pipe, and looking at me and saying, "Simon, what have you been doing with yourself?"'

In her memoir, *Things I Don't Want to Know*, Deborah also recalled her father coming home: 'My father is standing in the garden. His face is pale grey, like dirty snow. Only his eyes move. His arms hang stiffly by his sides. Dad is back, so very still and silent.

He looks like he has been hurt in some way. Very deep inside him. "Daddy, the cat died while you were away." He squeezes my hand with his cold fingers [and says,] "It's lovely to be called Daddy again."'[2]

The government banned Norman from teaching and restricted his movements, so, two months after his release, the family followed Leon and Lorna into exile in England, which is where the couple's third child, Jessica, was born.[3]

In exile, Norman worked for a clothing shop and then won a fellowship to the London School of Economics to complete a PhD on migrant labour in the gold mining industry. He was a professor at Middlesex University when Mandela was released from prison in 1990, and Norman packed his bags and returned to South Africa, where he reinvented himself and launched a new career developing policy.

As Norman put it: 'I was an old dog but I relished new tricks.'

Norman helped design affirmative action frameworks, and Mandela appointed him to the Presidential Review Commission, which looked at reforming the public service. He was then appointed 'professor extraordinary' at the University of the Western Cape's School of Government until he retired in 2011.

Leon returned to SA in 1997 and joined the Commission for Conciliation, Mediation and Arbitration, where he is credited with saving countless jobs. He retired from the commission on his 89th birthday.

Leon received the SAJBD's Rabbi Cyril & Ann Harris Human Rights Award in 2015.

'The name of Leon Levy has an honoured place in the history of the liberation struggle,' said Ann Harris, who presented the award to Leon. 'Tonight, the Jewish community recognises and lauds you for the part you played in bringing freedom to our beloved country.'

Throughout it all – the detentions, torture, bannings, exile – the twins remained hopeful.

---

2   *Things I Don't Want to Know*, Notting Hill Editions, 2013
3   Norman and Philippa divorced in 1974, and in 1991 he married Carole Silver

'We were always optimists,' said Leon. 'I always believed we were going to win. What spurred us on was that our values – in terms of human rights – were indestructible. Our cause was invincible.'

Norman agreed, and said that even in the grimmest of times they never gave up hope. 'We believed,' he said. 'We always believed. I kept my faith in the struggle.'

'Are you recognised as struggle icons?' I asked them.

'Are we struggle icons?' enquired Norman.

'I learnt modesty in England,' Leon replied. 'One of the most wonderful things about the English is their modesty, and I have taken a leaf out of their book. I leave it to others to sing my praises,' he joked, then added: 'I think we are recognised as people who made a good contribution to the struggle in South Africa. We enjoy telling people what we remember of our struggle so that other people can take over from where we left off.'

After Norman retired he wrote *The Final Prize*, a memoir in which he reflected on his personal and political experiences of the decades he spent in the anti-apartheid struggle.

For Norman, the 'final prize' was South Africa's liberation.

'But we're not quite there yet,' he insisted.

'I'm too old to be politically involved, but I read and think and talk to people. I've got a lot to say about politics. I'm not sure people listen,' he said.

Just before we logged off the Zoom call in June 2020, Leon asked when the profile would be published. I told him I wasn't sure.

'Well,' said Norman. 'Remember, we are 90, so don't leave it too long.'

After the profile was published I received separate messages from the twins, inviting me for tea and a slice of cake after the COVID tide had turned.

Leon offered cheesecake and Norman offered Madeira cake ('You can have two slices for that article,' he wrote).

In April 2021 I went to visit Norman to claim my slices of cake and to give him a copy of a book I'd written about apartheid-era spies. Norman's conviction in 1964 was largely because of the testimony of the Special Branch mole Gerard Ludi, who had infiltrated the SACP. Ludi was one of the spies I had written about.

In between mouthfuls of cake, Norman talked about the torture he endured and the endless interrogation sessions at the hands of the Special Branch.

As he handed me my second slice of cake he told me that his interrogators had brought him a cake on his birthday; it was a cruel stunt to make his comrades think he was being rewarded for cooperating.

Norman had refused to divulge information and, as he wrote in his memoir, he would rather have died than give up the names of his comrades. Recalling the incident was painful.

Norman and I stayed in touch, exchanging WhatsApp messages. One morning he forwarded me a meme with the word *'Maandagga'* written on a background of reggae colours. While I was scratching my head wondering what an appropriate response would be, he wrote: 'This went in error! Sorry!'

His daughter Jessica told me her father was obsessed with his cellphone and was more of a teenager than any of his grandchildren.

'He couldn't put his phone down and was constantly looking at his messages,' she said.

'His phone never stopped pinging. We'd be at the table about to eat and I'd say "Dad, can you get off your phone?" He'd send his grandchildren really profound philosophical conundrums to answer on WhatsApp. When he discovered emojis he would send messages full of them.'

In June 2021, a year after I had interviewed the twins, I sent Norman a message asking if I could visit him again. A response came only much later – and it wasn't from Norman, but Simon, who told me his father was very ill.

Norman had been diagnosed with lung cancer and his health was deteriorating rapidly. I arranged to visit him. It was a cold winter's morning and rain was lashing Cape Town.

Norman was in a wheelchair. He was wrapped in a blanket – only his head peeked out. His eyes were closed. His face was gaunt and grey. It was in the same room that we had sat a few months before and, barring the painful anecdote he shared, we had spent the time laughing and having a spirited discussion about politics and the fate of the nation.

We chatted for a while on that rainy day, but Norman was confused and found it difficult to concentrate. I knew it was the last time I would see him. I wanted to say something profound. I wanted to tell him that ever since I had encountered him and Leon I had been moved by their courage and humbled by their sacrifices. I wanted to tell him I was in awe of their commitment and blown away by their good-natured humility. I wanted to tell him that I was inspired by their idealism and that they had made me want to become a better person; a mensch.

I opened my mouth, but I couldn't find the words.

'Take care of yourself,' I said. It sounded feeble and I felt so inadequate.

Norman looked at me. 'I will,' he replied. 'Take care of yourself too.'

Four days later Norman died.

When I phoned Leon to send my condolences he told me that he hadn't yet come to terms with the death of his identical twin; they had always been separate, but inseparable.

CHAPTER 2
FINDING JOCK

Jock Isacowitz fought for equality and freedom, and was banned and jailed for his activism. He was the head of the Springbok Legion, the brains behind the Torch Commando and a key figure in the Liberal Party. More than half a century after Jock's death, his son Roy went on a quest to 'find' his father and record his place in South Africa's political history.

Roy Isacowitz was 10 when his father Jock died. Jock was a prominent anti-apartheid activist and a fierce opponent of the National Party government, but not much has been written about his life, and, to a large extent, his contribution to the freedom struggle has gone unmarked.

He died young – when he was 46 – and Roy and his siblings Tessa, then 12, and Steven, who was six, grew up with only hazy memories of their father. As Steven puts it, 'We all grew up with this huge hole in our lives.'[4]

So when Roy, a journalist who left South Africa to live in Israel, retired in 2017 he decided it was time to fill in that hole and 'discover' his father.

His quest took him to various archives and libraries dotted all over the country and resulted in his meticulously researched biography, *Telling People What They Don't Want to Hear – A Liberal Life Under Apartheid*.

'My father was always a mystery to me,' says Roy.[5]

A major part of what Roy set out to uncover was what motivated Jock to get involved in anti-apartheid politics in the first place.

'Many of my conclusions are suppositions, but I think they are well based. I think I now understand what it was that got him involved. Many people who look at it from the Jewish angle call it a Jewish sensibility, but I don't buy that at all because I don't think Jews are more likely to support underdogs than the bully.'

Roy believes his father got into anti-apartheid politics due to his liberal home environment – Jock's father, who came from Lithuania, read widely.

'The people who read in those days tended to support the left, and that's what happened to him. From a very young age my father had a liberal bent and he became radicalised.'

Jock, who was born in Benoni in 1915, moved to Joburg after he completed high school to study pharmacy.

Jock's political coming of age coincided with the rise of fascism in Europe. He participated in anti-fascist activities, hung out in cafés and bookstores favoured by leftists, and came under Marxist influences.

---

4   Interview with Steven Isacowitz, July 2021
5   Interview with Roy Isacowitz, July 2021

Jock joined the South African army to fight the Nazis in 1941 and served with the artillery in East Africa. A few months after the German invasion of the Soviet Union, he joined the Communist Party.

'I assume, but don't have any proof of this, that he didn't join the Communist Party earlier because of the Molotov-Ribbentrop Pact, but once the Soviet Union was on the side of the good guys, he joined the party,' explains Roy.[6]

Jock was one of the founders of the Springbok Legion, a radical anti-racist veterans' group. It was in the Springbok Legion that people like Joe Slovo, Rusty Bernstein and Wolfie Kodesh cut their revolutionary teeth. Jock was elected national chairperson in 1942, a position he held for 10 years. The Legion fought for the rights of servicemen and campaigned against the discrimination suffered by black soldiers. It was a considerable force in the South African liberation movement.

At that time Jock was an anti-Zionist, says Roy. 'However, I think that once the true dimensions of the Holocaust became clear to him, he questioned his anti-Zionism and became a socialist Zionist. In fact, he was very active in putting together the South African contingent for Machal, the group of overseas volunteers who fought alongside Israeli forces during the 1948 war. He also joined the SA Jewish Board of Deputies and was elected to the executive.'

While Jock moved towards Zionism, he distanced himself from the Communist Party. In a letter to then justice minister CR Swart in 1954 asking for his banning to be lifted, Jock pointed out that he had resigned from the party in 1946 because of its stultifying influence on thought, which was contrary to his democratic beliefs.

'He objected to the Communist Party's Big Brother totalitarian character,' says Roy. 'He was to an extent a Marxist in theory, but not in practice.'

Jock also became increasingly out of step with the Springbok Legion, which had become a front for the Communist Party and no longer had public credibility. Together with the United Party and non-aligned veterans, Jock and some other Legion leaders covertly

---

6 On 23 August 1939 Germany and the Soviet Union signed a non-aggression pact, agreeing not to take military action against each other. The pact fell apart in June 1941 when Nazi forces invaded the Soviet Union

established an ex-servicemen's organisation with mass appeal – the Torch Commando – in 1951. The Torch Commando took on the National Party over its plan to disenfranchise coloured people in the Cape, organising massive street protests, torchlight processions and even a motorcade to Parliament in Cape Town to defend the constitution.

After leaving the Communist Party, Jock looked around for amenable comrades, people who thought the way he did. He found Jack Unterhalter, a renowned advocate who represented political prisoners, and the two of them established a liberal association in Johannesburg.

Jock and Jack subsequently got together with other liberal groupings around the country – including people such as Peter Brown and the author Alan Paton in Natal, and Donald Molteno and Margaret Ballinger in the Cape – and together they established the Liberal Party in 1953.

Jock was one of the more radical, idealistic and energetic liberals in the party. Most of the Cape liberals were paternalistic, but Jock and Jack were an entirely different sort of liberal – they were 'more in touch with the mood of black political opinion and more flexible over policy and strategy'.[7]

Jock was elected vice-chairperson of the Liberal Party and chair of the Transvaal branch. The Cape liberals thought he was still a communist and didn't trust him.

'Jock had become anti-communist and had very good reasons, but the Cape liberals were knee-jerk anti-communists,' says Roy, who found a letter from Alan Paton to Jock saying he should be the one running the party. Jock replied that that would split the party because the Cape liberals would leave.

In 1954 Jock became the first member of the Liberal Party ever to be banned.

'Though he was never given a reason [for the banning], it was in the context of the Suppression of Communism Act,' states Roy, who adds that he believes his father was targeted because of his involvement in protests against the forced removals in Joburg's Sophiatown.

---

7   Moffatt, Debra: From 'conscience politics' to the battlefields of political activism: the Liberal Party in Natal, 1953 to 1968, University of Natal, 1999

'There were a few black people banned at the same time as he was, mainly ANC people who were also active in Sophiatown, so I think that was what triggered it, because the government was trying to get [the residents] out of there.'

On 21 March 1960, police opened fire on a group of black protesters who had gathered outside Sharpeville police station to demonstrate against the pass laws, killing 69 people. Sharpeville township was under siege, and Jock and other activists brought food and blankets to the community and filed legal actions against the government on their behalf.

The government embarked on a clampdown in the wake of the massacre, declaring a state of emergency and rounding up the leaders of the liberation movements. Jock was one of the people arrested.

Roy says that after 60 years it's difficult to know which memories are real and which are manufactured.

'Quite honestly I can't say if my memories are what I remember or what I heard from my mother or my uncle Issie (Jock's younger brother), or what I've read and taken on as my own; that's just the nature of memory.'

However, he does recall the security police arriving to arrest his father. 'I remember the cops searching the house while we were sitting in the lounge. I remember them escorting my father to his room to get dressed because he'd been in pyjamas, and I remember that he kissed us before they took him away,' he says.

Roy also recalls going to visit him in Pretoria Local Prison, where he was held with many other activists such as Joe Slovo, Harold Wolpe and Rusty Bernstein.

'I have a specific memory about a black prisoner who was cleaning the floor. We were sitting at the table and he was cleaning the floor around us, and for some reason I found this incredibly frightening. I remember my father taking me on his lap, calming me down. He bought us big bars of chocolate from the prison canteen. I'd never seen such big slabs of chocolate.'

Steven, who was just five, also recalls the visit. 'I still have the memory of the door and the lock,' he says. 'It was the sort of lock where you had to rotate the key twice. That's the sort of stuff I remember. I can hardly remember my father but I was overwhelmed by the intricacy of the locks.'

After a number of months Jock was released.

Roy says that something in his father had changed when he came out of prison; he was subdued and didn't have his old energy. Within a year of his release he was diagnosed with leukaemia and died shortly afterwards.

Roy matriculated in 1969, completed his national service in 1970, and moved to Israel in January 1971. When he landed in Israel, the immigration officer looked at his passport, grabbed him and kissed him on the forehead because he was Jock's son.

Being 'Jock's son' is something that Steven also grew up with.

'In high school when I went to friends' houses and their parents heard my surname, they asked "Are you Jock's boy?" He was a household name in the 1950s and 60s, but that generation of people who knew him are gone and he's now a forgotten man. It's just a sadness for me knowing the loss. I become emotional when I talk about it,' he adds.

Steven thinks that after Jock died, their mother, Eileen, decided that her children mustn't grow up in a home that was full of tears, so, besides the occasional anecdote about Jock, he 'was sort of an ignored subject'.

Whenever a new publication on South African politics was published, Steven would rush to the bookshop, find the book and open it to the index to see if Jock was mentioned. 'I spent a lot of time looking for him in the index of books.'

As far back as Roy can remember, he intended to understand and know more about his father and put it down in some sort of form.

'It took me so many years to do it because of my bringing up a family and pursuing my profession, and it was only when I retired that I decided to devote myself to the book.'

Roy and Steven, who joined his brother on the quest, spent many hours poring over letters, digging through archives and going over minutes of meetings as they pieced together their father's legacy. There were a number of surprises along the way – one being the realisation that Jock was 'quite a militant liberal'.

'I regarded myself as a radical lefty at university and I wasn't impressed with liberals and the soft left,' says Roy. 'I came across a book about liberalism in South Africa which described the Torch Commando converging on Cape Town, and at some point Jock apparently tried to persuade his colleagues to storm Parliament and take power. That impressed me.'

Roy isn't sure how Jock's politics would have turned out if he hadn't died so young.

'It's all hypothetical. For many years I thought he would have joined something like the African Resistance Movement, but I no longer think he would have turned to violence. My feeling is that if he had lived he would have left the country, like so many people did, but I really don't know what would have happened.'

Roy says it would be an overstatement to say he discovered the father he didn't know during the process of writing his book, but he did find out a great deal about Jock's role in the struggle against apartheid.

'I have a much better idea about his contribution and, to an extent, what motivated him, but the warmth of human contact isn't going to come from archives. For me he's still only a person on paper.'

CHAPTER 3:

BROTHERS IN ARM

The large number of Jews among the trailblazing generation of white activists is difficult to miss. There were 23 white defendants among the 156 accused in the Treason Trial – 16 of them were Jewish – and Jewish involvement was even more disproportionate in the Rivonia Trial. All six of the white activists arrested in the 1963 police raid on Liliesleaf Farm, the ANC armed wing's underground headquarters in Rivonia, were Jewish, with three eventually being among the accused at the ensuing trial.[8] While the contributions made by ANC/SACP Jewish activists have been recorded in multiple books, they, like the rest of the Mandela generation of activists, are slowly slipping away from the country's collective memory. Meanwhile, another group of Jewish activists can't be forgotten, because they aren't remembered. These activists played a dramatic albeit little-known role in the fight to make South Africa a better place, but their contribution is

---

[8] The 16 Jewish defendants in the 1956-1961 Treason Trial were Jacqueline Arenstein, Ben Turok, Sonia Bunting, Brian Bunting, Lionel Forman, Ruth First, Joe Slovo, Hymie Barsel, Lionel Bernstein, Leon Levy, Norman Levy, Yetta Barenblatt, Ronnie Price, Sydney Shall, Isaac Horvitch and Dorothy Shanley. Those Jews arrested as a result of the Liliesleaf raid were Lionel Bernstein, Denis Goldberg, Harold Wolpe, Arthur Goldreich, Bob Hepple and Hilliard Festenstein.

being lost in the mists of time. These activists were involved in the African Resistance Movement.

The African Resistance Movement (ARM) started in prison and ended four years later with most of its members behind bars. One of its members was Roman Eisenstein[9], who says ARM was a consequence of the Sharpeville Massacre, where police fired on unarmed protesters on 21 March 1960, killing 69 people.

The government clamped down on the liberation movement and responded with a state of emergency that saw thousands of activists detained.

Among the detainees held at Pretoria Local Prison was a group of 'dissident leftists', which included Monty Berman and his wife Myrtle.

At that time, the resistance to apartheid was chiefly non-violent defiance. However, according to Roman, while in prison, Monty resolved that the only way to confront apartheid was by doing something 'more drastic than just talk'.[10]

'The Communist Party also came to the conclusion that non-violence was no longer practical,' Roman says, 'but the two wouldn't work together because the Communist Party was very Stalinist.'

So Monty and Myrtle, along with other activists who weren't members of the Communist Party, formed the National Committee for Liberation, which later became ARM, to embark on a sabotage campaign.[11]

'And I was part of that,' says Roman.

Roman was born in Warsaw in 1936. As a child he witnessed beatings and killings by the Nazis, and when he was three, his mother hid him in a laundry bag when a death squad raided the Warsaw Ghetto.

The family escaped through city sewers in 1943 and went to live in France, before coming to South Africa in 1955.

---

9   Roman Eisenstein was then known as Raymond
10 Interview with Roman Eisenstein, June 2021
11 Info on ARM also obtained from Andries du Toit's thesis, The National Committee for Liberation 1960-1964: sabotage and the question of the ideological subject, 1990

'I acquired a strong dislike of Nazism,' Roman tells me. 'When I arrived in South Africa I realised I didn't like the [apartheid] system. I went to Wits University to study economics and joined the Student Fellowship Society, a non-racist group that believed in democratic values.'

Roman was introduced to a member of the society, Baruch Hirson, a physics lecturer at the university, who had been a member of the socialist Zionist youth movement Hashomer Hatzair and had set up the International Socialist League, a clandestine Trotskyist group. Hirson was also a member of ARM.

Roman decided to join ARM and get involved in protest politics because, after Sharpeville, 'prospects were very dark'.

ARM embarked on its military operation in 1961, making it the first group to launch a sabotage campaign against the apartheid state.

'We did a lot of things, not only sabotage,' says Roman. 'We took people out of the country and rescued people who had been banished to remote areas.'

They also smuggled a group of black nurses to Tanzania in a King David school bus (more about this later).

Roman stole dynamite from a mine quarry, which he used to blow up a number of pylons.

'We took a stick of dynamite, put a timer on it, and then got out of there as quickly as possible,' he explains. 'The ANC took credit for everything we did, but it didn't bother us.' Roman says the sabotage campaign was a symbolic protest against apartheid, although some ARM members believed it was the first step towards a full-on guerrilla war against the government.

Not long after the sabotage campaign began, Monty was charged with breaking his banning order and handed a three-year suspended sentence. He and Myrtle decided to go into exile in Britain, from where they shipped explosives to ARM.[12]

ARM's three-year operation came to an abrupt end on 4 July 1964 when Adrian Leftwich was arrested.

Adrian, who was from a prominent liberal Jewish family, had been president of the National Union of South African Students,

---

12 Bell, Terry: Death of a largely unsung heroine, Terry Bell Writes, 9 December 2016

and had joined the Liberal Party before being recruited into ARM. He cracked under interrogation and gave up the names of most members of the group.[13]

The police started rounding up activists, who tried to reveal only what they guessed the police already knew. The problem was that the cops knew everything.

Baruch was arrested at a roadblock on his way back from a conference in Durban. Roman, who was then 27, was working as a business journalist at the *Rand Daily Mail* when the police arrived at the newsroom.

'I wasn't surprised. I expected that things would crash down,' he says. 'I was treated very badly. I was beaten up. My face was made into pulp, and I was forced to stand for hours on end.'

Hugh Lewin, another member of ARM who was detained, wrote about being interrogated in his book *Stones Against the Mirror:* 'At one stage the door opened and they brought in Raymond Eisenstein – Tom[14], also detained a fortnight before – his face puffy and red, bruises around the eyes. "You know each other," they said. We looked at each other and said nothing. They dragged him out again, into the passage, and I heard the one man (whom I met in Pretoria later, named Van der Vyver, scream: "*Staan op, Jood* (Stand up, Jew)," and there was a scuffle, with the sounds of thuds and hits.'[15]

A 1972 United Nations report on the maltreatment and torture of prisoners in South Africa confirmed that Roman 'was punched steadily on one spot on his arm for three hours until it was swollen. He was also forced to stand for 28 hours. He then sat down and was kicked and beaten. He was seized by his testicles, lifted up bodily, taken to the window and threatened with dropping. He then made a statement, which was false.'[16]

---

13 Three weeks after Adrian Leftwich was arrested, ARM member John Harris set off a bomb at Joburg's Park Station that killed an elderly woman and maimed a girl. Harris was convicted and hanged, the only white resistance fighter to suffer this fate

14 Tom was Raymond/Roman Eisenstein's nom de guerre

15 Lewin, Hugh: *Stones Against the Mirror: Friendship in the time of the South African Struggle*, Cape Town, Umuzi, 2011

16 UN General Assemply report of the Special Committee on Apartheid: Maltreatment and torture of prisoners in South Africa by rapporteur Barakat Ahmad, 26 September 1972

Within two weeks after the arrest of Adrian, who turned state witness and testified against his comrades, ARM had been effectively crushed.

The state charged Roman; Baruch; Hugh; Frederick Prager, a Jewish Austrian-born photographer; and Joburg businessman Alexander Cox with conspiring to commit sabotage, which carried a minimum sentence of five years in prison.

Roman's mother gave evidence in mitigation of sentence for her son, testifying about his childhood in the Warsaw Ghetto, and how he was sickened by South Africa's racial politics and found himself forced by his conscience to get involved in the resistance.

Baruch, Roman and Hugh were found guilty. The other two were acquitted. Baruch was handed a nine-year jail term while Roman and Hugh each received seven years.

Roman's mother was refused permission to see her son before he started his sentence at the notorious Pretoria Local Prison, where white political prisoners were held.

When Roman arrived at the prison there were so many Jewish prisoners, they could have had a *minyan*.

Roman rattles off a list of fellow Jewish prisoners: Lewis Baker, Baruch Hirson, Norman Levy, Eli Weinberg, Issy Heymann, David Ernst, Rowley Arenstein, Jack Tarshish, Paul Trewhela, Ben Turok, David Kitson and Denis Goldberg.

The Jewish prisoners received food parcels on Pesach and Rosh Hashanah, which they shared with the others, even though the authorities tried to prevent them doing so.

'Conditions were bad; we were in prison, which is nasty, but it wasn't totally harsh,' says Roman. 'We could talk – we talked politics, literature and even talked about love – so it wasn't terrible from that point of view.'

He says he coped because he broke all sentimental attachment to the outside world.

Meanwhile, Roman's mother put pressure on the authorities to release her son, apparently camping outside the office of the Minister of Justice BJ Vorster every day, demanding that her son be let out of prison.

The government finally relented and in June 1967, three years after he'd been arrested, Roman was released from jail and taken straight to the airport and deported.

More than half a century after he walked out of prison, Roman says he doesn't regret his involvement and doesn't mind that his sacrifice hasn't been acknowledged.

When Adrian Leftwich started spilling the beans about ARM, two members who managed to get out of the country in time were student leader Neville Rubin, the son of one of the Jewish founders of the Liberal Party, Leslie Rubin, and Michael Schneider, who had been dubbed the Pimpernel by the press when he managed to evade the security police's dragnet.

As a teenager, Michael had a strong Jewish and Zionist identity and was the national treasurer of the Young Israel Society. In his early 20s he was recruited into ARM, where he was trained on how to fell electricity pylons.

'We made a solemn pledge not to target civilians, not to hurt people,' he says.[17] 'My garage in Sea Point had all the equipment – detonators, plastic explosive, gelignite. We once knocked out five signal points on the suburban commuter train line between Cape Town and Simon's Town, bringing Cape Town's commercial district to a complete standstill.'

One day Michael was asked to 'borrow' the King David school bus to transport 20 African nurses to the newly independent Tanzania, as a present from the ANC.

'With a forged letter ostensibly from State President CR Swart, I was disguised as an Anglican priest, and we picked up the nurses in Sophiatown in Johannesburg. An ANC member and I took the King David school bus to the Bechuanaland border (this was before it became independent Botswana). We were met in the middle of nowhere – there was a table and tablecloth, and they sang *Nkosi Sikelel' iAfrika*. We drove back to Joburg and got the bus back in one piece before school opened on Monday. The school was an unknowing fellow conspirator.'

Some time after Adrian had been arrested, Michael was returning to his flat in Sea Point when he saw 'two huge guys in raincoats' at the entrance of the building.

'They looked strange, and I feared they were from the Special Branch. I went to the first floor and left the building via the back

---

17 Information about Michael Schneider comes from an interview by Steven Gruzd with Michael in *Jewish Affairs*, Vol 66, Rosh Hashanah 2011

entrance. We had evaded capture for so long because the police didn't suspect that most of us were white ... but the game was up.'

Michael continued to evade the police, who launched a huge manhunt for the Pimpernel.

'I planned to head for London, where I knew it would be cold, so the next day, I went to buy a coat – maybe that was my Jewish grandmother's training – and bought a plane ticket to Joburg. At the entrance to the plane was a huge Afrikaner policeman. As I passed him to board the gangway, I realised I'd left my new coat on the chair. I was scared, but wasn't going to leave that coat! So I risked going back to fetch it, and boarded the plane again.'

Michael managed to get to Swaziland, where he spent six months working on an apple farm.

'A friend provided me with a fake passport, then drove me across an unguarded border to Bechuanaland and provided me with a scooter, which I drove to Francistown. I was picked up in a huge truck with 50 guerrillas from Swapo (South West Africa People's Organisation, the Namibian liberation movement). They were en route to Kasane, separated by a 400-metre ferry ride across the Zambezi River to Kazungula, the border crossing into Northern Rhodesia (present-day Zambia). The Swapo guys were off to Tanzania to be trained. It was unheard of that a white man could be anti-apartheid in those days, and many suspected I was a spy.'

Eventually, the Swapo leader agreed to take him across the river, and Michael promised to pay a £50 fee to Swapo when he arrived in London.

'At the border post, the official stamping us went to the toilet, so I quickly stamped my own passport and entered Northern Rhodesia. I boarded a train to Lusaka and sought refuge at the British High Commission there. I was helped by someone who bought me a ticket to London. At Heathrow I applied for political asylum. I spent a few days in Brixton Prison. I was released, and given £15, compliments of Her Majesty's government.'

In London, Michael went to see Sam Nujoma, the Swapo leader in exile and later Namibia's first president.

'I thanked him for the role he played in my escape by his guerrillas, but I was embarrassed that I wasn't able to pay the debt of honour of £50 to him. I haven't seen him since. I intend to visit him sometime and hand over the money!'

Michael went on to have a distinguished career in Jewish communal affairs, inter alia serving for many years as Executive Vice-President and Chief Executive Officer of the American Jewish Joint Distribution Committee and as Secretary-General of the World Jewish Congress from 2007 to 2010.

A WELL-MEANING REBEL

CHAPTER 4

THE WELL READ (AND WELL RED) FANNY KLENERMAN

A lifelong rebel, trade unionist, naturist and Trotskyite, the indefatigable Fanny Klenerman owned the iconic Vanguard Bookshop, a favourite haunt of Joburg leftists from 1931 to 1974. The shop's history has never been told, and its eccentric owner has been largely forgotten.[18]

Born in 1897 at Lutzin in Vitebsk province, Belarus, Fanny Klenerman came to South Africa at the age of four or five with her mother and older brother to join her father, who had arrived in Johannesburg in the late 1890s. With money scarce during the South African War (1899-1902), Fanny's mother operated a small store, selling herring, *kvas* (a drink made from the juice of fermented bread), pickles and brown bread.

After the war the family moved to Kimberley, where Fanny's father opened a men's outfitting store. An accomplished Hebrew scholar, he lost his religion but not his Jewish identity. Although they never belonged to a synagogue, Fanny's mother insisted the family attend services on the high holidays so that the children should not 'grow up to be savages'.

The family supported Jewish organisations but were not Zionists. Theirs was a Yiddish-speaking household. Fanny remembers going to school not knowing a word of English. She soon picked it up, and by the age of seven or eight was an avid reader. She was exposed to socialist ideas by her father, who imported liberal and socialist newspapers from Britain. He and his friends were dedicated to changing society, and he discussed these issues with Fanny.

After matriculating, Fanny went to the University of Cape Town, where she graduated with a degree in English and history. She taught at Wynberg Girls' School but found the atmosphere stuffy and repressive.

She returned to Kimberley but couldn't find work because of her outspoken political views, expressed in letters to the local newspapers. Shortly after the Rand Revolt in 1922, Fanny left to work for

---

18 This is an edited version of an essay by Veronica Belling that appeared in *Jewish Affairs*, Vol. 72, #1, Pesach 2017

THE WELL READ (AND WELL RED) FANNY KLENERMAN

the Labour Party in Johannesburg. Within a year she broke with the party because she objected to its industrial colour bar.

Years later she recalled: 'Here we've come to a country the British stole from the Africans ... They haven't got money to go anywhere, and you're excluding them from society and bringing them down to the level of serfs. And I said "I can't take it".'

Fanny joined the Communist Party of SA, the only multiracial party at the time, and distributed *Umsebenzi* (*The Worker*) newspaper in Soweto on Friday afternoons. However, she was expelled from the party in 1935 for being critical of its policies.

After the 1922 strike, wages fell sharply and there was a large movement of women from the country into the cities, where poverty was rife. The average monthly wage for working women was impossible to survive on.

Following the strike, the trade union movement was in chaos, and Fanny and her friend Eva Green, who like Fanny was also a teacher, humanist and socialist, formed the South African Women Workers' Union.

They took trams to factory yards and spoke to the women on their breaks, often in the face of strong resistance from the factory owners, who threatened to set their dogs on them.

They explained to the women their rights as workers.

In January 1927, Fanny married Frank Glass, a journalist and trade unionist. The couple had financial problems and were forced to give up their house and move to rooms with a shared bathroom and not much privacy.

To bring in some money, Fanny gave English lessons to Russian Jewish immigrants, who were arriving in South Africa. Her main goal was to teach them to read the English newspapers so that they could know what was going on around them.

Work was hard to find in the depression years, and Fanny and Frank took over a small tearoom, which Fanny managed. Frank also opened a bookshop, selling socialist and radical books.

To drum up customers, Fanny would drag a heavy suitcase full of books to potential clients. She was an avid reader – mostly of American books on politics – and subscribed to many American magazines.

Fanny and Frank's relationship ended when Frank decided to travel to China. Fanny remembered standing broken-hearted at Park Station watching him depart.

Fanny took over the bookshop and renamed it the Vanguard Bookshop, after the Vanguard Press, an American left-wing publishing house that published books on radical topics.

The new bookshop opened on 17 April 1931 and remained in Hatfield House in Eloff Street for a number of years. It became a centre for radical intellectuals and was for many years the only supplier of left-wing literature in South Africa.

Fanny became notorious when she and seven of her female friends were arrested for bathing nude in a secluded mountain pool near Witpoortjie in Roodepoort. The women were taken to a police station, fingerprinted and released on bail of £500.

The incident made headlines, and the women's names and addresses were published as well as the fact that Fanny was the owner of Vanguard Bookshop. On sentencing them to a fine of £2 each, the magistrate declared that society had done its utmost to instil in them a sense of propriety.

Fanny succeeded in having the verdict overturned on the grounds that the place where they had bathed was remote and inaccessible and could hardly be considered to be in the public eye. It transpired that the cops who arrested the women had spied on them through binoculars from an adjacent ledge.

Fanny was disgusted by the narrowness of officialdom in South Africa, pointing out that nude bathing was commonplace in Europe. She and her friends continued to bathe nude in mountain pools, 'observed only by monkeys and baboons'.

Many felt this incident would harm Fanny's business, but she had no regrets. 'I have always tried to maintain my true opinion against those obscurantists and conservatives. And so far, people of intelligence have accepted me. They regard me as a well-meaning rebel, but certainly not immoral ... [Our] real customers – who also became friends – all respected me as the owner of the best bookshop in South Africa.'

Fanny met Joe Moed, a Belgian national. When the steel company Joe worked for closed its Johannesburg branch, he moved into her home.

'That,' says Fanny, 'was the beginning of our "more-than-friendship".'

Fanny acquired a reputation as a discerning bookseller. She stocked the European classics, and made contact with distinguished publishers, who sent her books that might otherwise never have reached South Africa.

Fanny introduced the books of the Left Book Club and subscribed to the *Moscow News*, an English language newspaper, and the Russian-language newspapers *Izvestia* (Star) and *Pravda* (Truth). The readership was small but some students became devotees.

Apart from distributing these books, Fanny, with a few others, organised a Left Book Club discussion group. They hired a room in the Johannesburg Public Library and held regular meetings. Fanny often spoke there herself.

Fanny's bookshop drew numerous book lovers to its one room on the second floor of Hatfield House. Many patrons became her ardent supporters.

'This was more than a shop – it was a forum for informed political ideas, and also for the latest currents in philosophy, literature and art,' wrote activist Baruch Hirson.

While most customers were white, the shop attracted black shelvers, some of whom found a niche in journalism in the post-World War II years in publications like *Drum*. One, Todd Matshikiza, wrote the lyrics for the musical *King Kong*, while another, Bloke Modisane, wrote the book *Blame Me on History*.

In his book *Wasteland*, journalist David Robbins quotes the reminiscences of a former Vanguard employee: 'During the war I got a job in a bookshop. Vanguard, it was called, and it was run by perfectly crazy people – they were Trotskyites actually. During those days we were heavily dependent on imported culture, on books from London and America. When consignments of new books arrived, everyone who was anyone came to browse. The shop stayed open on Saturday afternoons, and it was like a social occasion. I could name you at least 50 top people around today who had accounts at the Vanguard... And of course the Vanguard was an important meeting place for black and white intellectuals. It was probably the only place they could meet in those days.'

Fanny believed very strongly that children's books displaying any form of racial discrimination should be banned, and was distressed that Helen Bannerman's book *Little Black Sambo*, which portrayed a southern Indian child in a deprecating light, was available in South Africa.

When the Hatfield House premises became too small, Fanny moved to Warwick House at 51 Von Brandis Street. Here, the shop occupied a large ground floor area with two very large windows for displaying books. When war broke out, her landlord, the real estate and cinema chain mogul IW Schlesinger, pressured her to leave as somebody wished to move into the adjoining shop and take over her space as well. Unable to persuade him to allow her to remain, she approached a cabinet minister, who agreed to invoke legislation protecting tenants from being given notice during the war. Although she continued in the premises for quite a while, she realised that once the war was over, she would be given notice again, so she began to search for new premises.

Opposite them was a dilapidated building that the Johannesburg Building Society was looking to restore. It was near their old premises and the rental was very reasonable. The new shop had a small ground floor, but was mostly in the basement.

In 1952 Joe became a director of the bookshop. He and Fanny were avid readers. They had an immense knowledge of books and became expert in tracing them.

Fanny would read all the reviews in the British newspapers: *The Observer*, *The Sunday Times*, *New Statesman*, *Encounter*, *The London Magazine*. Then they would discuss them and order the books.

Publications were imported from many countries. They subscribed to *The Monthly Film Bulletin*, *Sight & Sound*, *Theatre Monthly*, and *Polemics*, a theatre magazine, and also to architectural publications from Brazil, Bulgarian publications about the film industry, as well as magazines on sex and how to explain sex to children.

Needless to say, they had to do battle with government officials on the prowl for material that would destroy society's moral fibre, and in 1964, officials came into Fanny's bookstore and seized Thomas Hardy's *The Return of the Native*.[19]

The book tells the story of an Englishman who returns from the city to his home on Egdon Heath. But, as Fanny explained to a *New York Times* journalist, in race-obsessed South Africa, the authorities must have thought that 'native' meant a black man [and not a person born in a specified place].

Another book that was banned was Agatha Christie's *Caribbean Mystery*. The clampdown followed a protest from the Dutch Reformed Church's morals committee.

---

19   Censorship Rises in South Africa, The New York Times, 25 November 1964

THE WELL READ (AND WELL RED) FANNY KLENERMAN

It was sometimes impossible to get into the shop because it was so crowded. Some of the students who spent many hours in the store became world-renowned scientists, architects and writers.

The shop flourished until the owners of the building were made an offer by American Express.

Fanny and Joe scoured the city, looking for new premises with adequate space for their thousands of books. Desperate, they settled on a building in Commissioner Street under construction with heaps of sand and rubble outside and still without windows.

They moved in at the end of December 1966, storing crates of books in the basement.

'The move to Commissioner Street was to be the downfall of the Vanguard Bookshop,' Fanny wrote.

It was hoped that the Carlton Hotel, which was being built, would bring an influx of tourists that would improve business. Unfortunately the building was delayed for several years, the street was dead and business was slow. Even when the hotel opened and business improved, the expense of running a shop on two levels was great. They were forced to employ more staff, and found that even highly educated staff didn't necessarily know that much about books. Then came a slump. People began to spend less money on books. In addition, the shop was plagued by theft of money and books by staff and customers. Fanny felt that to be a socialist and to be a boss was a contradiction in terms. As she put it, 'As an employer I should have taken strict measures to stop the continual frivolity among my staff, but as a socialist it was difficult to become a tyrannical employer. I didn't really want to be a boss and I think that is why I failed.'

The shop closed down in 1974, and Fanny died in 1983.

WORKING-CLASS HEROES

CHAPTER 5

SACHS APPEAL

Solly Sachs earned a reputation as one of the most remarkable trade unionists of the 20th Century. When Nelson Mandela addressed the congress of the SA Jewish Board of Deputies in 1993, he said Solly's name was indelibly inscribed in the history of the country's labour movement because of the contribution he made to the struggle for workers' rights.

When I was 12 years old I would sneak into my father's study, open his drawer and take out a giant pair of scissors. I loved holding it in my hands. These were scissors unlike any other I had ever seen. The heavy metal scissors resembled two swords crisscrossed. I can still feel the weight of them in my hand. They were also sharp, and I was sure they could cut through steel.

Like many Jewish children in the 1970s I grew up on stories of the Holocaust and persecution, and devoured books like *When Hitler Stole Pink Rabbit*, *Friedrich* and *The Diary of Anne Frank*. These books had a profound impact on me, and 40 years later I still remember them vividly.

As a boy I often wondered who would hide my family if the Nazis came for us. I collected foreign coins in case we needed to escape to another country. I had decided that if we had to flee I would take my dog, my coin collection and the giant pair of scissors. It wouldn't be the first time these scissors had fled persecution.

The scissors, which are still in my father's drawer, had made their way from Poland to South Africa almost a century ago.

The scissors had belonged to my grandfather, Chaim Ancer, who was one of many Jewish tailors who left eastern Europe for refuge in South Africa at the turn of the 20th century.

Chaim was born in Poland on 4 February 1900. He was the youngest of 11 children. When he was 12 – the same age as I was when I would sneak into my father's study to play with the scissors – he was sent to become an apprentice to a tailor. He was a servant. In fact, he was little more than a slave.

He woke up before the family he served got up so that he could make a fire for them. He cleaned the home and got the tailor's children washed and dressed. In between all his household tasks he learnt his tailoring. When he was 18 he was conscripted into the Polish army for three years.

My grandfather subsequently met and married Tauba Bella Pieterkovski.

Life was tough. Jews were banned from becoming professionals, and there were frequent pogroms that left many dead, women were raped, and people's meagre possessions were stolen or destroyed. Chaim sought sanctuary in South Africa, where he managed to find a job as a tailor and machinist in a clothing factory.

The conditions were terrible and he earned a pittance. It took him six years to save enough money to bring Tauba Bella to South Africa. She managed to get out before the Nazis invaded Poland.

The rest of their families perished in the Holocaust. Chaim worked as a tailor, and for his entire life he was a member of the Garment Workers' Union (GWU).

They were led by one of the most successful trade unionists in South Africa's history – the colourful and controversial 'Jew Communist' Emil Solomon 'Solly' Sachs, who was considered the paragon of organisation.

My grandfather was a great believer in Solly. Many of the eastern European Jews were drawn to socialist ideology, and the artisans threw themselves into the struggle for better working conditions. They had a romantic notion that socialism was the answer to antisemitism; they thought it would spell freedom not only for the Jewish people, but the whole world. For them, Russia was the utopian ideal.

My father remembers my grandfather having a discussion about Russia with a friend. The two spoke about how there were no prisons in Russia, because in Russia every person has a job and there is no reason to steal.

Every week my grandfather would make his way to the Yiddishe Arbeiter Klub (Jewish Workers' Club), a social and socialist hub, where Solly was also a member. My grandfather idolised him.

'I am a Jew. I have a rough voice and a Lithuanian accent. I am ugly,' is how Solly described himself.[20]

He was also a brilliant, passionate and effective unionist, who had a difficult personal life and found himself in conflict with the bosses, the government, his own comrades and members of his family, yet he was generally admired for his spirit, courage and sense of humour.

Solly was born in the Lithuanian village of Kamai, but we don't know when exactly. He decided it was 11 November 1900. He made up the date because the actual date wasn't known.[21] He was the fourth of five children of Abraham and Hannah Saks (the surname was later changed to Sachs).

---

20 Joseph, Helen: *Side By Side: The Autobiography of Helen Joseph*, Zed Books Ltd, New York, 1986
21 Verwey, EJ: *New Dictionary of South African Biography Vol 1*, Pretoria: HSRC Publishers, 1995

Solly was a sickly child and could still not speak or walk by the time he was four. His brother Bernard Sachs described him as 'an amorphous mass of flesh'.

'His head drooped to one side as he sat day after day in his chair until his mother carried him to bed. His face bore an expression of pain ... as if he had entered the world unwillingly,' Bernard wrote.[22]

But Solly blossomed into a lively and precocious boy, who at 13 was the best pupil in the village and impressed everyone at the local *cheder* with his knowledge of the Talmud.

In 1914 the Sachs family moved to South Africa and settled in the Johannesburg inner-city suburb of Ferreirasdorp. Solly left school in Standard 5 (Grade 7) and began working as an assistant in a shop, where he cut his trade union teeth by organising shop assistants. Bernard Sachs says the Talmud was so ingrained in his brother that long after Solly embraced socialism and renounced religion, people still called him The Rabbi.

While Solly was connected to Judaism through culture and history, he became increasingly drawn to revolutionary politics.

He opened a provisions store but was far too preoccupied with politics to make a success of it. Political journals and books were piled high on the counter. While he was running the shop he was given a £20 fine for some technical offence. He went to court and lost, and then appealed – and won.

Solly developed a love of litigation and was in thrall by the logic of the law, becoming embroiled in more than 20 different trials throughout his life. A young advocate who cut his teeth appearing for Solly in many matters was Sydney Kentridge, who later became a famous counsel in Johannesburg and London.

Solly established a group to study what he considered 'the classics' – Marx, Engels and Lenin – and when he was 19 he joined the Communist Party of South Africa.

Informally, Solly studied global revolutionary movements and British trade unions and, formally, he studied law and economics at Wits University.

---

22 Sachs, Bernard: *South African Personalities and Places*, Kayor Publishers, Johannesburg, 1959

He became secretary of the Witwatersrand Middlemen Tailors' Association and then in 1928 became secretary of the GWU – and that proved to be his life's course.

The GWU may have started with Jewish tailors, but Solly was instrumental in recruiting black and coloured women who worked in clothing factories into the union.

He also felt great sympathy for the plight of the poverty-stricken young Afrikaans women who fled the rural areas during the Great Depression to work in factories, and he recruited them too.

The Afrikaans women were the daughters of the Boers who rebelled against the British – and Solly referred to them as 'the rebels' daughters'.

Solly mentored two of these women, Anna Scheepers and Johanna Cornelius, who became very prominent trade unionists. He was also a major influence on Lilian Ngoyi, another GWU member, who would go on to play a massive role in the broader political struggle. Helen Joseph, who, with Ngoyi, led the Women's March in Pretoria in 1956, worked for the GWU's medical aid fund.

Under Solly's leadership the GWU became the most militant and active union of its time.

Solly married Ray Ginsburg in 1926 and they had two sons, Albie and Johnny. In 1937, with the marriage in trouble, Ray took the boys to live in Cape Town and worked as a typist for the then general secretary of the Communist Party, Moses Kotane.[23]

'I had a father who was in the news a lot,' Albie told *The Guardian* newspaper.

'My emotions were mixed. It was mainly pride. In many ways he was the guy behind the newspaper – I saw the top of his head sticking out and his knees underneath.'[24]

In 1941 Albie received a postcard from his father that read: 'Dear Albert, congratulations on your sixth birthday. May you grow up to be a soldier in the fight for liberation.'

23　Dzur, Albert: A talk with Albie Sachs, *The International Journal of Restorative Justice*, Issue 2 2018

24　Barkham, Patrick: Albie Sachs: 'I can't tell my son everything', *The Guardian*, 8 October 2011

And that's exactly what happened. Albie became a lifelong freedom fighter, and was a major architect of the post-apartheid constitution and a much revered judge of the Constitutional Court.

Albie remembers his dad as a man of integrity.

'He used to play cards with the bosses who had come out on the boat with him as a kid. They had been tailors and had now become factory owners, and people used to say: Solly, how can you play cards with the class enemy? And he'd say: Class struggle is class struggle, and poker is poker.'[25]

Solly then married Dulcie Hartwell, who was a leader in the GWU, and had another son and a foster son. This marriage also fell apart.

While Solly wasn't having much success in his romantic unions, he was faring much better with life in the trade unions.

He secured better wages, improved working conditions, job security, more paid leave (from three days to 10), and morning and afternoon breaks. And he negotiated May Day as a public holiday – the first in any industry in the country. He also established a sick fund.

He led the GWU through several successful strikes,[26] including two general strikes in 1931 and 1932, which put him in the firing line of the staunchly anti-communist Oswald Pirow, the then minister of justice and an admirer of Adolf Hitler, who banned Solly for 12 months.

Solly challenged the restriction order in court and lost.[27] It was one of only two cases that he ever lost.

For Solly the courts were another battleground where he could fight for workers' rights, and he won numerous cases against Afrikaner nationalists who tried to wrest control of the GWU from 'the Jew communist Sachs' and neutralise his influence on the 'rebel daughters'.

In June 1939 Charles Harris, the Jewish secretary of the South African Mineworkers' Union, was assassinated by a right-wing extremist.

---

25 LRC Oral History Project: Interview with Albie Sachs, 5 August 2008

26 GWU public relations handout. As quoted in Martin Nicol's thesis Riches from rags: bosses and unions in the Cape clothing industry 1926-1937

27 General Jan Smuts revoked his banning order when he succeeded Pirow six months later

Solly received numerous death threats, and people often greeted him by saying: Are you still alive?

Solly wasn't at war only with the bosses, the government and extremists; he also had ideological differences with his own comrades, which saw him being expelled from the Communist Party for 'right-wing deviationism'. He was accused of sabotaging the trade unions' revolutionary activities.

One of his 'crimes', wrote former trade unionist Johnny Copelyn, was that he had chosen to take workers on a picnic and not to the Communist Party's May Day rally.[28]

He may have been expelled from the Communist Party, but according to the Nationalist Party, once a communist, always a communist, and during the 1948 elections the NP played the Rooi Gevaar card, highlighting Solly's role in the GWU.[29]

The government used its Suppression of Communism Act to ban Solly and force him to resign as the union's general secretary.

Solly was outraged. So were thousands of garment workers. Their hero who had led them to victories for 20 years had been suddenly and summarily removed.

In defiance of the banning order, Solly marched with a group of elderly Jewish men and young coloured, Afrikaans and black women to the Johannesburg City Hall, which is where he addressed the peaceful crowd.

His brother Bernard Sachs says that for someone who had derived all his strength from books, Solly's courage was immense, and he stood his ground in the face of the heaviest odds.

One of the people in the crowd was my own father, Bernard Ancer, who was 12, and had been taken to the march by my grandfather.

My father remembers the bespectacled, fiery, red-haired and blue-eyed Solly standing on the steps.

'As he started to speak,' my father tells me, 'the doors of the City Hall swung open and a troop of policemen with shiny new pickaxe handles came out. There was nowhere to run. The police arrested Solly and then they started swinging their pickaxes like batons.'

---

28 Copelyn, Johnny: *Maverick Insider*, Pan Macmillan, Johannesburg, 2016
29 Verwey, EJ: *New Dictionary of South African Biography* Vol 1, Pretoria: HSRC Publishers, 1995

My father was hit on the shoulder. My grandfather also received a thwack.

Helen Joseph was among the protesters, and she described it as a horrifying sight.

'Women and a few old men, with bleeding heads, scrambling to their feet to get away. I had not known that police could act like this,' she wrote in her autobiography.[30]

According to Albie, the joke afterwards was that hundreds of women followed his father as he was being led to the police station, shouting 'We want Sachs! We want Sachs!', which sounded a lot like 'We want sex! We want sex!'[31]

Solly was released on bail, and again, in defiance of his ban, tried to address workers, and was again arrested. He was found guilty on two charges and sentenced to six months' hard labour on each charge.

He appealed against the convictions, which he argued himself with Albie, who was then a second-year law student, in the Appellate Court. The judges commended his argument that his banning orders were void for vagueness, but rejected it. They did, however, suspend his sentence.

Solly was bitterly disappointed, though. He was forced to give up the GWU – the union he had dedicated a quarter of a century to building. He decided to go into exile, and in 1953 left for England, where 'the most remarkable trade unionist of the 20th century'[32] helped to start and build the anti-apartheid movement.

Solly died in London on 30 July 1976.

At his funeral, the anti-apartheid lawyer and former Communist Party MP in the SA parliament Sam Kahn said he was sure that if God exists, Solly is arguing with him right now.[33]

***

---

30 *Side By Side: The Autobiography of Helen Joseph*, Zed Books Ltd, New York, 1986

31 LRC Oral History Project: Interview with Albie Sachs, 5 August 2008

32 This is how the Times Literary Supplement described Solly in its review of his book *Rebels' Daughters*

33 LRC Oral History Project: Interview with Albie Sachs, 5 August 2008

SACHS APPEAL

The 1950 Suppression of Communism Act sparked a witch-hunt that cut short the political lives of many activists. The Act gave the government the power to 'name' communists. The definition of a communist was so crude that anyone with anti-apartheid sympathies could be declared a communist, who could then be banned. Over the years, more than 1,600 men and women were named as communists. Many of them were trade unionists, such as Ray Adler, who had been a shop steward for the Garment Workers' Union, and Ray Alexander, who had founded the Food and Canning Workers' Union.

On 21 March 1960 policemen shot into a crowd of thousands of people who were protesting against the pass laws in Sharpeville. When the bullets stopped, 69 people lay dead. The government declared a state of emergency, outlawed political organisations and unleashed a new reign of terror on activists. The state's iron fist drove the anti-apartheid movement underground and into exile.

While the ANC regrouped outside the country, the union movement entered a 'decade of darkness' until a wave of strikes, involving thousands of African workers, erupted in Durban in 1973. A number of Jewish activists were among the army of fiery unionists who emerged in the labour movement's renaissance in the 1970s and 80s. They included Mike Morris, Johnny Copelyn, Alan Fine, Merle Favis, Judy Favish, Taffy Adler, Neil Coleman, Dave Lewis, Di Cooper and Bernie Fanaroff.

CHAPTER 6
SWAPPING THE UNIVERSE FOR THE UNION

Photo: South African Radio Astronomy Observatory (SARAO)

Bernie Fanaroff could have got a job at a university anywhere in the world as a top-flight physicist, but instead he joined the union movement during the thick of apartheid and remained right through to the bitter end. Bernie made invaluable contributions to science, social justice and the public service – a trifecta of extraordinary achievements.

Bernard 'Bernie' Lewis Fanaroff was born in Johannesburg in 1947. His father Isaac came to the gold mining town of Benoni from Latvia as a child in 1910. His mother Fanny was born in the town, but her father and mother came from Lithuania.

Isaac and Fanny were teachers who never cared much about money. They established and taught in night schools in townships and were both associated with trade unions.

From the time he was born, Bernie 'absorbed' politics.[34] Ever since he could remember, Bernie listened to his parents and their friends talk about political developments in South Africa and the world.

'Politics was never pushed on me. It was never a case of you must do this or you must believe that, or this is right and that's wrong; it was just the environment I grew up in,' he says.

The environment was a political and a Jewish cultural one, but the family weren't religious or Zionist.

'I've been an atheist since I was born, although I've always been very happy to be Jewish,' says Bernie.

'My parents mostly spoke Yiddish at home. It was their home language, so I understood a fair amount even though I couldn't speak it. My father loved Yiddish poetry and Yiddish literature. My parents had both tried to trace family members in Latvia and Lithuania after the war, but they had all perished in the Holocaust.'

Bernie's parents taught him about being open and honest, and instilled in him humanist values and a lifelong love for learning, reading and acquiring knowledge. They encouraged him never to stop questioning.

While Bernie was at school he mapped out a long-term vision. He didn't have much detail, but he was interested in physics and decided he would get his PhD and then become involved in political activity. He didn't know what exactly, but he knew he wanted to oppose apartheid in some way and help improve the lives of all South Africans.

After matriculating, Bernie made his way to Wits University and registered for a BSc. He didn't view campus politics as being particularly relevant and kept his distance from student activities so that the security police wouldn't have a file on him. However, he did teach maths to black workers at the Wits night school.

---

34 Interview with Bernie Fanaroff, October 2020

He graduated with an honours degree in theoretical physics in 1970, and told the head of the department that he would like to be a cosmologist, which is the branch of astronomy that studies the origin and evolution of the universe.

The professor told him he wasn't clever enough to be a very good cosmologist and suggested he try radio astronomy instead, which is what he did.[35]

Bernie received a prestigious Isaac Newton Studentship to study for a doctorate in radio astronomy at the University of Cambridge. While he was completing his PhD, he and his colleague Julia Riley pioneered the classification of radio galaxies.

It might not sound like much to people who don't know their asteroid from their elbow, but to radio astronomers it's one of the most important developments in the field, and is still used today.

Bernie returned to South Africa in 1974 to lecture at Wits, conduct research at the Hartebeesthoek Radio Astronomy Observatory, and see what was available in political activism.

'I didn't fancy the ANC underground. I didn't particularly fancy the ANC and I had a very jaundiced view of the Communist Party, so that didn't appeal. I looked and looked, and after a year I'd pretty much given up, so I applied for a fellowship in the UK.'

Bernie was awarded the fellowship, but before he took it up, fate in the form of the Wits history professor Phil Bonner intervened.

Bonner told Bernie about the Industrial Aid Society (IAS), which was a Johannesburg front for the developing African unions. Bernie was intrigued.

The IAS offered worker education classes, and Bernie volunteered to teach labour law.

The society began to organise the Johannesburg branch of the Metal and Allied Workers' Union (Mawu), and Bernie worked with the emerging union in his spare time, going with organisers to meetings in Soweto to recruit workers for the union.

A number of the trade union organisers were banned in the wake of the June 16 Soweto Uprising in 1976, and Bernie asked Wits for two years' unpaid leave to work in the union.

---

35 Scientist, unionist and now star of the SKA show, *Mail & Guardian*, 5 July 2012

They refused, so he resigned and became an organiser for the Trade Union Advisory and Co-ordinating Council, which was at the forefront of the rise of black worker power.

The TUACC had been established to unite the new militant unions that had been formed after the widespread strikes in Durban. Bernie's focus was on building Mawu.

A day or two after he started, a lieutenant from the Special Branch turned up at the office and 'invited' Bernie to have a chat with him at John Vorster Square.

'Well, do I have an option?' Bernie asked him. The captain shook his head.

'He took me to John Vorster Square, and when we went into the lift he said, "You know, people fall out the windows here." We got up to the ninth floor and he hauled out a thick file, which I knew must either be bogus or about my parents, because I'd kept my hands clean. More than anything else he wanted to know who was paying me. I told him the unions pay me. I was being paid R140 a month, which was just enough to pay my rent and buy a bit of food, but he couldn't believe that a white man would work for such a low wage.'

Bernie, like his parents, wasn't motivated by money.

The lieutenant eventually let Bernie go.

Being an organiser in those days meant building a strong factory-floor presence. Bernie travelled from factory to factory with the other Mawu organisers and, trying not to be seen by the management, talked to individual workers when they came in and out of the plants.

The strategy was for every worker they recruited to recruit another worker, who in turn would recruit another worker, and so on, and gradually they would get the majority of workers in a factory to join the union.

Bernie would explain to the workers that as individuals they had no power, but if they all joined, they would have power.

It was difficult work because the history of the SA Congress of Trade Unions, which had suffered repression by the apartheid state and collapsed, and which had in some cases left members hanging out to dry, was still fresh in workers' minds, and many were afraid to join a union.

Another difficulty was that black labour unions didn't have legal status, and companies would dismiss any worker seen talking to a union organiser.

'People had very few rights in those days,' explains Bernie.

'They could be fired for anything. If the foreman didn't like your shirt he could fire you. Remember, there was no CCMA or Labour Relations Act, no industrial court. If they dismissed you, that was it.'

Bernie also had to be on the lookout for the security police because the management was quick to call the authorities if they thought there was any union activity going on.

'We had to be quite careful,' says Bernie. 'We would organise people outside the factories and then have meetings in people's homes in Soweto or Katlehong or Alexandra or Daveyton or Thokoza.'

Sometimes the Mawu organisers would travel with workers on buses to their plants to recruit them. Bernie would also pick workers up after they knocked off and transport them to and from meetings in the evenings and on weekends. He drove all over the Witwatersrand and often got home after midnight.

Mawu made progress in individual plants, and bit by bit the union spread across the Transvaal, from Benoni to Witbank to Lydenburg to Roodepoort, which meant Bernie's area of work became larger and his working hours longer.

During the day when members were at work he would follow up on complaints, dismissals and any other labour issues. His office was his Volkswagen Beetle, which he was in the whole day, and his daily nightmare was making – or, at least, trying to make – phone calls.

Cellphones were still the stuff of sci-fi movies and it was almost impossible to find a phone booth that hadn't been vandalised.

Mawu was a militant union and members would often down tools. 'We held the record for the number of strike days in South Africa for many years,' Bernie says.

In the early days, management refused to negotiate with the union, and Bernie recalls the Steel and Engineering Industries Federation (Seifsa) as particularly hostile in the 1970s.

'Seifsa was run by Anglo American with an iron fist, and the director said he would recognise black unions over his dead body. So, although Harry Oppenheimer portrayed himself as the saviour of democracy in South Africa, it wasn't like that in the early days. Anglo led the fight against the unions in those days.'

Black workers in industry had few rights, were paid poorly and were treated badly.

As an example of how workers were typically treated, Bernie points to Dunswart Iron and Steel in Benoni, where employees had little safety equipment.

'Workers often got burnt by red hot rails or rods coming off the mills, but management wouldn't allow them to go to hospital. They kept them at the company's premises and [Dunswart chairman Frederick] Zoellner got his GP in to treat them because otherwise Dunswart would have had to pay more to workman's compensation. That was the kind of treatment people got. It was completely inhuman.'

When Bernie wasn't at factories recruiting workers, dealing with complaints or organising strikes, he attended meetings – general meetings, union meetings and shop steward council meetings.

'We were very strict. The shop stewards had to report back to their departments every week and after every meeting with management, and there had to be a monthly general meeting. I think those things have broken down now, but we were insistent on worker democracy. Workers had to be involved in all decisions. That was another thing we insisted on: organisers didn't own the union; workers owned the union.'

Bernie attended branch executive committee meetings that started on Friday afternoons and went through until Saturday mornings. There were also national executive committee meetings that started on a Friday night and continued until Sunday.

Union work was exhausting and Bernie was hardly ever at home. And even when he got home his work didn't stop. He'd be phoned at home around midnight because that's when night-shift workers had a meal, and if the foreman wasn't there, they'd go into his office and phone Bernie to tell him about their problems.

'It was seven days a week and late every night,' he says. 'Luckily my wife is very forgiving.' Bernie married Wendy Vogel, a specialist in child and adolescent psychiatry, in 1980. Meeting her was one of the defining moments of his life.

When Bernie started to organise at Siemens, the personnel manager told him that Siemens worldwide had less than 15% union membership, and there was no way Mawu would be successful. But Mawu managed to get about 90% membership in the various Siemens plants around the country. Bernie recalls sitting outside a Siemens plant in Pretoria West to recruit workers when the police arrived.

'We were bolshy with the police and they went away,' he says, 'and when workers saw that we could chase away the police, they joined.'

The security police kept their eye on the unionists, and one night Bernie was taking workers to a train station after a meeting when the security police arrested them.

When Bernie asked why they were being arrested, the police said they had information that there was a shipment of arms.

'It was all bullshit. They just wanted to intimidate us,' says Bernie.

Bernie was also arrested at a number of strikes after the management called the security police, and he was taken in for questioning.

'I was once kept in John Vorster for three days, that was the most, so I don't have much "street cred",' he chuckles.

Mawu unionists were in the line of fire. In May 1986 a grenade was tossed through the window of the home of Mawu organiser David Moedimeng. He was injured in the blast; his wife Joyce was killed.

Bernie gave a speech at Joyce's funeral and said: 'As we stand here now there is a one-day stoppage in every Mawu factory in South Africa to make it very clear to the system and our allies that we will not stand for our people being murdered. We will defend ourselves, and we will not stand for force to be used against the workers' democratic movement.'[36]

Bernie's parents had gone to live in England, and whenever they read anything about South Africa, his mother would phone to find out if he was okay.

Although they worried about their son's safety, they understood and supported his involvement – after all, he had followed in their political footsteps.

The ANC had always been suspicious of Mawu and of Bernie (whom they had labelled a workerist). The feeling was mutual.

'I was expecting that we'd be able to create a worker-controlled state and was very suspicious of this two-stage-revolution stuff and "colonialism of a special type". Never believed in it. I still don't,' he says.

---

36 Forrest, Karen Anne: Power, independence and worker democracy in the development of Numsa and its predecessors: 1980–1995, Wits University, 2005

Bernie remembers standing outside Mawu's Port Elizabeth office in the early 1980s, arguing with some of his union comrades against pursuing a connection with the ANC.

'I remember saying, "You know, the change won't come for another 30 years. We've got plenty of time to build socialism [before the ANC takes power]." I was wrong.'

Despite ideological differences, Mawu forged important links with the ANC-allied United Democratic Front (UDF) from 1984, and the two came together to organise boycotts and stayaways.

The union wasn't involved only in the fight against unfair dismissals, retrenchments, poor wages and shoddy conditions for workers; it also made an important contribution to the national liberation struggle and took up social, civic and political issues such as rent increases and lack of services in the townships, unequal education and forced removals.

For example, in 1984 the UDF and the unions embarked on a stayaway, with 800,000 workers downing tools to demand the removal of SA Defence Force troops from the townships and reforms to the system of Bantu Education.

Mawu's membership had grown from around 6,500 workers in the 1970s to about 350,000 a decade later when its general secretary, Moses Mayekiso, was detained in 1985 and charged with high treason.

In 1987, when the union merged into the National Union of Metalworkers SA (Numsa), one of the largest and most influential unions in the country, Bernie played a role as a national secretary responsible for collective bargaining. He also became a member of Cosatu's executive committee.

Bernie had a doctorate, but he says it was as a unionist where he learnt some of life's most valuable lessons.

'I learnt to deal with people, to listen to people and to value people. You know, when you're young you're very arrogant, you think you know the answers to everything, but you quite quickly learn in the unions that you don't know very much.'

Organising taught him to confront issues early and get everything out in the open. He also learnt the art of negotiation: how to negotiate, where to negotiate and when to negotiate.

'We learnt how to establish good bargaining positions, how to think strategically, how to talk to people, run meetings, and get people to understand and accept a position,' he says.

Being a unionist wasn't just a job; it was a way of life, and the unionists developed tight bonds.

'We worked very closely and we trusted each other,' says Bernie.

Being a unionist was immensely stressful and extremely exhausting, and I ask Bernie what kept him going.

'We just never contemplated that we could fail. That's what drove us. We were not unrealistic. We always looked at what the problems and setbacks would be and assessed the risks realistically, but at the same time we were always convinced that we were going to win in the end,' he says.

Bernie didn't know when 'the end' would happen, he just knew it would happen, and so it was just a question of slogging on.

'At times it was exhilarating, but it wasn't always fun, I must say that. The first time I was involved in a big strike where everybody was dismissed, which was at Toyota, I didn't sleep for a week, worrying about everybody losing their jobs and trying to get them back. But you get used to it and ultimately you learn to live with it. It was hard work and tiring and stressful, but the motivation was in the long-term view.'

Bernie was out by about 30 years in his estimation of when liberation would come – and when freedom arrived, he was taken completely by surprise.

His surprise turned to awe.

'I attended Nelson Mandela's inauguration at the Union Buildings, and when the air force flew overhead, showing the colours of the new flag, I said to myself, "Wow, that's our air force now! That's our air force!"'

Post 1994

Bernie left Numsa in 1994 to work in President Nelson Mandela's office, and was the head of the Office for the Reconstruction and Development Programme. When the office closed, he joined the civilian safety and security secretariat, which lasted until police commissioner Jackie Selebi suggested Bernie become a divisional commissioner in the SAPS. Bernie didn't see himself as a policeman and left to establish a consulting business. He returned to radio astronomy as the director of the Square Kilometre Array project in 2003, bringing the world's largest radio telescope to

Africa. His contributions to science and society continue to be recognised on a global scale, and he has a string of honours, including the Order of Mapungubwe and the National Research Foundation's Lifetime Achievement Award. He has also been elected as a Fellow of the prestigious Royal Society of London. He has seven honorary doctorates to go with his blood-sweat-and-tears doctorate from the University of Cambridge. The University of Manchester holds an annual lecture series titled The Fanaroff Lectures. There's also 'Fanaroff-Riley 1 and 2', ensuring his name lives on in perpetuity after he and fellow astronomer Julia Riley identified two classes of radio galaxies.

Yes, despite the acclaim and accolades, he remains humble. For someone who played such a crucial role in the world's largest radio telescope, Bernie doesn't relish his considerable achievements being placed under the microscope.

When asked about his awards, he's quick to point out that he appreciates the recognition, but the awards reflect the achievements of the teams he has worked with.

The *Daily Maverick* described him as the country's most modest national treasure. His friend Judge Dennis Davis agrees, saying: 'Bernie is a *mensch* in the classic sense. He is utterly remarkable and totally humble.'[37]

You could say Bernie reached for the stars, yet has remained down to earth.

---

37 Interview with Dennis Davis, July 2020

THE ART OF PROTEST

CHAPTER 7

JEWS, JAZZ AND JOY

The Jewish contribution to South Africa's performing arts has been significant. But at 7.30 pm on 2 February 1959 when the curtain opened on a sparkling production at Wits University's Great Hall, something magical happened: a black cast and a Jewish production team came together to defy the colour bar and produce one of the most remarkable performances in the history of South African theatre.

The performance was *King Kong* – the township afro-jazz musical that celebrated the smoky sounds of the sax and the sharp sound of the penny whistle. Miriam Makeba was the female lead. Abdullah Ibrahim was in the orchestra and so was Hugh Masekela, who played on a trumpet given to him by jazz legend Louis Armstrong.

'The impact of *King Kong* was just incredible,' theatre doyen and Mr Computicket Percy Tucker tells me.[38]

The musical launched the careers of a number of very talented black actors and musicians – and it also broke down racial barriers.

At the time, the director, Leon Gluckman, said: 'There has been genuine co-operation between black and white in this venture and in a small way it has brought understanding, which is much better than the fear which informs the relations between the two sectors.'[39]

---

38 Interview with Percy Tucker, September 2020
39 Slier, Lionel: King Kong and the Jewish Connection, *Jewish Affairs*, Volume 61, #4, Chanukah 2006

The musical became Nelson Mandela's favourite show. In fact, it was just about everyone's favourite show. It was so popular that when the curtain came down at the end of the opening performance, the audience refused to leave.

Writing in the *Mail & Guardian*, journalist Hilary Prendini Toffoli explained why the show had captured the public's imagination: 'In a country where the majority of the population was being kept down and restricted by draconian laws, *King Kong*'s effervescent celebration of life, love and muscle was like nothing we'd seen before. It was a gritty musical depiction of [Sophiatown], a place and era whose annihilation by the apartheid government four years previously would remain a haunting element of our troubled history.'

It was, according to Percy, one of the greatest nights in the history of South African theatre

This is how Lionel Slier described opening night: 'The stage of the Great Hall exploded into life. The energy of the cast was electric, the music alternatively seductive, exhilarating and haunting. The final curtain fell to an ovation rarely heard in any theatre anywhere. The roars grew louder when Leon Gluckman finally appeared on the stage ... [Leon] stood for a moment facing the audience, then turned his back and bowed low to his 63 actors. It was one of the most memorable nights and those who had made it possible were rewarded with a monumental hit.'[40]

And, boy, was it a hit.

For almost two years, the musical, which narrates the tragic life of boxing legend and feared gangster Ezekiel 'King Kong' Dlamini, played to multiracial audiences, with repeat seasons in all the major cities. In February 1961, after more than a quarter of a million South Africans of all colours had packed out performances, the cast flew to London, where the show opened in the West End, bringing international fame to Makeba and Masekela.

The musical charted the rise and fall of Ezekiel against the backdrop of Sophiatown, a multiracial Johannesburg suburb that was known for its bohemian lifestyle and vibrant music scene until the government decided it should be a whites-only area.

Ezekiel was born in Natal in 1921, and left home when he was 14 to seek his fortune in Joburg. He survived on the streets by playing

---

40 Ibid

cards and dice, and was blessed – or cursed – with enormous boxing talent. He soon became a folk hero.

Then he murdered his girlfriend Joyce because she had spurned him. He was sentenced to 15 years' imprisonment and sent to the Leeuwkop farm colony, where, soon after his arrival, he drowned himself in a dam in March 1952. He was 32.

There had been a strong Jewish presence in the musical from the very beginning. A meeting between Jewish philanthropists Clive and Irene Menell and their friend, composer Todd Matshikiza set *King Kong* into motion.[41]

The Menells gave financial and practical support, and Clive wrote the synopsis of the story that Harry Bloom turned into a novel.[42]

The Jewish influence continued: Leon Gluckman was the director; Stanley 'Spike' Glasser was responsible for musical direction; the set and costume designer was Arthur Goldreich; and Percy Tucker was part of the production team. Even the backstage group was Jewish, wrote Lionel Slier, who was himself a member of the crew.

At the time, Leon said: 'I would like to say that the Jewish spirit has to some undefined extent entered into the production of King Kong.'[43]

Many of the cast members were budding musicians and artists, but few had any theatrical experience.

According to Percy, Leon, who was one of the country's most creative directors, had moulded raw talent into a professional production.

We know that Makeba and Masekela remained abroad and became international superstars. So, nu, what happened to these Jewish cultural activists from *King Kong*?

---

41   Anthony, S: The Jewish-backed musical that stood up to apartheid, The JC, 11 October 2017

42   Sulcas, Roslyn: Reviving a South African Musical That Once Promised So Much, The New York Times, 8 August 2017

43   Slier, Lionel: King Kong and the Jewish Connection, *Jewish Affairs*, Volume 61, #4, Chanukah 2006

Leon Gluckman

Leon didn't have time to bask in *King Kong*'s triumph. One week after opening night, he was on stage for the play *Long Day's Journey Into Night*.

He was particularly interested in fostering black theatre and felt strongly that black and white artists had a great deal to give each other if they were allowed to.

After *King Kong* and a series of other successful plays, he put on the satirical revue *Wait a Minim!* in 1962 with an array of international folk music arranged by the Tracey brothers, Andrew and Paul, and original songs by Jeremy Taylor, whose *Ag Pleez Deddy* is credited with putting *Wait a Minim!* on the map. The production included mime, song, dance, a number of parodies against apartheid and, according to Percy, 'general craziness'. It received international success.

However, because of the constrictions placed upon his work by the government, Leon left South Africa in 1964 to live in London, where he was very active on the West End. He died in 1978 at the age of 55 after a battle with cancer.

Three days after his death, South Africa's Parliament passed a law bringing about the desegregation of theatres.

In a tribute to Leon, Percy wrote: 'It was a sad irony that Leon, who had defied the law in casting a black and white actor together for the first time in *Blood Knot*, hadn't lived to see this day.'[44]

Harry Bloom

Harry was a respected attorney who became an internationally revered writer when his novel *Episode*, giving an account of an uprising in a fictional township, was published in 1956. The book was banned. Harry was arrested and held for six weeks, and his passport was confiscated.

When he got his passport back in 1963 he went to live in England, working as an academic and journalist. He married Sonia Copeland,

---

44 Tucker, Percy: Leon Gluckman – Gifted Trailblazer, *Jewish Affairs*, Volume 61, #4, Chanukah 2006

with whom he had two children, Samantha and Orlando, who is well known as the elf warrior Legolas Greenleaf in the epic film trilogy *The Lord of the Rings*. Harry suffered a stroke in 1976 and died in 1981 at the age of 68.

Arthur Goldreich

Arthur was a key figure in the ANC's armed struggle. His involvement with *King Kong* was particularly useful for the movement's leadership because he put his experience designing costumes for the musical into making disguises for ANC leaders who were being hunted by the security police.

Arthur and his family lived at the Rivonia farm Liliesleaf, which was the HQ for the ANC's military wing, Umkhonto weSizwe. Also living at the farm was David, aka Nelson Mandela, who discussed guerrilla warfare tactics with Arthur, who had fought with the Palmach, the elite fighting force of the Haganah. Arthur was arrested at Liliesleaf in July 1963 but managed to bribe his way out of prison along with fellow Rivonia Trial accused Harold Wolpe. The pair made their way to Swaziland and, dressed as priests, flew to Botswana. Arthur settled in Israel, where he had fought in the War of Independence, and pursued his career in art and design. He died in Tel Aviv in 2011 at the age of 82.

Stanley 'Spike' Glasser

Stanley, who studied music as a child, was prolific in many fields, composing dramatic works, orchestral and vocal music, as well as chamber and solo instrumental works. He was the first South African to compose electronic music.[45]

His deep love of African music saw him eschew apartheid segregation when he composed the first full-length multiracial South African ballet *The Square*. He snubbed the colour bar romantically too and, in 1963, he fled South Africa after his relationship with the

---

45   Potter, Keith: Stanley Glasser obituary, The Guardian, 19 October 2018

singer Maud Damons, a black woman, saw him being charged under the Immorality Act.[46]

Stanley went to live in England, where he became head of music at Goldsmiths College. His large collection of recordings is housed at the British Library. After Stanley's death, in 2018 at the age of 92, Stephanus Muller, director of the Africa Open Institute, wrote that Stanley's musical legacy is 'still in many ways unknown in the country he left under duress in 1963'.

The Menells

Irene has had a lifelong interest in the performing arts and education. One of the many organisations she founded was the READ Educational Trust, which was established in 1979 to promote education for black children. She was awarded the Order of the Baobab in silver for her community service and dedication to the educational empowerment of black youth. She also served on the board of the Nelson Mandela Foundation, and when she stepped down in 2017, her parting words to the staff were: 'Just be your best you. It's a cliche, but it's not a bad one.'[47]

Clive, the deputy chair of the conglomerate Anglovaal, founded the Urban Foundation in 1977 to help improve the plight of black South Africans in Soweto and other urban areas. After Nelson and Winnie Mandela separated, Nelson Mandela stayed with the Menells for several months, and when Clive died in 1996, at the age of 65, Mandela spoke at his funeral.

Percy Tucker

I met Percy at his home in Cape Town.[48] In between gulps of green tea and bites of carrot cake, he tells me his love affair with the theatre began when he was a boy living in Benoni.

'I was born in Benoni BC,' he says.

---

46 Muller, Stephanus: Stanley Glasser: A life of exile and bravely crossing musical boundaries, The Conversation, 9 August 2018
47 Tribute to Irene Mennel on the Nelson Mandela Foundation's website
48 Interview with Percy Tucker, September 2020

'BC?' I ask.

'Yes, BC ... Before Charlize.'

He then takes me on a tour of his memorabilia – books, awards, and photos at opening nights with some of the world's greatest stars, such as Liza Minnelli and Luciano Pavarotti. He also hobnobbed with Bette Davis, Sir Laurence Olivier, Dame Margot Fonteyn, Shirley MacLaine, Roger Moore, Johnny Mathis, Marlene Dietrich, Goldie Hawn and Elton John.

Percy tells me he couldn't sing or dance, and the only thing he was good at was selling tickets – which is the height of modesty because he was, in fact, the backbone of South African theatre for six decades.

But, yes, he was very good at selling tickets too. Percy was South Africa's first tech entrepreneur. He founded Computicket, the world's first electronic theatre-booking system in 1971 – considered one of SA's top inventions.

Percy also campaigned against segregating black and white audiences in theatres.

In 1969 he secured the rights for *Show Boat*, a musical with a black leading man and a black chorus.

'Then the trouble started,' he explains. 'The government didn't want blacks and whites to be on the same level so we built a platform so that the black audience members sat higher up than the whites.'

Percy was part of a three-person committee lobbying the government on behalf of the arts, a campaign that took them to Parliament. The committee was successful in negotiating the desegregation of theatre audiences and actors in all South African theatres.[49] The legislation that racially segregated theatres was abolished on 11 March 1978 – at the height of apartheid.

With his involvement in selling tickets for *King Kong*, Percy came to realise how large a potential audience was out there if black and white people were free to attend the theatre together.

Percy was at the airport on 7 February 1961 when the cast of *King Kong* departed for London. When the flight was announced, a sudden hush fell over the departure lounge and the cast members spontaneously sang *Nkosi Sikelel' iAfrika*.

---

49 RIP Percy Tucker, an industry pioneer and founder of Computicket, YEI website, 3 February 2021

We chat about *King Kong* and its wide impact. I tell him that my parents had also been caught up in the *King Kong* craze when the show opened in 1959. They owned the record, and, growing up in the 1970s, the songs were the soundtrack of my childhood. I didn't understand the story line, but I knew that King Kong was a boxer who everyone was scared of. I spent many hours shadow-boxing while humming *'King Kong brave as a lion… King Kong bigger than Cape Town… King Kong knocks any ape down… That's me, I'm him. King Kong.'*

When I got to the final *'That's me, I'm Him. King Kong …'* I would execute a lethal jab-jab-uppercut combination and raise my fists in pugilistic glory.

It was the memory of the Sophiatown era that motivated South African-born theatre producer Eric Abraham to embark on a 20-year quest to get permission to revive *King Kong*.

After more than 50 years, minus a two-day blip in 1979[50], the smash hit was coming back to the stage.

When *King Kong* came to Cape Town's Fugard Theatre in 2017, I booked my ticket and, finally, saw the iconic production that had hit theatre-goers right between the eyes more than half a century earlier.

Percy died in February 2021, five months after our interview, at the age of 92.

---

50 An attempt in 1979 to put on *King Kong* flopped. Percy wrote that 'to watch this insulting travesty of the original was a nightmare'

CHAPTER 8

BARNEY SIMON: CREATIVE THORN IN THE FLESH OF APARTHEID

Although Barney Simon wasn't involved with *King Kong*, he was a King Kong-sized figure in South African theatre and just as iconic as the musical. The country's greatest playwright, Athol Fugard, described Barney as 'unquestionably the most significant theatre talent to have emerged in South Africa'.

Early one morning in July 1963, Barney Simon parked his car in a dark street in Hillbrow, Johannesburg, got out and began relieving himself. It had been a long night, and a series of farcical misadventures had prevented him until then from performing this (by now, decidedly urgent) function. Having been mugged six months before, Barney was already feeling nervous, hence his alarm when he heard a rustle and realised someone was hiding in the bushes nearby. He leapt back into his car and began driving off, but then heard his own name being called.

'It was Harold Wolpe and Arthur Goldreich,' recalled Barney. The two activists had been arrested as a result of the police's raid on the Liliesleaf farm in 1963.

'What had happened was that they had escaped from Marshall Square by bribing a guard, but the getaway car they expected wasn't there. They had been wandering on the outskirts of Johannesburg unsure where to go. So they chose me. They chose my apartment because it was a place that Harold knew. They were en route there when they encountered me on this dark corner.'[51]

Barney took the fugitives to his apartment, where they remained hidden for the next few days while he made contacts for them in the anti-apartheid underground. After a few days, they were moved out and, following further hair-raising adventures, succeeded in making their way over the border to Bechuanaland – now Botswana – and safety.

This was just one of many stories that Barney told. According to director, scriptwriter and film critic Alan Swerdlow, Barney's entire

---

51 Suttner, Immanuel: *Cutting Through the Mountain*, Viking, 1997

life was devoted to the telling of stories, particularly those of the voiceless, the dispossessed, the homeless and the forgotten.[52]

'The word "guru" has been attached to Barney so many times as to almost require some kind of debunking of the myth that surrounds him, but the truth is that there is nothing to debunk. Barney was always Barney ... wise, perceptive, gentle and capable of extraordinary empathy,' wrote Swerdlow.

The son of working-class Lithuanian Jewish immigrants, Barney was born in Johannesburg in 1932 and grew up with a strong sense of Hitler in his childhood.

After school he began studying architecture but dropped out and went to London, where he worked for Joan Littlewood's Theatre Workshop at the Theatre Royal.

When he returned to Joburg he met Fugard. There was instant electricity, and the two started to make theatre free of the restrictions of apartheid.

Barney worked with Fugard on the very first production of *Blood Knot*, a powerful play about human beings trapped in the madness of apartheid. The play became an international triumph and launched Fugard's career as a dramatist.

He was an advertising copywriter in the day and directed and produced subversive plays with multiracial casts at Dorkay House, an old building in downtown Joburg.

Barney learnt isiZulu and isiXhosa, held drama workshops in the townships and taught health education in rural areas.

After Dorkay House was closed, Barney staged guerrilla theatre anywhere he could: in warehouses, storefronts, people's homes, student communes, community centres, church halls in the townships, and in the backyard of the home of an activist who was under house arrest so that the man could watch it out the window. He had one condition: he refused to play to segregated audiences.

Around this time, Barney and Mannie Manim established The Company, which continued to stage productions in unconventional spaces. They soon realised they would need a more permanent venue. They heard that an old Indian fruit market in Newtown was to be demolished, and they convinced the Joburg municipality to

---

52 Swerdlow, Alan: Barney Simon – His Enduring Legacy, *Jewish Affairs*, Volume 61, #4, Chanukah 2006

allow them to convert it into a theatre. The venue had been a marketplace, which, unbeknown to them at the time, meant it was zoned for multiracial use. The Market Theatre opened in 1976, and had its first performance only days after the Soweto Uprising.

The 'Theatre of the Struggle', as the Market Theatre was dubbed, became a space where black and white actors and directors shared the stage and performed plays that packed a political punch. The Market Theatre was one of the few places where whites and blacks could mix on equal terms, making it an island of integration in a sea of segregation.

Barney was friendly with SA Communist Party revolutionary Ruth First and a number of other political activists, but his commitment to challenging the National Party government was producing works attacking the hypocrisy of its apartheid policies.

Barney was never arrested, but he was once questioned by the Special Branch, and he would occasionally receive threatening calls from 'pretty rough-sounding voices', calling him a *'Jood'*.[53]

The world-renowned actor John Kani said Barney was the only man who would give a black actor like himself a job outside township church halls. The two men established the Market Theatre Laboratory to teach theatrical skills to aspiring directors, actors and playwrights.

Barney developed original plays through a workshop process of field research, improvisation and collaborative writing, sometimes with professional actors and, at other times, people entirely new to the theatre.

His most famous protest play was *Woza Albert!*, a creation with Percy Mtwa and Mbongeni Ngema that exposed the cruelty of apartheid. The play, described as acidic satire, tells the story of Jesus stepping off a plane and arriving in apartheid South Africa.

The actors slip in and out of dozens of characters, from a poor black worker to the then prime minister, PW Botha.

At the end of the play, the actors chant *woza* (rise up) Albert ... *woza* Steve ... *woza* Neil, to revive political heroes like Albert Luthuli, Steve Biko and Neil Aggett. They used first names to avoid problems with the security police, who were no doubt sitting in the audience with tape recorders in their pockets.

---

53   Suttner, Immanuel: *Cutting Through the Mountain*, Viking Press, 1997

Woza Albert! opened at the Market on 25 March 1981 and soon became a worldwide hit.

In an interview with *The New York Times* when *Woza Albert!* toured the US in 1984, Barney said the play reflected the horrors of South Africa, but also the strength of the black people there.

'It talks about the gift of life and the abuse of life. I hope my work can celebrate the gift of life without forgetting the abuse of life.'

Barney died of a pulmonary embolism on 30 June 1995. He was 63 years old.

Fugard said he couldn't think of a single playwright or actor, white or black, who didn't owe Barney a debt of gratitude, 'and that includes an old warhorse like myself'.[54]

---

54 Information about Barney Simon obtained from obituaries in *The New York Times*, *The Independent* and *The Guardian*, July 1995.

CHAPTER 9

A MAN OF LETTERS AND INTEGRITY

Lionel Abrahams, novelist, poet, editor, critic, essayist and publisher, made an enormous contribution to literature and put a colossal effort into nurturing black writing talent and publishing groundbreaking works that launched a number of literary careers. He is one of SA's greatest creative forces, a public intellectual extraordinaire, and an icon of classical liberalism.

A MAN OF LETTERS AND INTEGRITY

When I think of the brilliant literary talent Lionel Abrahams, I'm filled with shame. My parents and Lionel were friends and he came to our house for a few Pesach *seders* when I was a child. I remember the first time I saw him. I was five or six and I gasped in horror at the sight of him. Lionel was born with a rare form of cerebral palsy, and his jerky, stiff, involuntary movements, facial contortions and slurred speech frightened me. To my child's mind he was a scary aberration. I hid from him.

That wasn't my only memory of Lionel that fills me with shame. Years later, when I'd stopped being scared of him, he attended my barmitzvah and gave me a present – it was his book *The Celibacy of Felix Greenspan*. He had inscribed it with a message, congratulating me on my rite of passage.

Writing was an enormous physical challenge, and it must have taken an incredible effort for him to write that message. I glanced at the message, closed the book, put it on my bookshelf – and that's where it remained, unopened, for many years. I don't know what happened to the book. It vanished – without ever having been read by me.

In a way, Lionel, one of the most influential figures in South African literature, has disappeared. Despite his incredible achievements (in the face of tremendous physical adversity), he is hardly remembered outside literary circles.

This son of Jewish immigrants Bendett and Anna, who had come to South Africa from Lithuania, was born in Joburg on 11 April 1928. He learnt to walk when he was 11 – and then with much difficulty, due to his shaky movements and difficulty balancing.

According to his nephew Laurence Milner, he had a 'mixed childhood'.[55]

There were happy memories with his two sisters, parents, uncles, aunts and cousins who adored and doted on him, and then there were 'not particularly pleasant' memories at the Hope Home, a special-needs school for children, where he spent weekdays.

'He spoke about some of the people there being nicer than others, and some certainly not nice at all,' says Laurence. 'There was some bullying of the kids, but the main thing was that many of the people who worked there just assumed the kids were stupid.'

---

55 Interview with Laurence Milner, June 2021

In an interview with his friend Hillary Hamburger, Lionel added that at the home his Jewishness was 'a mark of difference', which tended to make his time there 'not altogether easy'.

It took a superhuman effort for Lionel to persuade people that he had an extraordinary brain.

A few teachers at the school saw beyond his physical disability and encouraged him with his academic studies.

The school went only up to Standard 8, and when he was 16, Lionel went to Damelin College to complete matric. The move changed his life because one of the staff members happened to be Helena Bosman. One day, the English teacher was absent and Helena roped in her husband, the great South African writer Herman Charles Bosman – often referred to as South Africa's Mark Twain – to give the class a poetry lesson.

Bosman had a huge impact on Lionel, and a great literary relationship and personal friendship developed.

What happened next could have come from a Bosman short story. Lionel's father Bendett scooped the Irish sweepstakes, not once but twice, and on one of the occasions won a vast sum of money. Unfortunately, a confidence trickster swindled him out of most of it. It might have been from the pre-looted winnings that Bendett paid Bosman to mentor and coach Lionel.[56]

Bosman saw Lionel's potential and nurtured his writing abilities. Bosman taught him about creative writing 'and thus', as Lionel said, 'about life'.

Lionel studied at Wits and did a BA and an honours in English, getting firsts throughout his degrees – phenomenal when you consider he couldn't take notes in lectures.

'He also had a very active social life and was popular,' notes Laurence, adding that people were drawn to his uncle's impish sense of humour.

Lionel's friend Anne Pogrund wrote that Lionel loved, honoured and delighted in language. '[He] could make it dance as he himself, severely disabled from birth, could not, and was master of the wittiest, often wickedest *bons mots* – which he might struggle to

---

56   We can only speculate that Lionel's father paid Bosman for tutoring Lionel out of his winnings, but Lionel did write that his father used some of his spoils to pay for him to tour Europe in 1961

splutter out, and which often caused him to giggle as much as his audience.'[57]

Laurence remembers his uncle being a lot of fun.

'He loved funny stories and was very witty. He was a tremendous intellectual, in the old-fashioned sense of the word. He knew about many things and was interested in learning about everything. His interests were broad. He wasn't limited to literature and the world of literature. He was brilliant at maths, and loved numbers and number patterns as much as he loved words and word patterns.'

According to Laurence, Lionel had a tremendous interest in Jewish culture.

'He felt particularly close and connected to the Jewish literary world, but he was interested in all aspects of Jewish culture. I remember Lionel and my grandfather going to visit Israel. It turned out to be a disastrous trip, because while they were there, the Yom Kippur War broke out.'

Another of his interests was politics. He liked to observe politics and talk about it, and had very strong opinions.

'He was opposed to apartheid and was a staunch liberal who believed strongly in human rights. He was a person of action from his principles. He had a lot of friends who were activists and a lot who were communists, but he wasn't a communist,' Laurence notes.

He adds that Lionel's actions were always on a personal level.

'He wasn't someone who would join a protest against Bantu Education; it was much more his thing to nurture and provide an opportunity for black writers.'

Lionel launched the literary magazine *The Purple Renoster* from his parents' home in 1957.

It wasn't his first magazine. At the Hope Home he founded and edited *The Pepperpot*, 'a dutiful little organ carrying reports of activities, occasions and treats, character sketches, a spook story and bit of verse'.[58]

---

57 Pogrund, Anne: Lionel Abrahams: Mischievous guru of South African letters, Independent, 10 October 2011
58 Abrahams, Lionel: The Purple Renoster: An Adolescence, English in Africa, Vol 7, #2, Rhodes University, September 1980

Lionel's father paid for the 500 copies of *The Purple Renoster*'s first issue. As it turned out, all the contributors of that issue, even the pseudonymous 'Gerhard Viljoen', happened to be Jewish.

Barney Simon, Lionel's closest friend, became the magazine's associate editor.

Although Lionel never considered himself politicised, he lost his political virginity when an amendment to the Suppression of Communism Act made it unlawful to quote or publish people 'named' as communists.

Several writers were among the people who were gagged.

'As writers they were annihilated so far as their own country was concerned,' Lionel wrote.

Two of the named people were Alan Lipman, who had given Lionel an essay on architecture, and the poet Dennis Brutus.

'*The Purple Renoster* can be said henceforth to have maintained a campaign against the gag, as I took every opportunity editorially to criticise it and to commemorate the names of the writers it sought to blot out,' Lionel wrote.[59]

Writing and writers were Lionel's brief, and he wrote an editorial in the magazine's fifth edition in 1964 attacking 'this repellent law'. He published five of Brutus's poems anonymously immediately after his editorial.

'My belief was that this gesture would either prove that the gag could be circumvented by means of anonymous publication, or would provoke a prosecution that would embarrass the authorities because the "crime" in question would be the publication of a few innocuous poems. I further believed that this embarrassment stood a chance of inducing the government to rescind a not very useful but very offensive law.'

The edition sold for 30c and 160 copies were printed. Soon after it went on sale, Lionel's parents' home was raided by the Special Branch at 5 am one winter's morning. The cops searched his room and removed seven books and his typewriter.

Two-and-a-half months later, Barney was summoned to the Special Branch offices and questioned in connection with *The Purple Renoster*.

---

59 Ibid

A few days later the Special Branch came looking for Lionel, and a security policeman questioned him about some of the edition's contributors. Lionel refused to answer, insisting that the responsibility for the whole magazine was his.

'The remarkable thing, however, is that he [the security policeman] refrained from asking the one question that cried out to be asked: Who was the author of the anonymous poems?'

The security policeman then quizzed Lionel about 'the pornography' they had identified in Barney's story *Dolores*, which was published in the magazine.

Lionel's mother couldn't suppress her amusement. The cop, however, wasn't amused.

Lionel recalled the conversation between his mother and the detective:

'"Have you read [the magazine]?" he demanded of her.

"I helped to collate it," she replied.

"Did you read this?" he persisted, thrusting one of Barney's "fuck"-sprinkled pages under her eyes, whereupon I said something to discourage her from reading it, which caused him to round on me with a triumphant, "Aha! You're ashamed to let your mother read what you publish."'[60]

Three months after the interrogation, the issue with Barney's 'offensive' story was banned and the unsold copies of the magazine were confiscated.

The next edition of the magazine boasted: 'The Special Branch, the Publications Control Board and 39 subscribers can't be wrong – *The Purple Renoster* needs looking into.'

The magazine's circulation remained below 1,000, and the 39 subscribers in 1966 increased to only 102 by 1972, when it closed after publishing its 12th issue. But it had certainly made waves in the literary world.

Lionel also founded the publishing company Renoster Press, which gave young up-and-coming black writers a platform and a voice.

He put a huge amount of effort into mentoring Oswald Mtshali and Mongane Wally Serote. At the height of apartheid, he published

---

60   Ibid

Mtshali's *Sounds of a Cowhide Drum* and Serote's *Yakhal'inkomo*, two works that heralded the emergence of black poetry in South Africa.

He also focused on his own writing and poetry. He published his autobiographical novel, *The Celibacy of Felix Greenspan*, in 1975. It describes with fierce honesty and ferocious humour the emotional, intellectual and sexual experiences of a young man suffering from cerebral palsy (I eventually bought another copy of the book, and this time I did read it).

In a hat tip to Bosman, who died in 1951, Lionel edited several posthumous collections of his mentor's work, allowing new generations of readers to find delight in the tales of Oom Schalk Lourens.

As the journalist Shaun de Waal noted: 'Such a job wasn't as easy as it may appear today, now that Bosman is well remembered. But for Abrahams, Bosman might have been forgotten as a writer.'[61]

Laurence says his uncle often had disputes with other writers, which consumed him.

'If he had a disagreement with someone he couldn't just let it go or compartmentalise it. He was a man of principle and he stuck to his opinions. He didn't like political correctness at all. He believed in the quality of literature and would never make an allowance for someone from a disadvantaged background who produced something he didn't think was first rate.'

As a result, Lionel became embroiled in a number of literary controversies, notably the PEN International saga in the 1980s. The Joburg branch of PEN International, a worldwide association of writers, had all but collapsed until Lionel and a number of other writers revived it in 1977 by getting it to defy the apartheid barrier and accept black members 'so that [white and black writers] could learn to know each other, learn from each other, and support and protect each other in resistance to the ravages of censorship and police bullying'.

The new nonracial PEN was successful, at first. Meetings – part poetry readings, part jam sessions – were held in townships, and white PEN members defied the laws that required them to obtain permits to enter a township.[62]

---

61 De Waal, Shaun: Fighting poet, 4 June 2004, *Mail & Guardian*
62 Lelyveld, Joseph: Breakup of a Community, 17 May 1981, *The New York Times*

The security police didn't pounce because they probably realised they would have looked ridiculous raiding poetry readings.

Lionel became increasingly outspoken at what he viewed as the rise of political motivations at the expense of literary standards by PEN members. He criticised 'political rhetoric' for masquerading as poetry. He, in turn, was denigrated by many for being either naive or elitist (or both). They argued that the message was more important than the art, but Lionel remained steadfast in his insistence on literary standards. He took a stand against political sloganeering.

As Anne Pogrund noted: 'Taking a stand against the injustice in South Africa was basically a simple black-and-white issue, but sometimes, standing up for liberal values, as Lionel did, demanded its own brand of courage and defiance.'[63]

Just as Bosman had inspired him, he inspired many aspirant writers. Bosman, according to Lionel, had fostered in him 'a capacity to find a proud, celebratory pleasure in the discovery of new talent'.[64]

Lionel helped writers get published and became a much-sought-after literary guru.

He held creative-writing workshops where aspiring authors would bring their work to be discussed, analysed and dissected.

According to the writer Jillian Becker, Lionel's loyalty was always unwaveringly to the work, which meant he was a rigorous critic.

'But though his criticism was unsparing, it was delivered with such concern for the work, respect for the effort and desire to bring out the best from the writer that none felt deterred, let alone offended, when it was adverse. Because he was effortlessly sweet-tempered, those who submitted their work to his judgment could be left feeling almost as complimented when he faulted it as when he praised it.'[65]

He took on huge amounts of work – poring over manuscripts – and never accepted payment. As he got older, his mobility deteriorated and eventually he became wheelchair bound.

---

63   Pogrund, Anne: Lionel Abrahams: Mischievous guru of South African letters, *Independent*, 10 October 2011

64   Abrahams, Lionel: The Purple Renoster: An Adolescence, English in Africa, Vol 7, #2, Rhodes University, September 1980

65   Becker, Jillian: Lionel Abrahams: A Voice For This Season, New English Review, October 2020

Lionel was a generous reader, a powerful poet, a writer's writer, and a wise and witty presence in South Africa's literary world. He had a remarkable intellect. Above all, though, he was profoundly humane. 'It was his humanness,' noted Anne, 'that he imparted as a teacher, editor and critic to the innumerable writers and artists whose work he influenced. His humanity infused and lifted whatever he did in his life.'[66]

As his friend David Friedland wrote, Lionel knew he would never run, but he believed he could fly.

Achievements and awards

Lionel Abrahams published several volumes of poetry: *Thresholds of Tolerance*, *Journal of a New Man*, *The Writer in the Sand* and *A Dead Tree Full of Live Birds*, as well as two novels: *The Celibacy of Felix Greenspan* and *The White Life of Felix Greenspan*. In addition to establishing *The Purple Renoster* and Renoster Press, he also edited the literary magazines *Bloody Horse* from 1979 to 1981 and *Sesame* from 1981 to 1992, and was a co-founder of Bateleur Press. He edited six volumes of Herman Charles Bosman's works and Ruth Miller's collected poems, and co-edited with Nadine Gordimer *South African Writing Today*. Lionel was awarded honorary doctorates from the universities of the Witwatersrand and Natal and received four prestigious literary prizes. Lionel met and fell in love with the writer Jane Fox and they got married in 1986. He died of kidney failure on 30 May 2004 at the age of 75.

---

66   Pogrund, Anne: Lionel Abrahams: Mischievous guru of South African letters, *Independent*, 10 October 2011

PURSUIT OF JUSTICE

CHAPTER 10

DENIS KUNY: AN ADVOCATE FOR HUMAN RIGHTS

Photograph: Nigel Sibanda, *The Citizen*

In a career that spanned almost six decades, human rights advocate Denis Kuny was involved in many momentous political trials. However, he also took on all sorts of cases that no one has heard of, defending untold ordinary people charged with a range of offences – from pass law breaches to high treason. He did them all without any publicity. Denis was in the trenches from the beginning of the struggle years right until the dawn of democracy. He also once had a most extraordinary chauffeur.

When I was a boy, my father, Bernard Ancer, an advocate at the Johannesburg Bar, would occasionally take me with him to his office on the 10th floor of Innes Chambers, opposite the Supreme Court (now the High Court).

Most of my time there was spent in the bathroom playing with the liquid soap dispenser. I would walk down the passage and see the names of the other lawyers stencilled onto their office doors: Adv M Horwitz SC, Adv J Browde SC, Adv D Kuny SC. The advocates behind the stencilled names would greet me cheerfully when they encountered me (usually in the bathroom).

It was only many years later that I realised that while I was playing with the soap dispenser, these lawyers were quietly and courageously taking on the might of the apartheid government: challenging discriminatory laws, protecting the vulnerable, exposing human rights atrocities, and engaging in lawfare in an attempt to hold the government to account – an impossible task.

My father's speciality was medical and personal injury cases, but he was also involved in political trials and was part of the legal team that defended the Soweto 11 – the young men and women accused of inciting the 1976 rebellion.

The case, which lasted eight months, made a big impact on our family. News about the trial's twists and turns dominated our dinner conversations, and my oldest sister Judith made cards and baked cakes for the accused on their birthdays.

About 15 years after the trial – sometime in the early 1990s – my father and I were walking in downtown Johannesburg when a voice from behind bellowed out, 'Bernard! Bernard!' We turned around. A bald, stocky man with a massive grin gripped my father in a bear hug.

My father beamed back as he accepted the embrace.

The man was the Soweto 11's Accused Number 4, Maffison 'Murphy' Morobe. The accused had been found guilty of sedition and received a range of sentences. Murphy was sent to Robben Island for three years. After he was released, he helped to establish the United Democratic Front.

When I saw Murphy and my father hug, I realised the incredible bond that lawyers and their clients had during the dark days of apartheid. Lawyers were often the only thing standing between the political activist and a lifetime behind bars (or worse, dangling from the business end of the hangman's rope).

Jewish lawyers were well represented in South Africa's human rights cases. Courageous attorneys and advocates such as Sydney Kentridge and his wife Felicia, Joel Joffe, Jules Browde, Ruth Hayman, Geoff Budlender, Gilbert Marcus, Isie Maisels, Shulamith Muller, George Lowen, Harold Hanson, Nat Levy, Harry Schwarz, Raymond Tucker and Arthur Chaskalson were involved in just about every high-profile political trial during the apartheid years.

However, if you asked any of these legal titans to single out one lawyer who personified the pursuit of justice, they would say Denis Kuny.

'He never got the credit for the contribution he made,' says Judge Dennis Davis. 'He did case after bloody case and was a very effective advocate. I've always had the greatest admiration for him.'

Before we enter the courtroom, let's go to a street in the Johannesburg suburb of Yeoville in 1962. This was where a secret meeting had been arranged. Denis wore his fanciest suit and tie and did his best impression of a wealthy businessman.

His Ford Anglia was a wreck, so, to look the part, he had borrowed a more suitable car from Arthur Chaskalson, his friend and colleague. Denis had been at the Bar for six years, but what he was about to do could have put him behind bars. A man in a uniform and wearing a chauffeur's cap emerged from the shadows and got behind the steering wheel.

Denis's driver was the country's most wanted man – Nelson Mandela, the commander of the ANC's recently formed armed wing, uMkhonto we Sizwe (MK). The security police were looking for Mandela, who had been dubbed the Black Pimpernel. Unbeknown to them, he was hiding out at Liliesleaf Farm in Rivonia.

Mandela had slipped out of South Africa to undergo military training and to drum up support for the armed struggle from African leaders. After his return, he needed to go to Ladysmith to brief the ANC leadership there. SA Communist Party leader and lawyer Joe Slovo told Mandela he would find someone sympathetic and reliable to help him. Slovo asked Denis.

'I sat in the back of the car and Mandela drove me,' recalls Denis 60 years after the trip.[67] 'It was just the two of us. I wasn't involved in

---

67   Interview with Denis Kuny, May 2021. Additional information from a transcript of an interview with Denis for the Legal Resources Centre's Oral

the political movement, so we didn't talk much.' The pair arrived in Ladysmith four hours later. Mandela went to meet his comrades and Denis turned the car around and made his way home again.

Denis would meet Mandela again. This time, after having served 27 years in prison, Mandela was driving the country's reconciliation process.

'There was a dinner function for lawyers, and Mandela was conducted around the table saying hello to people, and when he came to me, he gave me a knowing look,' says Denis.

Denis hadn't always intended to be a lawyer. He had thought he would follow in his father's footsteps and become a doctor. Denis, who was born in 1932, grew up in Edenville, a small farming town in the Free State, where his father was the GP. When he was five, his family moved to Springs, east of Johannesburg.

'My father Benjamin Isaac came from a Russian family who had settled in South Africa. His elder brother went to Scotland to qualify as a doctor and then came to South Africa at the time of the plague that swept the world in 1919. He went to Cape Town, contracted the virus and died. My father had qualified as a lawyer, and when his brother died, he switched from being a lawyer to a doctor,' explains Denis.

In 1924 Benjamin Kuny was one of the four first students to qualify from the Wits Medical School.

Denis had been part of the progressive Jewish community and had spent summers as a teen at the reform-shul camps, which is where he befriended Joel Joffe. Joel and Denis studied law together, and Joel would go on to become one of Mandela's lawyers in the Rivonia Treason Trial.

Denis switched from wanting to become a doctor to studying law when he saw how his father worked day and night and weekends and holidays.

He qualified as an attorney, got married and started a family, and moved to London, where he taught sports and music. After a year the family came back home, and Denis decided to become an advocate.

History Project, July 2008 and Ebrahim, Shannon: Denis Kuny: Unsung hero, IOL, 17 March 2019

Denis says he wandered into human rights law by accident. 'Political cases descended on me,' he shrugs.

'I arrived back in February 1960 and the Sharpeville Massacre happened on 21 March 1960. And then [prime minister Hendrik] Verwoerd was shot at the Rand Easter Show on 9 April. He survived but all hell broke loose politically. All sorts of legislation came in at that stage,' recalls Denis.

A state of emergency was declared, and some people who Denis had become friendly with, like Slovo and Ivan Schermbrucker, were arrested for being members of the banned SA Communist Party.

'I got involved in appearing for them at these trials. There was a lot of political work, including smaller things like people painting slogans. People got into trouble for objecting to the situation and I just automatically became involved in a lot of those cases. There was no conscious decision or awakening, it was gradual,' he says.

Soon after his and Mandela's trip to Ladysmith, Mandela, who was pretending to be a chauffeur for the activist Cecil Williams, was arrested near Howick and charged with leaving the country without a passport and inciting workers to strike. He was sentenced to five years' imprisonment. A few weeks after he was moved to Robben Island, the police raided Liliesleaf Farm and rounded up the leaders of MK. Mandela was brought back from the island to stand trial with his comrades.

The defence in the Rivonia Trial consisted of Joel Joffe, Bram Fischer, Vernon Berrangé, Arthur Chaskalson, George Bizos and Denis, the last surviving lawyer of the most important trial in South Africa's history. In fact, Denis is the last living link to the trial – the accused, the judge, the members of the defence and the members of the prosecution have all died.

Denis appeared for Accused Number 8, Jimmy Kantor, who has gone down in history as the trial's accidental accused.

Harold Wolpe, a leading figure in the SA Communist Party, had set up practice with Jimmy, his brother-in-law, who was a sought-after divorce lawyer. Harold had been arrested in the police raid on Liliesleaf and, with Arthur Goldreich and two others, had managed to escape.

'A movie should be made about their escape,' grins Denis.

Denis would have a cameo role in the movie.

After escaping from the Marshall Square police cells, Harold and Arthur simply walked into Hillbrow. They came to a park where, coincidentally, the writer, playwright and director Barney Simon, who had been driving home, stopped for a pee. Barney didn't know what to do with the two fugitives, so he took them to his flat and went to seek help from Denis, with whom he was friendly.

'I followed Barney to his flat and found them there,' says Denis. 'They looked like criminals at large, which of course they were. I went to Ivan Schermbrucker's house, and I told Ivan what had happened, and he took over from there.'

According to Denis, after the Rivonia raid, Jimmy had then gone to Liliesleaf 'to feed the chickens or something', and was picked up and put on trial only because he was in partnership with Harold.

'There was actually no case against Jimmy,' states Denis, who had teamed up with George Lowen and Harry Schwarz to defend Jimmy.

Harry and George were brilliant lawyers who courageously fought apartheid. Another thing they had in common was that they both fled Nazi Germany. Interviewed in 1991, Harry stated that, 'I know what the word "discrimination" means, not because I've read it in a book, but because I've been the subject of it.'

George, a much sought after Jewish lawyer in Berlin in the early 1930s, had taken on members of the Nazi Party in court and was preparing the defence of those charged with setting the Reichstag fire of 1933 when he was warned that the Gestapo was coming for him. He fled Germany and arrived in South Africa in 1935. He spoke no English when he landed in Johannesburg, and worked as a petrol pump jockey to fund language school and legal training.[68][69]

George was a suave lawyer and dynamic orator, who took on victims of the Group Areas Act. One of his most memorable cases involved Harold Rubin, a jazz musician and artist charged with blasphemy for his artwork, titled My Jesus, of a crucified figure in which he had replaced the words 'Father forgive them for they know not what they do' with 'I forgive you, O Lord, for you know not what you do' – a direct accusation against the Christian God. If convicted, Harold faced nine years in jail. George argued successfully for the

---

[68] Lowen, Mark: George Lowen: From refugee to black rights champion, BBC, 8 September 2013

[69] George Lowen appeared in many political cases and represented the Ngudle family at the inquest of ANC activist Looksmart Ngudle, the first person to die in detention. George died in 1969

right to artistic freedom, and after a protracted trial that drew international attention, Harold was acquitted. He then left the country in disgust and settled in Israel.

Reflecting on absurd censorship situations during the apartheid era, the actress Janet Suzman recalled the country's censors banning a children's musical based on Bible stories titled *Holy Moses and All That Jazz*, which was being put on by the Market Theatre.[70]

'[The Market Theatre] was defended by Denis Kuny, who was an accomplished jazz musician in his spare time,' wrote Janet.

'The major premise of the banning was the title; the censors held that association with jazz denigrated Moses. You have to remember that we were living under Calvinist rule. When it became clear that the Market was heading for another victory, the chairman of the appeal board asked Kuny if the theatre could please consider another title without the word "jazz". Which is when Kuny launched into a short history of the great musical art form, to waves of applause from the audience. When he turned dramatically to the board at the end of his highly informed peroration, the chairman had to concede that the case was won.'

Meanwhile, back at the Rivonia Trial: Denis left the case after a series of eavesdropping incidents.

At a tea break during Jimmy Kantor's bail application, Denis had overheard members of the Special Branch talking about how they were going to make sure Jimmy didn't get bail. Denis commented to his colleagues that the police would stop at nothing – and were even prepared to commit perjury – to keep Jimmy in jail. The Special Branch in turn overheard him and reported what he had said to the chief prosecutor, Percy Yutar.

'Instead of Yutar confronting me with this "accusation", he stood up in court and told the judge I had been spreading stories about the police,' says Denis, who still bristles at the prosecutor's behaviour more than half a century later.

Denis, whose friends describe him as mild-mannered and a lawyer who isn't easily ruffled, lost his temper. 'It got really ugly,' he recalls.

---

70 Suzman, Janet: Stage directions in South Africa: Post-apartheid theatre, Index on Censorship, Vol 43, issue 2, 11 June 2014

The atmosphere between Denis and Yutar was so fraught that the defence team felt it would be better if Denis left the trial, which he did.

Although Denis was out of the Rivonia Trial, it wasn't long before he was back in court – for the sequel to State versus Mandela and Nine Others. This time, in a case where the leader of the Rivonia Trial's defence team, Bram Fischer, was in the dock.

Soon after the Rivonia accused were carted off to prison, the security police began rounding up activists who were then charged with membership of the SA Communist Party and furthering the aims of communism.

The trial that followed was known as the State versus Fischer and Thirteen Others. One of the others was Norman Levy, who had this to say about Denis and the other lawyers who represented them: 'We trusted them with our lives and will always remember them for the passion with which they defended us.'[71]

The trial identified Denis as a lawyer for the Communist Party, although he was never a communist or a member of any political party.

Denis defended anti-apartheid combatants who had left the country for military training and were arrested on their return. He was involved in trials of banned and house-arrested activists charged with breaking their orders.

One trial involved Mary Turok, who had been banned from attending gatherings.

'One day there was a political gathering in the streets of central Johannesburg,' recalls Denis. 'Mary stood on the other side of the road watching and listening. She was charged with "attending" that gathering. Her presence across the road was found to constitute attendance and she was convicted!'

Among the political elite Denis represented were Black Consciousness activist Mamphela Ramphele, former health minister Barbara Hogan, former Gauteng premier-turned-reality TV host-turned-conspiracy theorist Tokyo Sexwale, and ANC activist-turned-fraudster and Jacob Zuma praise-singer Carl Niehaus.

---

71 Levy, Norman: The Final Prize, SA History Online, Cape Town, October 2010

Denis defended members of the Pan Africanist Congress; the 'Nusas 5' (university students and a lecturer accused of treason); trade unionist Alan Fine; journalism academic Guy Berger; and Helene Pastoors, a Belgian national who joined the ANC's armed struggle. He also represented the family of trade unionist Neil Aggett at the inquest into Neil's suspicious death in custody, and he defended Black Consciousness leader Steve Biko.

Denis's involvement with Biko happened after he had appeared for a number of black pupils who were charged with burning down a school in the Eastern Cape in protest against the government's Bantu Education policy.

'Various people had given evidence against these so-called arsonists,' notes Denis. 'All the children, who were 13 and 14, got into the box and, without fail, denied knowing anything about it. What the State thought was going to be a good prosecution turned out to be a complete failure. Subsequently Biko was charged with defeating the ends of justice because the State claimed he had induced the kids to lie about the fire. At his trial, all the kids denied that Biko had induced them to lie, and he was acquitted. A month later, Biko was dead.'

Denis himself was also a target for assassination – although the details remain murky.

'Geoff Budlender found a document that suggested I be knocked off in Botswana,' says Denis.

He confronted the intended assassin, Special Branch member-turned-whistleblower Dirk Coetzee, but he denied any knowledge of it.

Denis eventually retired from practising in 2018, when he was 85 years old, with a reputation as one of the country's most skilled and dedicated anti-apartheid lawyers.

For more than half a century Denis has dedicated his life to justice, and his contribution to the country's march towards freedom has been immense – yet he remains humble about his vast legal accomplishments.

When I contacted him to arrange an interview for this project, he told me he wasn't sure he fitted the bill.

The fact that he doesn't think he belongs in a book of unsung human rights champions is the very reason he belongs in a book of unsung human rights champions.

Denis died on 25 October 2021 just before the book went to print. He was 89 years old.

CHAPTER 11

MADIBA'S LAWYERS

To reflect on the impact of Jewish lawyers in the anti-apartheid cause, we just have to look at the many legal heavyweights who made an impact on Nelson Mandela's life.

The attorney Lazer Sidelsky employed and mentored Mandela, while another lawyer at the law firm, Nat Bregman, shared his sandwiches with the future president and insisted on using the 'blacks only' elevator with him in the building.

Mandela described Nat as his first white friend, and said Lazer was the first white man to treat him with respect.

Lazer encouraged Mandela to complete his law studies at Wits University. On the first day of lectures, Mandela, the only black person in the class, sat down between two students. One of them, Ballie de Klerk, a famed rugby player and National Party supporter, got up to find another seat because he refused to sit next to a black man. The other student was Jules Browde, and he and Mandela established a warm and enduring friendship.

Jewish lawyers defended Mandela in the two high-profile trials in which he was an accused. The 1956-1961 Treason Trial defence team was headed by Isie Maisels, who came on board in 1958 when the trial proper began, and also featured the remarkable Sydney Kentridge.

Mandela and the accused in the 1964 Rivonia Trial had in their corner Denis Kuny, Joel Joffe, Nat Levy and Arthur Chaskalson, the first head of South Africa's Constitutional Court.

Here are short profiles of three giants of South Africa's legal world: Isie Maisels, Sydney Kentridge and Arthur Chaskalson, who have all been honoured by the South African Jewish Board of Deputies. Arthur was the first-ever recipient of the SAJBD Human Rights Award[72] in 1999 and Isie and Sir Sydney received the Human Rights Award at the SAJBD's centenary conference in 2003. Isie received it posthumously and Sir Sydney accepted in person.

Take it Easy, Isie

An iconic South African photograph shows Isie Maisels being triumphantly carried shoulder high outside court after the conclusion of the 1956 Treason Trial. All the accused had been found not guilty of plotting to take over the country. The men are grinning and giving the black power salute. Isie, who had just emerged from the 'Non-European Only Entrance', has a shy grin.

'The only weapon we had was to fight by law, and we used every legal stratagem which we were entitled to do,' Isie said in an interview.

In a tribute to her father in 2020, Helen Maisels Trisk recalls how Mandela and the other accused in the trial came to consult with Isie at the Maisels family home in Houghton.[73]

Helen revealed some of the family's treasures, which include a Rosh Hashanah card signed by Mandela on behalf of the accused.

Isie was an observant Jew who was actively engaged in the community and served as chairperson of the SA Jewish Board of Deputies, Federation of Synagogues and the SA Zionist Federation.

The card goes alongside two other pieces of memorabilia: a 1961 letter signed by the trial accused when they heard that Isie had accepted an appointment to the bench in the then Rhodesia, and a card that Mandela sent from Pollsmoor Prison to Isie on his 80th birthday in 1985. The message from Madiba reads: 'Take it easy, Isie!'

In 2002, at the naming ceremony of Maisels Chambers in Sandton, Mandela said: '[Isie] defended us at considerable cost to himself. He was a giant of the legal profession, respected and admired as a great lawyer. Let us honour him for his leadership and courage

---

72 The SAJBD Human Rights Award was renamed the Rabbi Cyril & Ann Harris Human Rights Award in 2015

73 Maisels Trisk, Helen: Maisels and his 'most famous client', *SA Jewish Report*, 16 July 2020

and generosity of spirit. Only someone of the calibre of Isie Maisels could help us go forward. He served justice with distinction. His name will always be remembered by all our people.'

Isie emerged into prominence in 1932 as junior counsel to the great Harry Morris KC in the case of notorious serial killer Daisy de Melker, who was charged with poisoning her two husbands and her son.

In addition to the Treason Trial, he acted in other important political cases, such as the Ahmed Timol inquest, David Pratt's attempted assassination of prime minister Hendrik Verwoerd in 1960, many Group Areas Act cases and the farm labour prison scheme case. He was a judge in the then Rhodesia as well as president of the Court of Appeal of Botswana-Lesotho-Swaziland.[74]

In the foreword to Isie's memoir, *A Life At Law*, Sir Sydney Kentridge describes Isie's power as a cross-examiner.

'In some uncanny way Isie would, from the outset, achieve domination over the unfortunate witness, which usually enabled him to extract exactly the answers he wanted. A prime example of this was his cross-examination of Professor Andrew Murray, the prosecution's expert on communism in the Treason Trial. In that instance he used a weapon of cross-examination which young advocates are not advised to imitate, but which could be deadly in Isie's hands – good-natured humour at the expense of the discomfited witness. All in all, I have never seen Isie's equal as a cross-examiner in any jurisdiction in which I have practised.'

Sir Sydney added that Isie was a lawyer, not a politician, but his fierce detestation of apartheid was plain to see. 'Time and again he appeared in the courts to vindicate the rights of the individual against the oppression of the apartheid state. The reader may learn from Isie's life in the law what it is that goes to make a truly great advocate – legal learning, eloquence combined with lucidity, wise judgment, but above all, courage. We are fortunate to have had him among us.'

Isie retired in 1992, when he was 87. He died two years later. Mandela came to prayers and wore one of Isie's yarmulkes.

---

74 Suttner, Immanuel: *Cutting Through the Mountain*, Viking, 1997

Good Knight

Born into a liberal Jewish family in Johannesburg in 1922, Sydney Kentridge's father Morris Kantrovitch, later changed to Kentridge, served as an MP from 1914 to 1958, initially for the Labour Party and later for the United Party. Morris fought for workers' rights. He was also a strong voice in parliament against antisemitism, opposing the anti-Jewish immigration laws of the 1930s and fighting South Africa's pro-Nazi agitators.

Sir Sydney has won international fame (and a knighthood) for his work as a human rights lawyer – although he has also practised just about every form of law, including murder trials, corporate takeovers, media law, labour law and constitutional law. He had successful careers in both South Africa and England.

Sir Sydney marked his 90th birthday in 2013 at the UK Supreme Court, where he represented the Law Society in a constitutional case.

He was admitted to the Johannesburg Bar in 1949 (after having served with the South African forces in World War II) and became a senior counsel in 1965.

He has represented three Nobel Prize winners in court – Nelson Mandela, Chief Albert Luthuli and Archbishop Emeritus Desmond Tutu.

In an interview in 2013 shortly before he retired at the age of 90, Sir Sydney recalled a warning he received from a fellow defence lawyer concerning the struggle to win cases for black clients in front of politically appointed judges in apartheid South Africa.[75]

'He said: "When you're doing one of these [ANC] terrorism cases, you can be certain of three things. First, the witnesses have all been assaulted, or threatened with assault, by the police. Secondly, any statement made to the police by the accused has been obtained by torture. And thirdly, your client is guilty".'

The journalist asked Sir Sydney if it wasn't demoralising to work in a country where the odds were so stacked against him and his clients.

'You had to do what you could,' he responded.

---

75 Gapper, John: Lunch with the FT: Sydney Kentridge, *Financial Times*, 18 January 2013

And Sir Sydney did. He was a leading member of the defence team that successfully defended the accused in the 1956-1961 Treason Trial.

'All the accused were simply acquitted,' Sir Sydney told the *SA Jewish Report*.[76] 'Of course, I and the other members of the defence team felt elated about it. It was the most political of trials in a highly politicised country, but it showed that the judiciary was still completely independent. It was a great day for the South African justice system.'

Sir Sydney represented Ambrose Reeves, the Anglican dean of Johannesburg, as well as the Sharpeville community at the inquiry into the Sharpeville Massacre in 1960. He defended his colleague, SA Communist Party leader Bram Fischer, who was charged with furthering the aims of communism and conspiracy to overthrow the government, and journalist Benjamin Pogrund, who was charged under the Prisons Act for his *Rand Daily Mail* exposé of the dire conditions in the country's prisons.

Perhaps Sir Sydney's most well-known case was when he appeared for Steve Biko's family at the inquest into the death of the Black Consciousness leader in custody in 1977.

'There is indisputable evidence that Mr Biko went into the interrogation room alive and well … [but] he came out a physical and mental wreck. He died a miserable and lonely death on a cold prison floor,' he told the inquest.

Despite destroying the police's version of events, the magistrate wasn't prepared to make findings against the police and ruled that Biko had died of unknown causes, and no one was to blame.

The inquest was widely reported in England and the United States, and played an important role in revealing to the world what was happening in South Africa.

The inquest was made into a play, and the role of Sir Sydney was played first by Ian McKellen and then by Albert Finney.

'It was very, very odd to hear my actual words uttered by Finney and to have him standing on the stage when the magistrate on the stage called him Mr Kentridge, it was very odd indeed,' Sir Sydney

---

76 Moshe, Jordan: Sir Sydney Kentridge: real-life hero at the bar, *SA Jewish Report*, 7 December 2020

stated in a 2008 interview for the British Library's oral history project Legal Lives.

He was called to the English Bar in 1977 and seven years later was appointed Queen's Counsel. Sir Sydney is widely regarded as one of the world's most eminent advocates and was awarded a knighthood for his contributions to international law and justice.

'I thought it was a great day when I went to Buckingham Palace and was knighted by the Queen with a tap on the shoulder with a sword. I remember telling one of my grandchildren that the Queen taps you on the shoulder with a sword, and the question I got from her was, "Isn't that very dangerous?"' he told the *SA Jewish Report* after receiving the Lifetime Achievement Award at the Absa Jewish Achiever Awards in 2020.

Sir Sydney said receiving the award from the Jewish community was 'very unexpected'.

'I certainly value it, coming as it does from Johannesburg, which was my hometown for many years before I came to England. I had my barmitzvah at the Yeoville shul, and my late wife and I were married in the Wolmarans shul. I have a very Johannesburg Jewish background, which I greatly value.'

King Arthur

Arthur Chaskalson saved Nelson Mandela's life when he and the rest of the accused in the Rivonia Trial were spared the death penalty. Nevertheless, Mandela would jokingly introduce him by saying: 'Here is my lawyer, he managed to secure me 27 years in prison.'

Arthur was born in Johannesburg on 24 November 1931.[77] His parents were Lithuanian Jews who owned a mattress company. When he was four, his father died from a heart attack, and for most of his early childhood he was raised by his mother, who was active in Jewish charities. After matriculating he studied commerce and

---

77 Information on Arthur based on articles in *Jewish Affairs* (Davis, Dennis: Jewish Contributions to law in South Africa, Vol. 71, #2, Rosh Hashanah 2016); *The New York Times* (Martin, Douglas: Arthur Chaskalson, Chief South African Jurist, Dies at 81, 3 December 2012); GroundUp (Budlender, Geoff: A tribute to Arthur Chaskalson, 18 December 2012); and the Constitutional Court and the Constitution Hill Trust websites

law degrees at Wits, where he spoke out against the banning of black students from attending the annual Bar dinner.

It was during his university years that he cemented his view that there was a difference between law and justice.

Arthur established a flourishing commercial practice at the Johannesburg Bar, dividing his work between corporate clients and political trials. He shot to prominence when he joined the defence team for the Rivonia Trial, where leaders of the ANC were convicted of sabotage and sentenced to life imprisonment.

In 1979, at the height of his career as a senior counsel, Arthur left the lucrative world of corporate law to head the Legal Resources Centre to challenge apartheid laws and defend justice and human rights. The centre, which started out with a staff of two, became one of the world's most impressive public interest law organisations.

The litigation-driven centre concentrated on what Arthur called the 'impact laws'. Its first success was in the cases of Veli Komani and Mehlolo Tom Rikhotso, which challenged the legality of apartheid legislation seeking to establish influx control and pass laws, policies that resulted in a widespread breakdown of the family life of black South Africans.

In a tribute to Arthur, fellow advocate Geoff Budlender described his colleague as an advocate of extraordinary skill and spoke about the Komani case as an example of Arthur's legal weapons – precise and remorseless logic.

'He was, quite simply, the best arguer of a case that I have ever heard. I remember the Komani case in the Appellate Division in 1980. Mr and Mrs Komani had a simple yet profound desire. They wanted to live together. The pass laws forbade it. The law was plain, and it was against them. Arthur constructed a brilliant and novel argument which was so persuasive that Chief Justice Rumpff – hostile from the outset – became frustrated: "I think you are leading us down the garden path," he said to Arthur. But he couldn't find a flaw in the argument, because there was none. Ultimately, the Appellate Division unanimously decided in favour of Mr and Mrs Komani. It was the finest advocacy I have ever heard.'

Further victories followed over the administration of the Group Areas Act.

In a speech to the New York City Bar Association in 1985, Arthur noted that he was a double outsider in South Africa: not only was he not an Afrikaner, he was Jewish, which, he explained, helped him to identify with the powerless.

In 1989 he was a consultant in the drafting of a constitution for Namibia, and he then helped to write South Africa's constitution.

After the 1994 elections, Nelson Mandela asked Arthur to head the new Constitutional Court.

'The last time I was in court was to hear whether or not I was going to be sentenced to death,' Mandela said at Arthur's inauguration.

The court's first major decision was to abolish the death penalty.

Arthur served as judge president until 2001, when the title changed to chief justice, and swore in President Thabo Mbeki at his inauguration in 1999. When Arthur retired in 2005, Mbeki called him a giant among the architects of SA's democracy and thanked him for his role as a lawyer, judge and South African in shepherding the nation into a place where all citizens belong.

Arthur died on 1 December 2012 at the age of 81.

In a tribute to Arthur, former Constitutional Court judge Kate O'Regan said: 'Most memorable of all was his integrity. Arthur Chaskalson was that rare person whose values were reflected in everything he did. His commitment to using law as a means to achieve justice and a better life for all shone brightly in every sphere of his life.'

CHAPTER 12
CHOOSING TO BE PART OF THE SOLUTION

Human rights lawyer Ilan Lax's experiences of antisemitism as a child and his brother's spell in detention were important factors that made him want to stand up for the underdog and use the law to fight injustice.

CHOOSING TO BE PART OF THE SOLUTION

A student called Les Lax was among a group of Wits University activists who had formed an SA Communist Party cell and made posters celebrating the party's 60th anniversary. One of the students was arrested for putting up posters at a bus shelter, which led to the whole group being nabbed by the security police.

'Les spent seven months in solitary confinement,' says his brother Ilan.

'The family didn't want to tell my bobba that Les had been detained, worrying about how she would react. She kept asking me, "Where's Les? Why isn't he coming to visit me?"' Ilan remembers.

'Eventually, I said bugger this, I'm going to tell her the truth. I told her, and my bobba looked at me and said, "Well, what's the big deal? I was secretary of the local communist party in Lithuania and I was arrested too. What's the big story, you know, that everyone's afraid to tell me this is what's happening to my grandson?"'

Les was finally brought to trial and, after entering into a plea bargain with the state, served a further 10 days and was released. He finished his studies and went into exile.

'And that was the end of it,' says Ilan.

But for Ilan, Les's detention was just the beginning. It was one more reason for him to devote his life to human rights law.

Ilan's parents Mervyn and Dina met at the Hashomer Hatzair youth movement and made aliyah in 1955. 'I was born in Israel in 1956 on Kibbutz Nachshon, which my parents helped to start. Then my dad got very ill and they returned to South Africa.'

Ilan's maternal grandparents were from Lithuania and came to South Africa in 1928. His mother was born in Standerton in 1936.

Ilan's paternal grandparents were middle-class South African Jews. His great grandfather arrived at the Cape from England in 1878.

'They kept their heads down,' says Ilan. 'My grandmother was one of those travelling salesladies for Edgars. She would go from factory to factory, selling goods on appro. I remember in one of my school holidays going with my bobba in her little Ford Prefect to factories around Judith's Paarl, Troyeville and Mayfair.'

According to Ilan, the family weren't political but there was a strong sense of the importance of doing the right thing, treating people fairly and not saying racist things.

'What made me much more politicised was being subjected to lots of antisemitism as a kid at boarding school,' he explains.

Ilan's parents got divorced when he was five.

'Initially, we lived with my bobba and zaida in Bez Valley, and then moved to a flat in Hillbrow. I guess that for my mom, bringing up two boys as a single parent must have been tough, so sending us to boarding school was safer than having us mixing it up on the streets of Hillbrow.'

Ilan was eight and Les six when they went to boarding school. 'I was called "Jewboy" the whole time. The antisemitism was overt and the people told silly jokes to reinforce that you're not the same as them.'

Ilan matriculated in 1973 and worked as a stoker on steam engines in Durban in the six months between finishing school and going to the army in July 1974. It made him aware of job reservation because only white people could be stokers in those days.

'The propaganda we were fed in the army was so over the top that, for me, it was counterproductive and made me question everything. I'd see how the coloured guys were being treated and think that if these guys are prepared to fight for the country and they're being treated like rubbish, then there's something wrong.'

After completing his national service Ilan went to university in Durban to study a part-time law degree and simultaneously do articles at a law firm. However, he was unhappy at the firm and didn't like the ethos of corporate law.

'I had a bit of a meltdown, so I quit and wandered around for six months, thinking about what I might do. I tried a range of different things and eventually came to the realisation that I wanted to do law, just not corporate law. I wanted to focus on human rights.'

Ilan went to Pietermaritzburg in 1979, completed his degree in 1983 and managed to get a position as a clerk with one of the foremost liberal lawyers in Natal, Les Weinberg, to complete his articles.

'Les took me under his wing and I was articled to a very liberal lawyer called Pat Stilwell. I felt at home with the two of them. It was just the sort of work I wanted to do. Much of what I did was supporting organisations that were doing work in land rights issues.'

Ilan also defended anti-apartheid activists who were involved in various 'subversive' activities, such as possessing banned literature, and he acted for the Detainees' Parents Support Committee. Lawyers were the only people allowed to visit detainees.

'For example, I'd get a phone call to say the security police had raided the [education NGO] Sached office. I'd ask the police what they were doing, who they were arresting and why. Then I'd let the families know they were being detained. I wasn't involved in any famous cases, none that made headlines, just hundreds of little cases of ordinary people being detained left, right and centre, and of people being charged.'

Ilan kept copies of records from the Association For Rural Advancement, a land rights group focused on rural and farmworkers' rights, and the Detainees' Parents Support Committee, because even though the security police were a law unto themselves, they wouldn't dare raid an attorney's office.

'The security police appeared to have a grudging respect for attorneys. I think part of it relates to this idea that if you want people to respect your society, there are certain boundaries you can't cross publicly, even if they had this seriously twisted view of what a reasonable society entailed. The authorities wanted to be considered decent and law-abiding.'

When a protest march was planned, Ilan would apply for permits on behalf of the protesters. The permit would be denied and the march would happen anyway.

'My job was to negotiate with the police, keep them talking long enough for the march to happen and for everyone to disperse so nobody got arrested. If people did get arrested, I would attempt to negotiate their release on bail and the eventual withdrawal of charges. It was those kinds of strategies that I would do, week in and week out.'

Another strategy Ilan and his colleagues adopted could have come straight from the 'People's Front of Judea – Judean People's Front' skit in Monty Python's *Life of Brian*. When an organisation was banned, the members simply launched a new one and called it by a different name.

Ilan explains: 'When they banned the Detainees' Parents Support Committee we just renamed it something like the Detainees Aid Committee and carried on. And when that was banned we changed the name slightly and continued.'

The Security Branch knew who Ilan was and would try to intimidate him by walking up to him in public and saying, 'Hello, Ilan Lax, I know who you are and I know what you're up to.'

Ilan decided to beat them at their own game, so he found out information about some of the security policemen and used the same tactic on them.

'Mike Smuts was one of the local security cops. He didn't know that I knew who he was, and so the next time he greeted me and said "Hello, Ilan Lax" I responded by saying "Hello, Michael Smuts, I know what you're up to". After a while we started greeting each other normally and they left me alone.'

In 1986 Ilan and two friends started their own law firm, Volsum, Chetty & Lax.

'We funded our work by cross-subsidisation. We did ordinary commercial law to pay for the political work. We didn't care that we didn't have funding. We just did what we had to, and for the next 10 years I did human rights work of one kind or another.'

Ilan was commissioned by some of the big law firms in Johannesburg to hunt down witnesses and gather evidence.

'I'd interview mineworkers who'd been assaulted and whose friends had been killed. I'd be called in the middle of the night with a voice saying, "Ilan, we've got a witness. Can you hide him somewhere?" I would get in my car and head off into the dark, find the person in the township and take them to a safe place. It wasn't like all these huge and exceptional political cases, but looking back all these years later, it feels like it was something worth doing.'

Ilan was never arrested because he was careful not to overtly cross the line between being an activist and being a lawyer.

'I took the view that I was more valuable to my colleagues who were activists by remaining a lawyer, even though I supported everything they did. I knew that the minute I made myself vulnerable in that way, I couldn't help them anymore, so I never did anything patently underground.'

Battling the apartheid system took its toll, and Ilan had to be upbeat and resilient. 'But because I felt like I was part of a bigger movement, it didn't get me down much. I just got on with it.'

Ilan says he feels comfortable with what he tried to do in his life.

'Not in a complacent, pat-myself-on-the-back kind of way, because I'm sure I could have done more of this and more of that. I don't feel like I did the best I could, but I certainly didn't do the worst I could either.'

Ilan felt that as someone who was relatively privileged and who had benefited from a good education, he had a duty to contribute to the country and try to bring about change.

According to Ilan, when people are confronted with something that's patently wrong – like apartheid – the choice is either to practise a kind of cognitive dissonance or to get involved and do something. Ilan couldn't pretend that everything was okay.

'I guess that part of the conundrum of the Jewish community is that we've been victims for so long in so many ways, and so we're afraid to stick our necks out, but that's exactly what we have to do. That's the conundrum: by putting up with injustice, you either become a victim or you become part of the problem, but you don't become part of the solution. At some point we've got to choose to be part of the solution.'

SELMA & JULES

CHAPTER 13

THE BROWDE BRUNCH

When so many white South Africans buried their heads in the sand during the apartheid era, Jules and Selma Browde stuck their necks out. Selma made revolutionary advances as a radiation oncologist and advanced the revolution as an anti-apartheid activist. She brought electrification and basketball to Soweto, and established a host of community organisations, including Operation Hunger. Jules was one of SA's most admired advocates. According to former chief justice Ismail Mahomed, Jules was such a good lawyer that when lawyers needed a lawyer, they turned to him. His optimism was infectious, his generosity legendary and his integrity infinite.

My phone rang. 'Jonathan,' a gasping-rasping-breathless voice said.

'Yes,' I replied.

'I need you ... *wheeze-cough-splutter* ... to write my obituary.'

The voice belonged to Professor Selma Browde, who was phoning to say she couldn't make our interview because COVID had struck her down.[78] She was joking – not about COVID, but about my writing her obituary.

'It started off mildly *wheeze-cough-cough-gasp* but then it hit hard. You wake up in the morning *cough-cough* and think *wheeze-croak-cough-pant-gasp* you're okay, and then the next moment you feel terrible – so terrible. *Gasp!* It's a vicious beast. I've never been this ill.'

Selma had come to Cape Town for her great-grandson's birth, which coincided with the country's second wave in January 2021.

'Eight out of the nine of us have got it. For me it's okay; I'm 94, it's not important. It's something out of a science fiction novel,' she adds, 'and I don't like the author.'

Selma phoned later that day to say she had good news. An X-ray showed her lungs were clear, and although she was feeling weak, she could now concentrate on getting stronger.

'You won't have to write my obituary for a while,' she advised me.

Five months later, the recently vaccinated Selma and I managed to meet. While making me a cup of coffee using her 'secret' recipe

---

78 Phone call with Selma Browde on 5 January 2021

(Psst: she warms up the milk in the microwave before adding boiling water), she tells me she still experiences COVID 'brain fog'.[79]

Selma is extraordinary; she has had four full-time careers simultaneously: a doctor, a politician, a health activist and an academic.

In addition to her political and professional achievements, she's also the matriarch of the Browde Bunch (her fifth career, perhaps).

Selma is working on her memoir, and reads a quote by Bertrand Russell in which he summed up the three passions that governed his life: the longing for love, the search for knowledge, and his 'unbearable pity for the suffering of mankind'.

Selma plans to open her memoir with this quote because it fits her life too.

'From childhood I couldn't tolerate suffering. That's what dominated my life. It came naturally to me to worry about poor people, sick people, oppressed people. I can't bear people suffering, whether it's physical, emotional or psycho-social; any kind of suffering.'

Selma Meyer was born in Cape Town in 1926. Her father, a doctor, set up a practice in Maitland, which was then a coloured suburb in Cape Town. He was the only doctor who made house calls in Maitland, and Selma would often accompany him. His selfless service to poor people made a profound impact on her.

Growing up she read two very different books that affected her life dramatically.

The first was the *Socialist Sixth of the World* by the Dean of Canterbury, Hewlett Johnson – nicknamed the Red Dean of Canterbury because of his undying support for the Soviet Union.

---

79   Interview with Selma Browde on 3 June 2021 and additional information about Selma and Jules Browde from:

Browde, Daniel: *The Relatively Public Life of Jules Browde*, Johannesburg, Jonathan Ball, 2016

Chaskalson, Raphael: In conversation with Jules Browde, Aleh, November 2012

Minors, Deborah: Selma Browde: Passion and Compassion, Wits Review, October 2014

Romero, Patricia: Selma Browde: "Dear Colleagues, please come to a meeting", Profiles in Diversity: Women in the New South Africa, Michigan State University Press, 1998

Wits University honorary doctorate citations for Jules and Selma

Saks, David: Browde, legal and communal giant, passes on, *SA Jewish Report*, 1 June 2016

'I was 12 and I thought this was absolutely spot-on. This book became my bible. It described utopia. Communism promised everything. You could be a ballet dancer or an engineer, everything was open to you, and university was free. So I thought I was a communist,' Selma says.

The other one, *The Brown Book of the Reichstag Fire and Hitler Terror*, shook her to her core.

'It describes how Hitler's people, who weren't even in power yet, were going to all the Jewish households and torturing them. I still remember some of those tortures. I was terrified. I used to imagine being in a concentration camp in Cape Town and wonder how I would be tortured. It didn't make me a Zionist because, although I had a Jewish identity, I didn't believe in religion.'

Selma started high school at the beginning of World War II. After matriculating in 1943, she followed in her father's footsteps and studied medicine at the University of Cape Town.

'When I was a teenager I was so ugly that I decided I would never get married, and my plan was to be a missionary doctor in Umtata. Umtata was so far away it might as well have been in Ghana. I wanted to help people, but I didn't think about activism. My looks improved when I was 18 – perhaps because I stopped having perms. I still didn't want to get married, but I no longer wanted to be a missionary. I just wanted to be a doctor.'

Selma was in her third year of medicine in 1946 when she decided to attend a students' conference in Johannesburg. She stayed with an aunt and uncle, who invited her to their friend's daughter's engagement party.

Meanwhile Ida Browde had asked her son Jules to go with her to the engagement party of the daughter of her friend. Jules had returned eight months earlier after fighting for five-and-a-half years in World War II and had arranged to meet up with some of his army friends, but Ida had a way of twisting his arm (Psst: it's called Jewish mother's guilt).

But before we get to the party, let's go to the Joburg suburbs of Doornfontein and Yeoville in the roaring 1920s, which is where many Jewish immigrants lived. This is where Jules grew up and led a carefree life, going to King Edward VII School, playing soccer behind the local shul, attending the Talmud Torah, and becoming involved in the newly established Jewish scouts group Habonim. It was in the youth movement where he cooked over fires, slept in tents and learnt about Jewish history, philosophy and ethics. Habonim became a big part of his life from the time he was 13 until long after he stopped being a youth.[80]

In the outstanding biography *The Relatively Public Life of Jules Browde*, by his grandson Daniel Browde, Jules noted that although he was a diligent pupil, high school couldn't compete with his interest in Habonim.[81]

'I found in Habonim something I didn't find at King Edward School. We had discussions about *ideas* – ideas about the world and the future. And while I found school interesting, I was never inspired by what we were learning there in the same way as I was by the comparatively young people who were running Habonim.'

After matriculating, Jules went to Wits University to study law. He had just started his LLB in 1940 when France fell to the Nazis.[82]

He decided to go to war against Hitler and enlisted in the South African artillery. He took part in the successful Abyssinian campaign against the Italians and was then sent for further training for a year to Egypt. During this time, he was chosen to go on an officers' training course in Potchefstroom, becoming a lieutenant. He returned to the frontline and fought in the fierce battle of Monte Cassino, and in all the subsequent hard-fought campaigning as the Allies made their way up the boot of Italy.

Jules, a gifted raconteur, hardly ever talked about his time in the war. He had lost friends, and knew that all that separates a living war hero from a battlefield statistic is luck.

'If you're lucky in war, you survive, if not, you don't,' he said. Jules was lucky.

When he came back to South Africa he resumed his law studies and struck up a friendship with a fellow student who would go on to become the world's most famous political prisoner and then the country's first black president.

---

80 Jules was appointed Habonim's first *manhig* (honorary head) in 1950, a position he held for 25 years
81 Browde, Daniel: *The Relatively Public Life of Jules Browde*, Johannesburg, Jonathan Ball, 2016
82 Veterans Voices: *Jewish Affairs*, Vol. 70, #2, Rosh Hashanah 2015

To be a friend of Nelson Mandela in the late 1940s – or any other black person for that matter – was regarded by most white people as infra dig.

But Jules didn't care what most people thought. He did care what his mother thought, though, which is why he agreed, albeit reluctantly, to accompany her to the party in 1946, which is where Selma Meyer and Jules Browde met and forged a partnership that would last the next 70 years.

Selma relocated to Johannesburg and the couple married in 1947.

'Jules had an instinct for helping people,' says Selma. 'It's funny how we got together without knowing we shared a philosophy about helping people. When I married him I thought he's clever, he plays chess, he reads a lot, but I never thought to ask: Would he be a good father? Would he be a good husband? To me it was all intellect. What did I know? I had just turned 20 when I met him.'

Jules turned out to be a good father and husband and a lionhearted man, whose compassion shone through in everything he did.

Selma, who was then in her fourth year of medicine, applied to transfer to Wits, but the university was giving priority to the returning serviceman, so she went to look for work.

Jules qualified as an advocate and joined the Johannesburg Bar in 1948. He took on *pro Deo* cases – one of which was preventing Mandela and his law partner Oliver Tambo from being evicted from their office in downtown Joburg when the Group Areas Act came into force in 1952. He also defended black people who were charged with breaking pass laws.

'Jules was one of the most unusual people I've ever come across,' says Selma. 'He had no ego. He didn't need to make money to be somebody. He was a natural liberal.'

Selma did a range of non-medical jobs – from selling advertising space to launching an art-lending library – to support the family, which had grown with the birth of their sons Alan and Ian.

When Jules' practice took off, Selma reapplied to go to medical school and was accepted into third year in 1956.

'Eight years without one spoken word of medicine ... I didn't even remember the name of the femur,' she chuckles.

Selma qualified in 1959, and after the couple's third son Paul was born, she worked, and specialised, as a radiation oncologist. People used to say to her, 'Don't you find cancer depressing?' and she would respond that she finds what goes on in the world more depressing, 'because it's man's inhumanity to man that I can't tolerate'.

In 1972, when she was a senior consultant at the Johannesburg Group of Hospitals and lecturing at Wits Medical School, something happened that pushed her into politics: she discovered that an academic paper based on her research was being submitted to a medical journal with the names of seven male doctors as the authors.

'My name wasn't on it after all those years of work. I was so angry,' she recalls, her face turning red as the injustice stings her all over again.

Timing in politics is everything, and very soon after Selma's discovery, she answered a phone call from the plucky Progressive Party politician Helen Suzman. Helen told her the party needed a candidate to stand for a ward in the Johannesburg City Council, which was then run by the United Party.

Selma recalls the conversation: 'I said, "Hold on, I'll call Jules." Helen said, "No, we don't want Jules ... we want *you*." I said, "You are crazy." Helen told me she wasn't going to take no for an answer, and bang went the phone.' Selma was stunned.

'I was passionately anti-apartheid, but politics for me was like flying to the moon. I had three children, a husband, I was studying and working, I didn't have time for a career in politics.'

Jules convinced her to stand. He told her the campaign would be a distraction. 'You'll meet different people, you'll enjoy trying to change people's minds, and then you can go back to work and you'll have got over your hurt and anger.'

The 'when you don't get elected' was so obvious, it didn't need to be said out loud.

Selma agreed and went knocking on doors with the 13 other Progressive Party candidates standing in the election.

'I won,' she laughs. 'I couldn't believe it. Nor could my opponent from the United Party. He had three re-counts. I was horrified. I was the only Prog that got in, and when they announced I had won, you would have thought I was Jesus Christ. There were crowds and crowds of people. I was lifted onto a table to make a speech! Public speaking is one of my phobias. I remember saying to myself, "Just say thank you, just say thank you." I thanked this one and that one; it wasn't even two minutes. Suddenly I wanted to add one thing. I will never forget this, I said: "It is so wonderful to be out of the hypocrisy of academia and into the sincerity of politics." I meant it! I thought they were all wonderful people. They roared with laughter. They thought I was being witty. Helen nearly wet herself because she knew I was being serious.'

The next day Selma received a call from a *Rand Daily Mail* journalist asking for her opinion on a statement that the British prime minister, Edward Heath, had just made.

'I was now the official voice of the Progressive Party, but I didn't know what to say. I said: "Hold on a minute while I go and ask my husband." Later I was told that the journalist had rolled on the floor with laughter.'

According to Selma, the learning curve was so steep, it was like jumping from Grade 1 to matric.

The council consisted of 37 United Party members, 10 Nats and Selma, the lone Prog, who quickly became the unofficial representative of people in the townships.

One of the many issues Selma took up was lighting in Soweto. The council wanted to light up just one area of the township, but Selma insisted on the whole area. With the backing of the media, she launched a battle against the council, which eventually led to the electrification of Soweto.[83]

Selma was then elected onto the Transvaal Provincial Council. She resigned her post at the hospital but continued lecturing.

'One day a man, who didn't look very savoury, came to see me. He told me he knew about crookery in the council and wanted me to expose it. We arranged to meet in a garage – like how the Watergate journalists met Deep Throat – and he gave me amazing material. I asked him how he got it, and he told me it takes a thief to catch a thief.'

Selma's investigation took her to the United States, where she confirmed the whistleblower's story, but her attempts to highlight the allegations were repeatedly thwarted.

She eventually resigned from the council in frustration. She returned to the radiation oncology department and continued her community activism.

Her tireless campaigning didn't make her friends in the council but it won the confidence of many black community leaders.

---

83 Moshe, Jordan: The woman who lit up Soweto, *SA Jewish Report*, 13 June 2019

When Selma saw the anguish that malnutrition inflicted on poor South Africans, she recruited the help of Dr Nthato Motlana – a popular political activist – to establish Operation Hunger. The national feeding and self-help scheme became one of the most effective organisations in South Africa.

She also co-founded the Soweto Basketball Association; established Soweto's first basketball court; and was treasurer of the association for eight years.

In the meantime Jules, who was appointed a senior counsel in 1969, had earned a reputation as a brilliant cross-examiner who was skilful in all types of cases.

He used his legal skills to assist victims of apartheid and was a founding member of Lawyers for Human Rights, which confronted apartheid's racist laws through litigation.

He led the defence in a 1980 test case, State v Adams, against the iniquitous Group Areas Act spearheaded by Actstop, the organisation Selma had helped start in 1976 to fight against forced removals.

Jules argued that the Adams family couldn't be prosecuted for living in a whites-only area because there was a shortage of housing in the coloured and Indian areas and therefore no alternative accommodation was available to them in Joburg.

If Jules' 'defence of necessity' argument had succeeded it would have invalidated the Group Areas Act. It didn't, but all prosecutions under the Act were put on ice pending the outcome of the case, which took three years to make its way through the legal system.

The case played an important role in the Act's ultimate repeal when Judge Richard Goldstone ruled in 1985 that the availability of alternative accommodation had to be taken into account before someone could be evicted under the Act.[84]

Jules was an abiding optimist, but one case – the Trojan Horse Massacre – left him reeling.

On 15 October 1985, a group of mostly schoolchildren gathered in Cape Town's suburb of Athlone to protest against the government.

---

84   Judge Goldstone is among the world's most widely admired legal minds. He served on the Supreme Court and in the Appellate Division, where he chiselled away at apartheid laws, and was a judge of the Constitutional Court

A railway delivery truck loaded with crates drove through the protest, passing a group of children, who ignored it. The truck then turned around and drove back, which is when one of the children threw a stone at it.

When the stone hit the windscreen, 10 policemen hiding behind the crates sprang up and opened fire into the crowd, killing Jonathan Claasen (21), Shaun Magmoed (15) and 11-year-old Michael Miranda, and wounding many more.

An inquest found that the police had acted unreasonably, but the state refused to prosecute.

Jules, acting for the victims' families, led a private prosecution against the killers. And even though he produced video evidence of the vicious attack, the cops were acquitted.

'That was the worst thing for him,' says Selma. 'He never got over it.'

Selma has been talking for almost three hours. There has been no evidence of her COVID brain fog as she reached into her past to recall details about her and Jules' remarkable lives.

Jules died at the age of 97 in 2016, just shy of the couple's platinum wedding anniversary. 'Jules left a wonderful legacy,' Selma tells me.

After Selma retired in 1986 she continued her community activism, which included establishing Community Action to tackle HIV/Aids and TB, and the Palliative Medicine Institute to help relieve pain for all patients, whatever their condition.

As Selma explained when we first started chatting, like Bertrand Russell, she has 'unbearable pity for the suffering of mankind'.

This description, of course, also sums up her husband.

Jules and Selma may have worked in different spheres but were tireless in their efforts to end suffering and, through their burning commitment to justice and human rights, they made South Africa a better place.

WRITING WRONGS

CHAPTER 14

'FACTS, FACTS, FACTS, BUT WITH EMOTION'

During apartheid, Benjamin Pogrund made headlines, met deadlines, crossed colour lines and stood on the frontlines of press freedom. He was put on trial several times, put in prison once, and was considered a threat to the state by security police.

THE FINAL DEADLINE - that was the bold headline which ran across the front page of the *Rand Daily Mail* on Tuesday 30 April 1985. Those three words signalled the death of the popular morning paper. The reason given was that it had lost money and circulation, and could no longer be sustained.

The actual reason was that its anti-apartheid editorial stance and frequent exposés of National Party crimes had made it unpopular with its owners and, of course, the government. President PW Botha congratulated the mining houses that owned the paper when they closed it down.[85]

The *Rand Daily Mail* was founded in 1902 by the Jewish Johannesburg financier Harry Freeman Cohen, and it soon became Joburg's biggest-selling newspaper. Its closure 83 years later left a gaping hole in the news landscape because it was the only 'white' newspaper reporting regularly on the political and economic issues affecting black South Africans.

The paper's most famous journalist was Benjamin Pogrund, who had started as a rookie reporter in 1958 and worked his way up the editorial ranks. He was the paper's deputy editor when it bit the dust.

Benjamin, says professor emeritus Gideon Shimoni, was at the forefront of the relentless effort to maintain press reportage of the politics of the liberation struggle and the social carnage and human suffering wrought by apartheid.[86]

Benjamin's parents, Nathan and Bertha, came to South Africa from Lithuania in the 1920s.[87] The family lived in Observatory in Cape Town, where his parents had a grocery shop.

'We kept a kosher home and belonged to the Observatory Mowbray shul. Even as a young boy I was astonished at the solidarity in that community,' says Benjamin.

On his way to *cheder*, Benjamin would pass a fruit and vegetable shop where he'd buy sweets and encounter a boy his own age – that

---

85   Harber, A: The untimely death of SA's finest daily
86   Shimoni, G: Community and Conscience: The Jews in Apartheid South Africa, University Press of New England, Brandeis University Press, United States, 2003
87   Interview with Benjamin Pogrund, August 2020

lad was a future minister of justice, Dullah Omar. The two would meet up years later and strike up a friendship.

One of the most important moments of Benjamin's life happened during World War II when his father received news that the last of the family's known relatives had been murdered.

'I watched my father cry, and that imprinted something on my psyche which is there to this day. I became very aware of discrimination,' he says.

Benjamin was a member of the Jewish youth movement Habonim, where many of his values regarding human rights and social justice were formed.

Training for a future on a kibbutz in Israel, members spent school holidays in the middle of winter on a farm in the then Transvaal, sleeping in tents and taking cold showers. They spent the days hacking the ground and removing rocks, and nights listening to Beethoven on scratchy records and having debates that went on interminably about things like whether you could own your own shirt on a kibbutz.

When he was 16 and in matric, the movement's *shaliach* came to see his mother to arrange for Benjamin to go on *aliyah*. His mother said no.

'In those days one listened to one's mother,' says Benjamin.

So instead he enrolled at the University of Cape Town. In Benjamin's first year he started crossing racial lines and spent time with a group of Trotskyites. At one meeting he asked one too many questions, and a member of the group jumped to his feet and yelled, 'Liberal, liberal, liberal'.

'To them that was the ultimate insult,' Benjamin chuckles.

He became involved in student politics and was elected to the Students' Representative Council. He was also elected as director of research on the national executive of the National Union of South African Students (Nusas).

'When I came up for re-election at the annual conference, a close friend came to my room in residence, sat opposite me and cried. Unknown to me he had become a member of the underground Communist Party and told me that the party had ordered him to stand against me because I was a liberal. He said he had to obey party orders. I thought there was something very wrong with anyone who gave allegiance to a political party instead of a personal friendship. At that stage I'd been reading a collection of essays against communism and also Arthur Koestler's *Darkness at Noon*. I became bitterly anti-Soviet and anti-Stalinist, which played a colossal role in my life.'

After completing three degrees – in psychology and sociology – Benjamin made his way to Johannesburg. He had been on the Cape provincial committee of the Liberal Party. He went onto the Transvaal provincial committee and worked for the party in Sophiatown – one of Joburg's last suburbs where black people enjoyed the right to own land before bulldozers arrived to evict the residents and move them to Soweto.

While working in Sophiatown he got to know Nelson Mandela, Oliver Tambo and other prominent people in the ANC.

Benjamin, who was an executive trainee at African Explosives and Chemical Industries, then decided to pursue his interest in journalism.

'The *Rand Daily Mail* had been an absolutely awful paper when I got to Johannesburg. It was just a rag. Then suddenly articles started appearing in the paper under the name of Owen Vine, which electrified the country. These pieces were analyses of apartheid such as had never been seen before. Up to then, the late 1950s, the English newspapers were against apartheid, but it was because they were more anti-Afrikaner than anti-apartheid, and what they really wanted was a weaker form of apartheid.'

Benjamin says that when he joined the *Mail*, he had a very simple idea: He wanted to change the world. His reporting mantra was: Facts, facts, facts, but with emotion.

He also wanted to change the way black people were portrayed in the paper. Black people hardly featured in the mainstream press, and when they did it was mainly in stories about tragedies and crime.

A typical story would read, 'Mr Hennie van der Merwe and six natives died in a rockfall last night.' Black people were seldom named.

If it's a newspaper for the public, it must represent everybody, he believed. Laurence Gandar had become editor shortly before Benjamin started at the *Mail*, and he too wanted to change the paper's culture. Gandar was in fact Owen Vine – and he and Benjamin developed a close relationship.

'It was a relationship of trust,' remarks Benjamin. As the reader will see later on in this chapter, that was very important because, despite Benjamin 'destroying' Gandar's career, they remained close friends.

'FACTS, FACTS, FACTS, BUT WITH EMOTION'

Benjamin was sent to court where he covered the trial of hundreds of black women who had been arrested for protesting. Mandela was their lawyer. The magistrate barred the press from the proceedings, so Benjamin marched off to see the chief magistrate and warned him that if he didn't open the court to the media, he would lodge an urgent application in the Supreme Court that afternoon.

'I was bluffing,' says Benjamin. 'I had no power, but I was right, and they opened the court. Nelson never forgot this.'

That incident helped to seal the men's friendship.

Benjamin had been inspired by Leon Pinsker, one of the seminal thinkers in the rise of Zionism, who had enunciated the policy of self-emancipation.

'Pinsker argued that if Jews wanted to be regarded and accepted by the world, we must stand on our own feet and look people in the eye,' says Benjamin, 'and that was the same philosophy that underpinned Black Consciousness. I developed a special empathy with African nationalism and a close relationship with Robert Sobukwe, founder of the Pan Africanist Congress.'

At the *Mail*, Benjamin wrote about black people's lives and reported on politics, education, trade unions, health and injustice. He started covering Basutoland, Swaziland and Bechuanaland, and the growing African nationalist movements there.

He pushed for the *Rand Daily Mail* to be non-racial, and the paper's culture gradually started to shift. It hired several black reporters, first as tipsters and then as full-time staff.

In 1961, Mandela went underground to organise a countrywide stay-at-home. While the police searched for Mandela, aka the Black Pimpernel, he and Benjamin met regularly – usually sitting in Benjamin's car at night in a dark street on the edge of the city centre. Mandela briefed Benjamin about his plans, enabling the *Mail* to keep the public informed.[88]

Benjamin was in town one Saturday when he bumped into a friend, Robin Scott-Smith. Republic Day was coming up and the defence minister, Frans Erasmus, had announced that a document detailing a leftist plot to disrupt Republic Day celebrations had been discovered. Scott-Smith told Benjamin the plot was a joke and showed him the document, titled Operation Thunder Cracker.

---

88 Pogrund, B: The Mandela I knew, *SA Jewish Report*, 16 July 2020

'It was written in semi-military language and seemed obviously to be satire,' says Benjamin, who thought it was very funny that the defence minister had fallen for a prank. He decided to write about it. His story appeared on the Monday on the bottom of page 1, where the humorous stories were placed. Two days later, Benjamin was at home suffering from a migraine when the office phoned to tell him that a policeman was there and wanted to talk to him.

'What about?' asked Benjamin.

'I don't know. Some story you wrote,' the person replied casually.

Benjamin stumbled into the office, and waiting for him was Hendrik van den Bergh, who was then a police detective but would go on to head the feared intelligence agency, the Bureau of State Security (BOSS).

'He was courteous,' recalls Benjamin. 'He told me the minister was very upset and wanted the name of my source. Van den Bergh explained that if I didn't he would serve a Section 205 on me.[89] I remember him telling me that I would have to go to prison, and it was the middle of winter and he would have to get extra blankets for me. It was all terribly pleasant,' says Benjamin.

Scott-Smith had asked Benjamin to keep his name out of the story, and Benjamin was committed to protecting his source and told Van den Bergh he wouldn't name names.

Benjamin appeared before a magistrate, and an hour later Van den Bergh escorted him to the Old Fort prison in Hillbrow.

'He shook my hand, wished me well, and I was locked up,' remembers Benjamin, who adds that his wife was heavily pregnant at the time.

There hadn't been a journalist in jail for many years. It was a particularly cold winter. While locked up he insisted on showering every day, and his time spent at Habonim camps had prepared him for the ice-cold showers.

The *Rand Daily Mail* lodged an appeal, and after eight days behind bars, Benjamin was taken back to court, where he made a declaration to the magistrate about journalists' ethics.

'The magistrate couldn't have cared less. There was I, talking about ethics, and he was just sending me to jail.'

---

89 Section 205 of the Criminal Procedure Act allowed the state to jail reporters who refused to reveal their sources

Benjamin was out on bail when his wife went into labour. He was standing outside the hospital when a car came screeching up. A policeman rolled down the window and told him he had been sent to take him back to jail. Benjamin's appeal had failed.

'I leaned in the window and told him I was going nowhere until my baby was born. The policeman said he would see what he could do. I got a call later saying I could stay out over the weekend.'

In the meantime Scott-Smith left the country and gave Benjamin permission to reveal his name, which he did.

Benjamin's next brush with the law would cost him four years of his life as he battled to stay out of jail.

'In those four years I must have been involved in about 20 or 30 court cases,' he says.

In 1965 Benjamin wrote a three-part investigative series on abuses in prison. He had spent months interviewing prisoners and warders. The series revealed how black inmates were beaten and tortured and how white political prisoners were mistreated.

The government hounded Benjamin and Gandar, charging them under the Prisons Act and seizing their passports. The case eventually ended when the pair were found guilty. Gandar received a R20,000 fine and Benjamin was handed a six-month jail term, which was suspended. Benjamin says it was a Kafka-like trial, with conviction certain from the start; their victory was in not being jailed.

Gandar had long been under attack by the newspaper's owners, and now lost his editorship.

After the four-year ordeal, Benjamin became the paper's night editor, then assistant editor, and in 1977 he was appointed deputy editor.

Benjamin says he never stood a chance of becoming editor. There was an unspoken tradition that no Jew would be appointed editor of the *Rand Daily Mail*, and Gordon Waddell, the former son-in-law of Harry Oppenheimer, who was in charge of the company that owned the newspaper, had told him openly, 'You're Jewish, you can't be editor.'

Early in 1963 Benjamin was in Cape Town on holiday and was walking past Parliament when out came Hendrik van den Bergh, the 'polite' policeman who had taken him to jail 18 months earlier.

'He greeted me like a long-lost brother and told me the then justice minister, BJ Vorster, had just appointed him the head of the security police. He said he wanted to talk to me. We later had lunch and he propositioned me, telling me how he was fighting against communists, and wanted me to help. I laughed and told him I'm not going to be part of protecting the apartheid government. I told him he was like a man with a spade walking behind a team of oxen and picking up their dung.'

Over the years, Van den Bergh and Benjamin met many times.

'I told him once that whenever someone said something rude about the government in our editorial conferences, they'd look up at the ceiling and say, "Sorry about that, general." Van den Bergh gave me a thin smile and said, "It's not in the ceiling."'

The government was keeping an eye on the *Mail* as the paper continued to bring the horrors and injustices of apartheid to its readers. Its political correspondent Helen Zille reported on the brutal death of Black Consciousness leader Steve Biko at the hands of the police in 1977, and two years later the paper broke news of the Information Scandal, which exposed how taxpayers' money had been used to launch *The Citizen* as a pro-government mouthpiece.

The paper had police spies. According to Benjamin, there were ones from Van den Bergh's BOSS, the security police, military intelligence, and possibly another unidentified shadowy intelligence organisation.

'I used to work on the basis that every one of those agencies had at least two spies in the newsroom,' he says, adding there was lots of finger pointing as to who these spies were, which endangered staff morale.

Benjamin was preparing for a PhD when the security police raided his home and seized many documents. He was charged under the Suppression of Communism Act, found guilty of possessing banned documents and given a suspended sentence.

The death of the *Mail* left many of South Africa's best journalists unemployed.

Benjamin says, 'I couldn't get a job. Someone suggested, seriously, that I should apply for a post as director at the Jewish old-age home in Joburg. In the end, England gave me sanctuary and I left South Africa to work on Fleet Street newspapers, and continued to write about apartheid.'

In 2019, President Cyril Ramaphosa awarded him the Order of Ikhamanga Silver for 'his excellent contribution to the field of journalism and to scholarship on the liberation struggle. His informative

'FACTS, FACTS, FACTS, BUT WITH EMOTION'

writing shone the light on our country during some of the darkest days in our history. He defied those who would deceive the world.'

Says Benjamin: 'It was one of the proudest moments of my life. I don't consider myself to have been an activist. I was a journalist. I did my job as I saw it, and the fact that the then government didn't like it was their problem, not mine. I did what I believed was the right thing to do.'

CHAPTER 15
THE INVISIBLE EDITOR

Anton Harber (left), Irwin Manoim (right)

Everyone told Irwin Manoim and Anton Harber that they were mad and their venture to start a newspaper couldn't possibly succeed. Nevertheless, in the midst of censorship laws, states of emergency and petrol bombs through their windows, the courageous newshounds launched the *Weekly Mail*, a newspaper that dared to tell the truth.

One of the other 'unemployable' journalists after the *Rand Daily Mail*'s closure was 30-year-old Irwin Manoim. Irwin had grown up in a liberal family in Johannesburg. His mother was a German refugee who had come to South Africa with her mother in the late 1930s.[90] His parents had been members of the Hashomer Hatzair youth movement, and Irwin remembers his parents as being open-minded and tolerant.[91]

In the 1950s they would do 'some kinds of mysterious good works in Alexandra township', and Irwin's father would occasionally tell his son about street fights with the Greyshirts.

Irwin went to Houghton Primary School and then King Edward VII School.

He was an avid newspaper reader, and read the *Rand Daily Mail*, *The Star*, *Sunday Times* and *Beeld*.

'I was an admirer of Helen Suzman, and a great accumulator of election-type information. I knew the names of all the major politicians, but was otherwise as politically naive as all the other pupils around me,' he says.

After matriculating, Irwin went to the army – it was a time when performing military service was a nuisance, but not yet politically contentious – and then enrolled at Wits University, where he studied art.

On 27 February 1973, his first day of university, the government banned eight Nusas students, which was followed by several days of street protests.

'Unlike everyone else's parents, mine were very sympathetic to the students,' he says.

Irwin became peripherally involved in Nusas but wasn't too enthusiastic about meetings, so rather spent his time at *Wits Student* – the popular campus newspaper that introduced the students to topics they wouldn't find in mainstream newspapers.

According to Irwin's former colleague Anton Harber, it was in the student media where Irwin got a taste for the alternative press.[92]

---

90 Suttner, I: *Cutting Through the Mountain*, Viking, Parktown, 1997
91 Interview with Irwin Manoim, July 2020
92 Harber, A: Honour outs revolutionary newsman, *Mail & Guardian*, 21 November 2013

Irwin was appointed *Wits Student* editor in 1976, a turbulent year in South Africa, and the paper was banned frequently.

'It was no big deal,' he shrugs. 'It didn't take much for it to be banned, so you weren't much of an editor if the paper wasn't getting banned once a month.'

The two major stories of his editorship were a referendum on the future of Nusas (which had been concocted by police spies) and the June 16 Soweto Uprising in 1976.

'Students went marching through town during June and we provided copious coverage and photos of how they were ambushed by both baton-wielding police and bicycle-chain wielding Afrikaans students from the tech,' he recalls.

Irwin was also part of the South African Students Press Union (Saspu), a national non-racial organisation representing student newspapers and radio stations throughout the country. He travelled from campus to campus presenting media training workshops to student activists, and was involved in the launch of *Saspu National*, a publication 'about the politics of oppression and struggle' that circulated off campus.

Irwin also helped to produce other semi-underground anti-apartheid newspapers, publications and pamphlets – mostly on kitchen tables late at night, using scissors, glue and Letraset.

After graduating, Irwin landed a job at the *Sunday Times* on the strength of the *Wits Student* coverage of the Soweto Uprising. He was soon removed from the newsroom and sent to the subs room; a move he describes as 'not overtly political but, yes, political'.

It was a move to get him out of the newsroom because he was active in the journalists' union and edited its publication, which was critical of the management and covered racial politics in the newsrooms. It also earned him the nickname 'Red Robbo', after Derek Robinson, a Trotskyite trade unionist active in Britain at the time.

Irwin's move to the subs room was perfect timing because electronic editing was just being introduced and the *Sunday Times* was the guinea pig.

Irwin showed remarkable talent for working with the new technology – coding as well as newspaper design.

'The other subs were over-the-hill Fleet Street hacks who never got the hang of computers. One guy would sit with a China marker and write on the screen. They didn't have a clue,' says Irwin, who became indispensable because of his computer skills.

Irwin and the *Sunday Times* editor Ken Owen got on well, and when Owen was appointed editor of the *Sunday Express*, which was in the same stable as the *Sunday Times* and *Rand Daily Mail*, he took Irwin with him.

Irwin became the production editor. Unfortunately for Irwin, his competency would cost him his job, because the *Express* went down with the *Mail*.

'It was gone in a week and forgotten in two,' he says.

One night, while mooching with Anton over many cans of beer, the pair decided it was time to launch their own newspaper.

'If we'd had any notion of what folly we were getting ourselves into, we would never have started, but our secret ingredient was that we were clueless,' says Irwin, who was 30 at the time.[93]

Anton, who was 26, had been the *Rand Daily Mail*'s political reporter and, according to Irwin, was 'cocky, opinionated and fearless'.[94]

Many people still regard Anton as cocky, opinionated and fearless – especially those who have found themselves on the wrong side of his pen.

While working at the *Mail* Anton had interviewed a young black activist who had threatened to make the townships 'ungovernable'.

Police demanded that Anton lead them to his source, which, like Benjamin Pogrund before him, he refused to do. Anton was about to be arrested when the activist fled the country, and the police lost interest.

Irwin and Anton had no experience, no capital and no business plan, but they had passion and energy and, most importantly, chutzpah by the gallons.

They wanted to produce a new critical voice to replace what had been lost. They recruited a number of others, combined their severance packages and managed to raise about R50,000. They hired a two-room office in Braamfontein on a three-month lease. The office had been a hairdressing salon and the walls were painted pink.[95]

---

93 Information from a talk by Irwin Manoim to Limmud UK, December 2019
94 Ibid
95 Manoim, Irwin: A few post-retrenchment beers … and a new paper is born, M&G, 11 June 2015

'The interesting thing about us,' says Irwin, 'is that although we had made no attempt to define ourselves as Jewish, all but one of our number were Jewish. Several of us had been at school together and in the same barmitzvah classes.'

The Jews who made up the early group became directors and managers: David Dison and Steven Goldblatt (lawyers), and Clive Cope (managing director). The other Jews were liberal business types who put up the money, most prominently Bennie Rabinowitz and (later) Joel Joffe, and a number of senior advocates.

Their first obstacle was registering the newspaper with the government. Irwin believed they didn't stand much of a chance because only the applications for innocuous or pro-government publications weren't rejected. Dozens had applied over the past 25 years and failed.

They had come up with a plan should the government reject their registration application.

'We set up a *Weekly Mail* Society, with a constitution and elected members. The *Weekly Mail* would be available only to members of the society, as an internal newsletter. That got around the registration rules which exempted organisational newsletters,' explains Irwin.

To their astonishment their application was quickly approved.

'The only explanation, perverse as it seemed, was this: the government's spooks had belatedly realised that losing the *Rand Daily Mail* had damaged their ability to keep a watch on the anti-apartheid movement. The government actually wanted us to publish.'[96]

Irwin and Anton formed a society of volunteers to help with fundraising phone calls and packing publicity flyers into envelopes. Irwin recalls looking around a room with 40 or so willing helpers and realising that most of them were Jewish, 'ranging from university students to iron-haired Yiddishe *bobbas*, trade unionists and socialists who had endured detention and house arrest and were still unbroken in old age'.[97]

With Irwin and Anton as co-editors, the team of young reporters and photographers worked long days and long nights, for little or no money. They were passionate about their mission to expose injustice and tell the stories that none of the mainstream newspapers

---

96   Info from a talk by Irwin Manoim to Limmud UK, December 2019
97   Ibid

was telling, and open the eyes of white South Africans to what was happening in the country.

Printers themselves could be arrested for producing subversive publications and the only printers prepared to produce the *Weekly Mail* was the Dannheisers, a Jewish family, who owned a community newspaper in Springs.

Putting the first edition together was utterly exhausting, remembers Irwin.

'Both the office furniture and the newspaper were being put together at the same time; phone interviews amid electric drills. My greatest anxiety was whether we could produce it at all. Since we couldn't afford a conventional editorial/typesetting system, I had taken the mad risk of cobbling together, with some help from kindly techies, a home-made computer network of cheap little proto laptops (laptops had not yet been invented) which displayed only two lines of text; the original Apple Macs (which had tiny screens and hardly any memory) and Apple Lisas (predecessors to Macs), and another brand new invention, an Apple laser printer which had to be shipped into South Africa from abroad (sanctions!) and arrived five days before we were due to publish. This rickety system had to be debugged and experimented with on the fly. It was the first example of a newspaper produced using desktop publishing, a term that had not yet been invented. That was quite apart from the small matter of the editorial. I didn't go home for four or five nights in a row.'

On 14 June, just six weeks after the *Rand Daily Mail*'s final edition, the first issue of the *Weekly Mail* was published. It went on sale for the princely sum of R1.

When Irwin held the paper in his hands for the first time, all he could see were the mistakes and what could have been done better.

'It took months before I could separate myself enough from the product to look at it dispassionately,' he says.

Almost everyone, including the paper's biggest fans, believed the venture would go belly up within three months. Before dawn on that Friday morning, staff members drove the streets of Johannesburg to distribute the paper.

The first lead story, headlined 'Detainees link SAP men to Renamo', was about breaches of South Africa's recent accord with Mozambique. This was scoffed at by the mainstream newspapers, which had ignored the story, but it was proved true. It raised the alarm with the authorities, and the most notorious security policeman of them all, Major Craig Williamson, paid them a visit.

'Williamson lumbered up a very narrow staircase with the intention of giving the place a once-over and perhaps intimidating the journalist, but almost everyone had gone home to sleep off the week and he found only a receptionist and the men putting the furniture together,' recalls Irwin.

Although the *Weekly Mail* was born from the *Rand Daily Mail*'s ashes, the two papers differed politically.

The *Rand Daily Mail* was the paper of the Progressive Federal Party, while the *Weekly Mail*, although it couldn't openly show its hand, had ANC/United Democratic Front sympathies.

The *Weekly Mail* carried innovative and creative stories and provided some of the younger staff with an outlet to produce the kind of reportage they had been unable to produce at the *Mail*.

The *Weekly Mail* also had a light touch, and readers could get a taste of the irreverent columnists, tongue-in-cheek satirists and its in-house political gossip Krisjan Lemmer before digesting the hard news.

However, it was its in-depth investigative features that cemented its reputation as a proudly progressive and fiercely independent publication. It wasn't long before its anti-government stance attracted the attention of the authorities, who had a twin approach to deal with the new rebellious publication: the government squeezed the paper with censorship regulations, and the security police pounced on its reporters.

The presses were raided, editions of the paper were seized, and reporters were detained and subjected to intimidation and harassment. Staff members had bricks and petrol bombs thrown through their windows.

Despite being the 'backroom boy' of the operation, Irwin was also a victim of these dirty tricks.

'The one direct personal experience I recall was when Molotov cocktails were flung through my bedroom window and two other rooms in the Yeoville house I shared with my brother,' says Irwin.

'My brother, a human rights lawyer, might also have been the target but it was my side of the house that got firebombed. Luckily we were both out of town when it happened. The security police, backed up by our neighbours, claimed there had been a noisy party and someone had dropped a cigarette. I'm still gobsmacked that the cops got the neighbours to lie,' says Irwin.

The neighbours' lie proved lucky for the Manoim brothers because the insurance company wouldn't pay for political violence but were obliged to pay for careless cigarette dropping!

Shots were fired through Anton's front door and his car brakes were tampered with.[98]

The paper took calculated risks to publish big stories, daring the authorities to take them to court – and the authorities did. According to Irwin, Anton spent almost as much time in the dock as he did at his desk.

There were several incidents that resulted in Anton and the paper's Eastern Cape correspondent Jo-Ann Bekker spending days in court over nonsense charges.

'Fortunately our lawyers managed to either trip up the prosecutors or cause enough public embarrassment for charges to be dropped,' says Irwin. 'One of the few charges to stick involved a failed attempt at amateur espionage. We were tipped off that a hit squad run by a notorious police officer met each week in a hotel room to plan their murderous attacks. We hired a private detective to bug the room. Alas, the PI proved a man of many thumbs but little grasp of the subtleties of espionage and was caught in the act.'

Anton was charged, found guilty and received a suspended sentence.

Prosecution was only one aspect. Harassment also took the form of warnings – three warnings and the paper was 'suspended', a euphemism for being closed down for a period. This also tied the *Weekly Mail* up in red tape and lawyers because they had to respond to the warnings.

Irwin, the paper's chief designer, earned a much deserved reputation as one of the world's top newspaper designers. He was responsible for some of the most powerful designs in South African newspaper history, including the *Weekly Mail*'s response to censorship that made the paper world famous following PW Botha's declaration of a state of emergency in June 1986.

---

98 Harber, A: *So, For The Record*, Jonathan Ball Publishers, Jeppestown, 2020

In addition to allowing for arbitrary and indefinite detention, the emergency regulations banned news reports about civil unrest and police action.

The *Weekly Mail*'s lawyers went through the edition, crossing out stories that fell foul of the new laws. They read all the proofs and put red lines through questionable words, phrases, sentences and entire stories. The paper was covered in red.

Irwin and Anton realised they would either have to redo the entire paper or publish and be damned and, because it would have meant permanent banning, go down in a blaze of glory. And then Irwin realised there was a third way.

'Looking through all those red slashes, it occurred to me that the best statement of all might be to turn those red lines into black lines, and to show the crossings out to the world: here is today's news.'

The paper was published with the headline: Our lawyers tell us we can say almost nothing critical about the Emergency ... But we'll try.

In a powerful act of graphic 'self-censorship', thick black koki covered any offending sentences and there were gaping white spaces where stories and photographs deemed unlawful had been removed. It was brave up-yours journalism, and the black blotches and white spaces became a powerful symbol of resistance. What the paper didn't say had said so much.

Unsurprisingly, the censorship of the censorship was banned.

The paper learnt to get around the emergency regulations. They manipulated loopholes in poorly written laws, causing government bureaucrats to scramble to plug them.[99]

'We spent years playing cat-and-mouse games with censorship, trying to tell stories that could not be told,' says Irwin.

One of these stories that couldn't be told was a five-part series on life on Robben Island, written by Thami Mkhwanazi, who had been a political prisoner. Publishing the story was a considerable risk because no one had dared report on prisons following Benjamin's investigation a quarter of a century earlier.

The paper's investigative journalists Eddie Koch and Chippa Molefe also created a stir when they 'bought' slaves who were victims

---

99 Irwin, I: *You Have Been Warned: A History of the Mail & Guardian*, Viking, Johannesburg, 1996

of the Mozambique war and were being sold to farmers. They lived in the newsroom for a week or two until Koch found them shelter. Koch also bought AK-47s on the black market, and photographer Kevin Carter, who would go on to win a Pulitzer Prize, broke into prison for a story. The *Weekly Mail* had exposed Stratcom, which was security police propaganda to manipulate the public by spreading disinformation and misinformation.

It was also the first newspaper to take seriously the accusation that the government had unleashed a third force to destabilise the country. The mainstream press had dismissed this as a leftist conspiracy theory. However, the *Weekly Mail* published a steady stream of articles exposing aspects of this third force, including the deaths of activists in suspicious circumstances, the fire bombings of buildings and interviews with confessed askaris.

In the run-up to the first democratic elections, the *Weekly Mail* covered the violence that erupted in the country in the 1990s and resulted in thousands of deaths. In 1991, the paper published a series of stories that revealed the government's covert support for Inkatha at a crucial time in the peace negotiations.

The *Weekly Mail* didn't publish only anti-government stories, and was one of the first publications to expose Winnie Madikizela Mandela and her 'football club'.

For five years the *Weekly Mail* had punched above its weight, and when Nelson Mandela was released from prison in 1990 it landed a knockout blow to the mainstream press: it was rewarded with Mandela's first newspaper interview.

The *Weekly Mail* won Irwin and Anton the Pringle Award for courageous journalism, the Missouri Medal of Honour and the International Press Directory's International Newspaper of the Year 1995.

When Wits University awarded Irwin an honorary doctorate in 2013, Anton described him as 'the invisible editor'.

'He was – and remains – a man of few words,' Anton wrote in a tribute to Irwin.[100] 'He kept a low profile. Few people knew about him. But he was the quiet, behind-the-scenes pioneer of the alternative press of the late apartheid era, driving innovation that made

---

100 The *Weekly Mail* was renamed the *Mail & Guardian* after the Guardian Media Group became the majority shareholder in the mid-1990s

these papers possible and allowed the penniless little *Weekly Mail* to become the substantial, international, digital *Mail & Guardian*.'

In its citation for Irwin's honorary doctorate, Wits University wrote that Irwin can be counted among those who fought in the struggle for democracy, and for freedom of expression and the press. 'He is a pioneering newspaperman who has made immense contributions to innovation and recreating how news and information are understood, produced, presented and consumed in the computer and digital age in South Africa and Africa.'

Irwin and Anton did what they believed was the right thing to do and, like Benjamin Pogrund before them, stood on the frontlines in the fight for press freedom.

Irwin and Anton eventually left the paper they founded and moved on to other jobs.

'There isn't a single Jew on the staff now,' Irwin notes. 'Nor is there anyone old enough to remember the paper's history, but the paper continues to needle and annoy those in power.'

THE HEART OF BUSINESS

CHAPTER 16

AN OFFICER AND A GENTLE RETAIL GIANT

David Susman was a brilliant businessman who built Woolworths into one of the country's largest retail chains. But for David being a good businessman wasn't just about making a profit; it was about doing the right thing. Under his leadership the company refused to bow to apartheid regulations, and David insisted on equal rights and opportunities for all.

David Susman described himself as 'a simple shopkeeper'. People who knew him agreed that at his core he was a person of deep humility, which sounds like an unlikely characteristic for someone who excelled in the cut-throat corporate world of commerce.[101]

David's son Simon says his father was first and foremost a businessman, but a businessman who believed that success comes with the responsibility of doing the right thing.

David's business journey begins when his father Elie Susman left the *shtetl* in Rieteva, Lithuania, in 1898 with 'half a crown' in his pocket to seek his fortune in Cape Town.

It was from his father that David learnt the art and heart of business. He admired his father's values, which were a unique blend of the tough-mindedness of the *shtetl* and what he called honourable righteousness.

When Elie arrived in Cape Town, his brother Harry was waiting for him. The Susman brothers – 20-year-old Harry and 18-year-old Elie – moved to Johannesburg, where they worked for *landleits*, the Yiddish term for people who come from the same place.

The brothers lived frugally, sleeping on the counters of the stores where they worked. One day they attended a meeting at the Johannesburg Town Hall, which was addressed by Cecil John Rhodes. The mining magnate spoke of the future of Africa and ended his speech with the stirring words, 'Go north, young men. Your future lies in the hinterland!'

The brothers heeded his call and headed north to the country named after Rhodes, making their way by train and ox wagon to Bulawayo. They set up a plant to process fizzy ginger beer, which they sold on the platform of the train station.

The success of their venture allowed them to gradually increase their capital, but more valuable than capital, it also built them a reputation for reliability and honesty, which became their most important asset throughout their lifetimes.

The pioneering brothers branched out into the cattle business in the western part of Zambia (then Northern Rhodesia) and forged a close friendship with the Barotseland king, Paramount Chief Lewanika.

---

101 Information for this chapter comes from an interview with Simon Susman in March 2021 and from *An African Shopkeeper: Memoirs of David Susman*, Fernwood Press, Cape Town, 2004

The king appointed Harry as 'special adviser to the nation', a position that entitled him to receive the royal salute. The honour, Harry would later say, was 'a *mitzvah* for a Yiddle from Rieteva'.

Simon says the king encouraged his subjects to trade with the Susman brothers because he trusted them. 'You're not going to be trusted if you're arrogant or if you're lording it over the people,' he adds.

By the time David was born in 1925, the Susman brothers' business exploits were legendary.

The importance of humility, honesty and trust was woven into David's business DNA, but it wasn't only business smarts that David learnt from his father. In his memoir, *An African Shopkeeper*, David wrote that his father taught him to have a deep respect for the human race, irrespective of colour and creed.

David spent an idyllic childhood in Livingstone, Northern Rhodesia. He went on field expeditions with his father and fishing trips with his cousin and enjoyed the companionship of his mother and three sisters.

'A small boy could not have asked for a better life,' he enthused.

When David was seven, the family moved to South Africa, first living in Cape Town and then settling in Johannesburg. He went to King Edward VII School but was sent to Kingswood College in Grahamstown (now Makhanda) for the final three years of his schooling. He was one of only six Jews out of the 700 boys in the boarding school.

'I had to learn to use my fists to rebut the frequent accusation that I had killed Christ,' he wrote.

After matriculating in 1942 David spent a year studying a BCom at Wits University – although what he was actually doing was 'drinking and ducking lectures'. He failed all four of his subjects, and decided to join the South African army and fight in World War II, where he took part in the Italian Campaign.

His home on the frontline was a slit trench, a foxhole measuring 6 by 4 feet square, which he shared for nearly five months with his friend Jeff Perlman.

David described life in the trenches: 'I can't think of a more trying test of a friendship. We were often in the same clothes for weeks at a time. There were dozens of points of friction, leading to acid and tight-lipped arguments. Boots had to be kept inside the trench since they would freeze hard if left near the opening. In the already fetid atmosphere of the trench, farting was an intolerable affront. Yet how could one refrain, given the baked beans and boiled cabbage in our rations?'

The soldiers patrolled at night, exchanging gunfire with the enemy.

David was only 20 when the war ended, and in the two years he spent in uniform he had witnessed a lifetime of destruction and misery.

'I had trembled in abject terror at moments prior to battle,' David wrote. 'I had killed a number of human beings and played a part in the death of many others.'

He also felt a sense of righteousness in having fought and beaten the evil that Adolf Hitler and his Nazis had inflicted upon the world.

He returned to Wits, and this time he took his studies seriously.

David spent his university holidays fly-fishing in the Eastern Transvaal and going to Sophiatown to teach black adults at Father Trevor Huddleston's church.

It was in Sophiatown that he met Nelson Mandela. Their lives would cross again when the future South African president was on trial for his life.

David's studies were interrupted when the Israeli War of Independence broke out in 1948, and he decided to put on a soldier's uniform once again and join the Israel Defense Forces.

During one skirmish he felt a hammer blow to his back, followed by a deafening crack.

'My tin helmet flew off my head, and the force of the bullet spun me around,' he wrote. 'I dropped to the ground, dazed, and lying on my right side. I was horrified to see a thick gout of blood flowing out of my mouth.'

The bullet, a dum-dum, had hit him just below his left shoulder blade and exploded out of his neck, tearing a large hole in it, destroying muscle and tissue in its way and knocking off his hat.

He recovered and returned to the frontline, managing to survive the rest of the war intact, reaching the rank of second lieutenant and platoon commander.

David's courage as a young man to get involved in two wars showed he had a strong sense of the need to commit to what he believed was right, and not just talk about it.

'His business life followed that philosophy,' says Simon.

AN OFFICER AND A GENTLE RETAIL GIANT

After the war, David married Ann Laski. The couple settled in Israel, which is where Simon was born in 1950.

David worked for Israel's Ministry of Foreign Affairs and did 'one or two minor jobs' for the Mossad secret service.

Says Simon: 'He didn't really talk about it [one doesn't talk about working for the Mossad], but he did tell us that he was assigned to track a Catholic priest who was behaving suspiciously and believed to have been a spy. After weeks of trailing him with all the best statecraft, he worked out that the priest was actually visiting brothels, which is why he was being secretive.'

Life in Israel after independence was tough. Food was scarce and Ann, who was from England, wanted the family to go to the United Kingdom. Ann was a niece of Sir Simon Marks – the founder of the upmarket retail giant Marks & Spencer.

It was always David's intention to go into retail, so when they arrived in England he joined the family business.

Simon Marks had been encouraged by Winston Churchill to invest in the colonies and had bought a share in Woolworths, which was Max Sonnenberg's business. At the time, Woolworths was a general retailer of a broad range of products, including food and groceries, homeware, clothing and haberdashery.

Simon Susman says: 'My grandfather worked for Woolworths at the time and one day Sir Simon Marks summoned my father and said, "This business that your father works for is a rubbish business. It doesn't make any money. I'm going to sell my shares."

'My father, who was all of 27 years old, responded: "But you've never sent anybody out there to make it a great business. It has the potential to be a great business." Sir Simon looked at him and said, "Exactly," and promptly sent him back to Africa. So we came back, and my father worked for the Sonnenberg family and slowly helped them to make Woolworths what it is today.'

Turning Woolworths into a success came naturally to David, with his business brain, but one of the most difficult challenges he faced was countering the inhumanity of apartheid's laws.

David's first target was the company's modest pension scheme, which provided only for white staff. He had heated discussions with Old Mutual, the company's pension providers, which ultimately led to all staff members being included, which is how Woolies became South Africa's first public company to operate a non-racial pension scheme.

The next issue was the thorny matter of whites-only fitting rooms in the stores. Woolworths opened these to all races in the large Pretoria store, which was deep in the heart of National Party territory. This was a breach of the core Separate Amenities Act, but the authorities turned a blind eye.

Woolworths received complaints from some aggrieved white customers and there was some resistance from their own store managers, but David was adamant that the policy must be rolled out at all their stores. They lost the business of a handful of diehard separatists.

Similarly, a number of white customers boycotted the chain when David scrapped the humiliating separate counters for black customers in country stores.

A more serious challenge to the Reservation of Separate Amenities Act took place when the company opened a new store in Cape Town's Adderley Street and was compelled to provide separate toilets and work and dining areas for each race group.

'Heaven forbid a white man should have to pee alongside a black man,' wrote David.

This law had earlier led to the establishment of eight sets of toilets in the company's Durban store: male and female for each of the white, black, coloured and Asian groups.

'We resolved to put an end to this preposterous practice. The Adderley Street staff quarters opened with two large, non-racial banks of toilets – one for men, the other for women. To reinforce the point, we provided one integrated staff dining room and a single, undivided general office.'

A few months later David received a visit from a senior official from the Department of Labour, who was investigating a complaint from a Woolworths staff member. The official suggested that Woolworths separate the toilets by way of 'a little ribbon'. David just laughed.

It wasn't only the separate toilets that David challenged. In defiance of laws not to employ 'non-whites' in certain occupations he appointed several coloured and black supervisors.

David recounted a story of a white customer going to the Stellenbosch branch of Woolworths sometime in the late 1970s or early 1980s and asking for a refund. When the coloured supervisor was called to approve the request, the customer said in Afrikaans, 'Can we not be served by someone of our own colour?' and asked to see the manager. A few minutes later the manager – a black woman – approached the customer and said, also in Afrikaans, 'Can I help you, madam?' The customer threw up her hands in fury and stormed out of the store.

David was delighted to hear that the customer returned to the store a couple of weeks later, which confirmed his view that 'self-interest overrides sterile ideology and dogma'.

The Group Areas Act prohibited black managers from buying homes in the more affluent white areas, so Woolworths launched a programme to purchase houses for black management in white areas.

'It wasn't strictly illegal,' explains Simon, who had followed his father into Woolworths. 'We said they were looking after the house for the company, so it was breaking the law without breaking the law.'

According to Simon, retail is a difficult industry to regulate, which frustrated the government.

'Retail is an industry that has a record of doing the right thing for its staff, for its customers and for society. Raymond Ackerman [SA's supermarket doyen who grew Pick n Pay into a retail behemoth] did similar things.'

According to Simon, one of the great lessons his father taught him is that business has a responsibility.

'It has a responsibility to make a profit – yes, that's important – but it also has a responsibility to be a good corporate citizen and to do the right thing.'

In other words, doing good is good business.

'The stance of doing the right thing made the staff happy and committed to doing the right thing. It's very much a virtuous circle.'

David didn't just pay lip service to these attempts to resist some of the evils of apartheid. It required constant vigilance and determination to ensure the policies were actually implemented.

Even though many Woolworths staff members were proud of the company's efforts, some resisted the resistance and attempted to sabotage them.

David wasn't a politician and didn't want to be a politician; he wanted to be a shopkeeper. But he became active in the political space because of his philosophy of doing the right thing.

'These weren't just words of commitment,' says Simon. 'These were acts of commitment.'

David was influenced by his friendship with Eulalie Stott, who was active in the Black Sash, an anti-apartheid organisation.

Simon remembers Eulalie visiting the Susman family and talking about the injustices occurring in the townships.

David also had a close friendship with the fierce opposition member of Parliament Helen Suzman and Jimmy Kantor, a lawyer whose law partner and brother-in-law was the ANC and SA Communist Party activist Harold Wolpe.

Harold was arrested after the Rivonia raid, and he and fellow activists Arthur Goldreich, Abdulhay Jassat and Mosie Moolla escaped from prison by bribing a guard.

Furious at the jailbreak, the police arrested Jimmy and held him in Harold's place. Jimmy became the Rivonia Treason Trial's accused number 10.

Jimmy's wife Barbara was due to give birth, and when they were sitting in the dock, he passed a note to Mandela that read: 'Barbara and I have discussed godfathers at length and we have come to the conclusion that, whether the baby is a girl or a boy, we would consider it an honour if you would agree to accept this office as an adjunct to the more disreputable positions you have held in the past.'

Mandela sent Jimmy a note back that said: 'I would be more than delighted, and the honour is mine, not the baby's. Now they dare not hang me.'[102]

Tanya was born on 30 January 1964.

Tanya had two godfathers: Nelson Mandela and David Susman.[103] Jimmy had also asked David to do godfather duties.

In the 1960s and 1970s, friends in the Black Sash and the Progressive Party would ask David to find employment in Woolworths for newly released political prisoners, who were confined to a single magisterial district under draconian laws. He always did.

David never forgot his roots and was very conscious of being a Jew.

'That was really important to him,' says Simon.

---

102 SA History Online

103 Jimmy Kantor was discharged from the case without having to present evidence. He left South Africa after the trial and died of a heart attack in England in 1975

Simon says his father felt that because of the persecutions and pressure the Jews had been under for thousands of years, they had an obligation to the broader society, particularly if they were successful.

'If the Jews could make themselves successful and run large organisations which carried weight, then they should use those for the greater good so that what was done to their parents and grandparents and great-grandparents should not be done to others. It was his Jewishness that brought him to that conclusion. He was not religious but he took a value system out of the Jewish community that stood him proud all of his life.'

Woolworths was established in Cape Town by Max Sonnenberg. David's father Elie Susman started the northern division in the then Transvaal. David joined the company in 1952 and was appointed director two years later. He retired in 1993. Simon Susman followed in the Woolworths footsteps of his father and grandfather, and on 28 November 2019 retired as chair after a 37-year stint with the company. David also played a leading role in the Jewish community, serving on a number of boards, including the Cape Jewish Aged Home, United Herzlia Schools, ORT-Tech (he was a former national president of ORT South Africa) and the IUA-UCF Welfare Campaign (now the United Jewish Campaign), and was chair of the Cape Town Holocaust Centre. He married Ann in 1950 and the couple had four children: Simon, Jennifer, Daphne and Peter. David died on 11 May 2010.

SERVING WITH DISTINCTION

CHAPTER 17
THE HUMAN BEING

Franz Auerbach came to South Africa as a refugee in 1936 to escape Nazi Germany. He knew from experience what can happen when people are demonised. He had a wide range of interests, but it was in the field of teaching where he made a giant impact. Franz worked quietly and tirelessly to agitate for equality in education and equip all children with knowledge, tolerance and hope for a brighter future.

To the apartheid establishment Franz was 'The Poisonous Spider', but he defined himself, simply, as a human being. A writer, educationalist and staunch optimist, Franz dedicated his life to fostering ties of friendship between all South Africans.

Where a person ranked in apartheid South Africa's racial pyramid determined where they could live, work or go to school, whom they could sleep with and which bench they could sit on. In the Kafkaesque world of racial categorisation upon which the National Party's policy of separate development was anchored, people were classified, reclassified and re-reclassified, with whites being transformed into coloureds, coloureds into Asians, and Asians into Bantus – as the groups were defined.

The laws tore families apart, and turned law-abiding people into criminals and neighbours into enemies. One of the worst examples of this was the story of Sandra Laing, daughter of three generations of white ancestors, who was expelled from school when she was 10 because of her dark skin and frizzy hair.

It was after encountering one of these irrationally cruel situations that Franz Auerbach embarked on a solo crusade to be classified as a human being. Franz's colleague, a gifted teacher, lost her post as a biblical studies lecturer at the Soweto College of Education because of this petty bureaucracy. The woman – classified as African – had married a man classified as coloured.

She applied to be reclassified as coloured so that she could live with her husband in a coloured area. Her application was successful, but what the government gave with one hand it took away with the other. The education department she worked for – the Department of Education and Training – employed only Africans, and now that she was considered coloured, she lost her job.

THE HUMAN BEING

Franz wanted to be proud to be a South African, but was ashamed of the suffering inflicted on his fellow citizens with whom he shared a common humanity.[104]

'What divides us most is my race classification,' he argued. 'I now wish to give that up. I do not wish to be racially classified at all.'[105]

In October 1988 Franz wrote to the Department of Home Affairs and asked to be reclassified as a human being. After a befuddled bureaucrat scratched his head for three-and-a-half months, Franz finally received a reply to say his 'request to be designated a human being cannot be entertained'.

Franz didn't give up. He wrote back and asked to be reclassified coloured because, according to the country's perplexing laws, a person who was coloured was not black and not white. This time the department didn't even bother to respond, so Franz returned his ID and asked that it be cancelled.

'I want nothing more to do with it,' he told the authorities.

For Franz, the attempt to be reclassified was worth making because it demonstrated that one person could show up the absurdities of the whole system. It was satire of Evita Bezuidenhout proportions and, as the journalist Irwin Manoim noted in the Fourteenth Annual Franz Auerbach Memorial Interfaith Lecture in 2018, Franz had made a serious point about the dangers of depriving people of a shared humanity.

It was just one of Franz's many personal battles against the apartheid system.

Franz gave a talk to a group of students at Wits University in 1990, and spoke about his childhood in Nazi Germany and how his experiences had led to his revulsion for institutionalised racism and an undying commitment to human rights. I was in the audience and listened to this inspiring talk from a man whose passion for justice was contagious. His principled stance made a profound impression on me, and 30 years on, I'm still struck by his quiet courage.

---

104 Franz expressed his views in an article in *The Star*, Why I don't want to remain 'white'

105 Auerbach, F: *No Single Loyalty, Many Strands One Design: A South African Teacher's Life*, Waxmann, Munster, 2002

Franz, one of the country's most eminent educators, had been an outspoken critic of the wicked Bantu Education system and of injustice in general.

In his autobiography, *No Single Loyalty: Many Strands One Design*, Franz explained that he didn't see himself belonging to a single human group to the exclusion of all others but was made up of many strands and was best defined as 'a human male named Franz Auerbach, born 1923'.

Some of his strands were: a teacher, a Jew, a humanist, and a South African of German heritage. He was born in Germany to Jewish parents – Erich and Alice – and spent his childhood in the menacing shadow of Nazism. Erich was an electrical engineer and Alice was a dentist. She headed the municipal dental clinic in the city of Wuppertal until she was fired because she was Jewish.

Franz arrived home one day to find an SS stormtrooper outside the entrance to the building where the family lived. It was a memory that stayed with him for the rest of his life.

Franz's parents left Germany in March 1934, a year after Hitler came to power. They went to Luxembourg to train to become farmers so they could get into Palestine, where they had intended to settle.

After three years the Auerbachs had still not received clearance to enter Palestine, so when Erich managed to get a berth on the SS Stuttgart to South Africa, they decided to seek a new life on the tip of the 'Dark Continent'.

Antisemitism in South Africa was on the rise and the authorities were tightening the country's immigration laws, effectively closing its doors to Jews fleeing persecution. The relief organisation Hilfsverein der Deutschen Juden chartered the SS Stuttgart to transport Jewish refugees to South Africa before stringent immigration regulations came into effect on 1 November 1936.

Erich was one of the 537 passengers on board the ship that set sail on 8 October 1936. When it docked in Cape Town harbour three weeks later, members of the Nazi-supporting Greyshirts were waiting for the ship's arrival so that they could spit antisemitic venom at the new arrivals. One of the demonstrators was a Stellenbosch University professor named Hendrik Frensch Verwoerd, who would go on to become the country's prime minister.

Franz and his mother followed Erich nine months later.

THE HUMAN BEING

The only English that 14-year-old Franz knew were the nursery rhymes *Hickory Dickory Dock* and *See Saw Margery Daw*, which his grandmother had taught him.[106]

Alice and Erich were unable to work in their professions and could only get manual jobs. Alice found work sewing dresses at a clothing factory – a job she did for the next 11 years.

Erich bought polony from a butcher he befriended and, putting it in a basket on his bicycle, he went door-to-door in Doornfontein, Yeoville, Berea and Hillbrow selling the meat to other refugees. Franz remembers how tired his father was when he came home and his bitter disappointment when someone who had promised to buy 'next week' had let him down.

Franz attended the Spes Bona Intermediate School and helped augment the family income by teaching English – earning a shilling an hour – to other immigrants whose English was even worse than his.

Despite the language barrier and the enormous physical and psychological upheaval of fleeing Europe, Franz came top of the class in his second year. He enjoyed writing English essays and admired his teacher, who inspired him to become a teacher himself.

In 1939, when he was in Standard 8 (Grade 10), Franz was selected head prefect. Spes Bona was a technical school and only went to Grade 10. When World War II broke out in September, Franz offered to step down as head prefect because he was German and South Africa was at war with Germany. The principal brushed his offer aside.

Franz left school and joined the Waygood-Otis Lift Company as an accounts clerk, while going to night classes to complete his matric and then doing a BA degree by correspondence.[107] It was also where he met his future wife Noreen.

In 1946, a friend invited Franz to the Mayibuye African Night School, and Franz signed up to become a volunteer, giving adult education classes to black adults, many of whom were illiterate. It was the start of his enmeshment in politics, and his association with

---

106 Suttner, Immanuel: *Cutting Through the Mountain*, Viking, 1997
107 Franz would go on to get three more degrees, including a PhD from the University of Natal

African night schools lasted until the government shut them down in white areas two decades later.

Franz obtained his teaching diploma in 1947 and taught English and history in white schools by day and was active in education for black adults at night.

Because of the experiences of his youth in Nazi Germany he felt strongly that all South Africans were his fellow citizens. The government's Bantustan policy of making black people foreigners in their own country appalled him.[108]

Franz couldn't understand how a person could suddenly be told they must have citizenship of a homeland 'somewhere else'.

Franz's daughter Margaret says her father identified with that because it had happened to him. 'My father spoke a lot about how proud his own father was of having served in World War I and had got a medal for it, and how he loved his country and was suddenly told he was no longer a German citizen,' says Margaret.[109]

Franz was committed to South Africa because it had given him and his parents refuge, but for Franz to be committed to the country meant to be involved in its problems, and not turn a blind eye to injustice.

His determination not to close his eyes to injustice landed him in hot water with the education establishment.

In 1957, while teaching at Athlone Boys' High School in Johannesburg, Franz enrolled for a part-time course at Wits University. A visiting lecturer from London, Professor Joseph Lauwerys, gave a seminar and said South Africa was the only country in the world that used its education system to keep its citizens divided.

Franz wondered if this was true and decided to investigate. The research changed his life.[110]

Franz found a disturbing trend of how the education system was promoting racial prejudice. He felt it was important for his findings to become public, so he leaked the story to the *Sunday Times*.

The Transvaal Education Department hauled him before a disciplinary hearing and found him guilty of misconduct.

---

108 Villa-Vicencio, C: *The Spirit of Freedom: South African Leaders on Religion and Politics*, University of California Press, Los Angeles, 1996

109 Interview with Margaret Auerbach, March 2021

110 Suttner, Immanuel: *Cutting Through the Mountain*, Viking, 1997

Nevertheless, Franz's research grew into a master's thesis and was published in 1965 in an authoritative book titled *The Power of Prejudice in South African Education*.

According to Professor Jonathan Jansen, it was unusual to find such a critical account of racism in school books from someone inside the education fraternity.[111]

'[Franz] must have realised that such a publication would come at great risk and that it could cost him his career,' said Jansen.

Die Transvaler, a right-wing Afrikaans newspaper, lampooned Franz and quoted education inspector JJ van Tonder, who had this to say about Franz: *'Waar die by sy heuning uitsuig, suig die spinnekop sy gif uit.'* [Where the bee sucks out its honey, the spider sucks out its venom.] The meaning of this Afrikaans proverb is that some people always think the worst of others and draw the worst conclusions.

The mean-spirited description of Franz couldn't be further from the truth and prompted one of Franz's sons to put his tongue in his cheek and jokingly refer to his father as 'The Poisonous Spider'.

Franz was also smeared in Parliament by the National Party MP Piet du Plessis (who would go on to be a cabinet minister) and was a victim of a disinformation campaign spearheaded by the security police.

Nevertheless, his ground-breaking work on racism in textbooks exerted a considerable influence in bringing about changes.

Franz didn't only take on the education system, though. He was also appalled by the 'second-class bus stop' signs designated for black people, and in 1965 he took on the Johannesburg City Council in a quest to have the signs scrapped.

Three years and many letters from Franz later, the signs disappeared. There were still separate signs for 'whites' and 'non-whites', which remained objectionable, but Franz felt that referring to people as 'second class' was particularly offensive. It had echoes of the Aryans and non-Aryans signs of his youth.

Margaret says her father often talked about his experience growing up in Nazi Germany and how difficult it was for him when he visited Auschwitz in Poland as an adult.

---

111 Jansen, Jonathan: Protest, but don't become the enemy – UFS, *The Times*, 25 May 2015

'You know, he was so humble,' says Margaret. 'He could have claimed reparations but he refused because he felt it wasn't right to claim it because he hadn't suffered as much as many other people.'

She says Franz was always determined to do the right thing, so much so that when he bought something at a flea market and the vendor told him he didn't have to pay VAT, Franz would say that wasn't right, and would insist on paying VAT.

'He was very, very honest,' says Margaret.

When Franz was teaching at Hyde Park High School in Johannesburg, he was elected president of the Transvaal Teachers' Association (TTA) – a liberal union of mostly English-speaking teachers.

Despite his excellent teaching ability, qualifications and experience, he was never promoted and his attempts to be appointed vice-principal were blocked.

He left the Education Department in 1969 and took up a part-time position with the TTA to train teachers, and so began 20 pioneering years teaching teachers in the Teacher-in-Service education programme he ran.

He arranged overseas lecturers, published booklets on educational methods, introduced teachers to innovations and alternative methods in education, and ran courses on creativity.

Franz launched the Teachers' Centre in 1974 and began to include black teachers in its programmes.

The centre didn't have premises, and when Franz wanted to run a course he had to ask a school's principal for permission to use their facilities. He couldn't invite black teachers to courses at government schools, so he went to meet the chairperson of the board of governors of Saheti – an independent Greek school in Johannesburg – and asked if he could hold courses at the school that black teachers could attend.

'Of course,' replied the chairperson.

The chair of the board was the renowned human rights lawyer George Bizos.

Franz believed that merely saying you opposed apartheid wasn't enough. If you believed that racial discrimination was evil then you could not be apathetic; you had to fight that injustice wherever it was and whatever the consequences.

Over the years, Franz wrote copious letters to the press.[112] He was also a prolific writer of scholarly articles, including for *Jewish Affairs*, and authored a book on the Holocaust, *World on Fire* in 1998.

Although his life was devoted to the anti-apartheid cause, Franz never joined a political party. He did, however, become a member of Jews for Social Justice (JSJ) when it was launched in 1985. The organisation aimed to build bridges between white and black communities and show a committed Jewish presence in the anti-apartheid movement.

JSJ members got involved in various issues, such as fighting against the detention of children. Franz was elected JSJ chair in 1989 and represented the organisation as part of a 115-strong Five Freedoms Forum delegation of white South Africans to meet with ANC leaders in exile.

Unlike many Jewish activists who had either renounced their religion or were detached from it, Franz's anti-apartheid convictions were premised on Judaism. Being part of JSJ meant he could get involved in human rights issues as a Jew.

His experiences of Nazi Germany engendered a repugnance for institutionalised racial discrimination[113] and he couldn't understand how Jews who had been persecuted for centuries could be indifferent to racism.[114]

'My father felt that Jews should be part of the struggle against apartheid because of our history,' says Margaret. 'He believed that by getting to know each other, things would change. He was trying to break down walls and barriers and get people to communicate with each other.'

Franz promoted Education for Peace, in which teaching attitudes and values is extremely important. It was the theme of the Eighth Desmond Tutu Peace Lecture he had been invited to deliver at a conference of religious leaders in 1992.

---

112 These letters have been collated and archived at the William Cullen Library

113 Shimoni, G: *Community and Conscience: The Jews in Apartheid South Africa*, University Press of New England, Brandeis University Press, United States, 2003

114 Villa-Vicencio, C: *The Spirit of Freedom: South African Leaders on Religion and Politics*, University of California Press, Los Angeles, 1996

In his lecture, Franz explained that citizens must be allowed to have hope for a better tomorrow. He argued for feeding schemes at schools, saying hungry children can't learn properly. He called for the need to promote 'certain educational truths' that could make for a more peaceful world, and stressed the importance of teaching positive attitudes and values, recognising that 'what is caught is more important than what is taught'.

'Children are not born prejudiced ... little children play together quite happily with children who look different. Prejudice is generally acquired; it is learnt.'

For Franz, one of the joys of teaching was being treated to young people's sense of idealism and hope.

Franz was a liberal in the best sense of the word. He listened, thought and reflected; he was tolerant and open to hearing views that were different to his own – as long as they weren't discriminatory.

He lived by the words of Anatole France, who said: Hate nothing but hatred; be intolerant of nothing but intolerance.

Margaret says Franz and Noreen's tolerance of their children's 'idiosyncrasies and quirks' ensured that she and her three brothers – David, Raymond and Ronald – had a happy childhood.

'We all grew up in completely different ways that challenged my parents, but they always accepted whatever our new thing was; whether it was keeping snakes or being a lesbian, it was all fine,' she recalls.

Margaret says growing up in the household was wonderful because the six Auerbachs had lots of animated discussions about what was happening in the world.

'We were always arguing and everyone had different viewpoints. We all talked a lot, and mostly at the same time.'

Franz and Noreen participated in rallies and attended funerals in Soweto.

'They were at the first Gay Pride march and cheered my partner Liebe and me along the way,' Margaret notes.

She says there was a lightness to her father.

'He was humorous and playful and would often recite the Lewis Carroll poem: "You are old, Father William," the young man said. "And your hair has become very white; And yet you incessantly stand on your head – Do you think, at your age, it is right?" My father would tell people, "Well, I like to stand on my head." They would laugh and he would go and stand on his head.'

Margaret says her father was always optimistic and never dwelt on difficulties.

'He was always positive that things would come right,' she says, adding that when everything did come right in 1994, Franz was over the moon.

'It was so wonderful that he was alive to see the transition to democracy and to be part of that because that was what he fought for all his life. He felt a great euphoria about the whole thing.'

After asking the authorities to cancel his identity document in 1988 because the government wouldn't classify him as a human being, he eventually applied for a new ID when an interim government was set up to manage the transition to democracy. His racial-classification-free ID arrived just days before the April 27 elections. Franz died in 2004 at the age of 81. There was an outpouring of tributes from his colleagues and friends, who described him as a gentle, brave, humble and committed teacher whose life was dedicated to conciliation, bridge-building and opening people's eyes. Above all, though, Franz was a thoroughly decent human being (yes, despite what the apartheid classification board decreed, he was first and foremost a human being).

Franz held many positions over the years, including president of the SA Institute of Race Relations, president of the SA National Yad Vashem Foundation, and executive member of the World Conference on Religion and Peace. He served on the national executive council of the South African Jewish Board of Deputies, which posthumously honoured him with its biennial Human Rights award in August 2005. Beit Emanuel in Johannesburg holds an Annual Franz Auerbach Interfaith Lecture.

CHAPTER 18

SCHOOLS OF THOUGHT

Since the inception of apartheid, many Jewish South Africans have attempted to deliver better education to black people. Many worked as volunteers in the African night schools in the 1950s. During the height of the education crisis in the 1980s, a 'temporary' school was established to provide hope to a group of matric pupils. The school turned out to be not-so-temporary. Meanwhile, the name of a Jewish philanthropist is attached to a school at the centre of a momentous – and painful – political event that put South Africa on the path to freedom.

When Sylvia Schrire was 20 years old she opened a night school at Cape Town's harbour for dockworkers. Sylvia came to South Africa from London in the 1940s, when she was 13.[115] Soon after arriving, she joined the Jewish youth movement Habonim.

'That's where I learnt how dreadful the apartheid regime was,' she says. After matriculating she went to the University of Cape Town and completed a degree in foreign languages. It was also where she mixed with people of various races and attended a meeting of the Congress of Democrats.

When she graduated she started teaching for the Cape Non-European Night Schools Association as a replacement teacher. The association was launched after World War II with volunteers from

---

115 Sylvia Schrire was interviewed in 2019 by Mohale Selebi

UCT to run literacy classes for black adults in an attempt to help alleviate the grave imbalances in apartheid education.

'I taught wherever I was needed. I enjoyed being able to help,' she recalls.

The association asked Sylvia to open her own night school in the harbour compound at the Cape Town docks, and she ran classes ranging from Grade 1 to Grade 8.

'It wasn't a huge night school,' says Sylvia. 'We would get 25, 30 people three nights a week from 7 pm to 9.30 pm. They were dockworkers and would come straight from work, which was very physical, and they wouldn't have had a meal.'

The conditions were difficult. Sometimes there was no electricity and she had to run classes by candlelight.

'I was very impressed with the students' devotion to trying to improve themselves and their education,' she notes. Sylvia established a library and was devoted to ensuring that the students enjoyed some education.

Sylvia had to find the teachers herself. 'One of the teachers seemed to me old, which means she was probably about 40. When you're 20, 40 looks very old. She was prim and proper, and wore stockings, high heels and gloves. We sat at trestle tables and I remember once we were so crowded that there was no space for her, so she climbed on top of the tables, which took quite some effort. One day there were so many people, we opened all the windows and had people crowded around each window, listening and trying to get something out from what we were teaching.'

In her master's dissertation, Daphne Wilson points out that in the early 1950s the association was run predominantly by Jewish volunteers.[116]

'As time went on, the need for more and more teachers and fundraisers to match the expanding number of night schools was one that was met in the 1950s by Cape Town's closely knit Jewish community, even to the extent of inspanning the occupants of the Jewish old-age home in Gardens to pin the thousands of flags needed for the annual fundraising street collections.'

---

116 Wilson, Daphne: The African Adult Education Movement in the Western Cape from 1945 to 1967, UCT, 1988

When Daphne asked the people she interviewed about this 'striking phenomenon', many agreed that the Jewish experience of discrimination and persecution before and during World War II had motivated them to give of their time and energy to people who were likewise suffering.

Two prominent Jewish night schools principals in the early 1950s were Raymond Ackerman and Ronald Segal. The two differed ideologically (Raymond the moderate liberal, Ronald the radical rebel) but both were key drivers of the schools' success.

According to Daphne, Raymond, who had started teaching when he was a teenager and still in high school, played a major role in building the association and was behind the rapid expansion of a growing number of schools around the Peninsula.

Raymond went on to become head of the retail giant Pick n Pay, while Ronald, who launched the anti-apartheid magazine *Africa South* and was the founder of the Penguin African Library, drove ANC leader Oliver Tambo in his mother's Vauxhall into exile in Botswana.

Well-organised night schools had been running throughout the country for over 10 years until they were taken over by the Department of Bantu Education. New regulations were introduced, including that all night schools must be registered with the department and that volunteer white teachers in Cape Town were forbidden from going into townships to teach at schools.

The Cape Non-European Night School Association was forced to discontinue its four schools in the townships, and a night school in the white suburb of Rondebosch was refused permission to continue. Sylvia's dockworker night school was also closed.

A report by the SA Institute of Race Relations records that following repeated representations by the association, the Department of Bantu Education agreed to the revival of Sylvia's school, but 'on condition that it is staffed exclusively by African teachers'. The department had ruled that 'help by white voluntary workers is no longer permitted'.[117]

---

117 Horrell, Muriel: A Survey of Race Relations in South Africa, 1962

Sylvia's night school, which had been staffed by white teachers, was effectively closed[118], and the government implemented its wicked Bantu Education system, which was conceived by the then minister of native affairs and a Nazi sympathiser, HF Verwoerd.

Bantu Education is apartheid's bitter legacy. Designed to keep black people enslaved and ignorant, it had profound and far-reaching consequences. The policy was for black people to have just enough education to work as unskilled labourers – anything else was seen as a waste. As Verwoerd stated: 'There is no place for [the Bantu] in the European community above the level of certain forms of labour ... What is the use of teaching the Bantu child mathematics when he cannot use it in practice?'

Black schools had inferior facilities, teachers and textbooks, and tensions boiled over in 1976 when Verwoerd introduced a regulation that Afrikaans be the medium of instruction. Thousands of pupils from all over Soweto marched to Morris Isaacson High School in defiant protest.

But who was Morris Isaacson and how did his name end up on one of the country's most significant educational institutions?[119]

Morris, a Jewish philanthropist and visionary, came to South Africa from Lithuania in 1896 when he was a teenager. The young man tried his hand at about a dozen different occupations: a smous, a shop assistant, working in a mineral factory and selling insurance, and eventually established himself as a trader.

According to his friend Richard Feldman, Morris was 'a born socialist' who took part in the 1913 strike and played a prominent role in the 1922 Rand miners' strike. Morris had been elected to the national executive of the SA Labour Party.

By the end of World War I, Morris was a prominent Jewish leader, president of the Jewish Guild, treasurer of the Jewish War Memorial Fund and, later, chairman of the SA Jewish Orphanage. He didn't

---

118 Sylvia continued her involvement in education, teaching at a school for autistic children and then working at the Grassroots Educare Trust, which helped empower communities to start their own preschool facilities

119 Information about Morris Isaacson from *SA Jewish Report* articles by Suzanne Belling: Morris Isaacson School – the legacy lives on (3 March 2017) and Just who was Morris Isaacson? (15 June 2017); and 'Soweto's Morris Isaacson School and the man who made it possible' by Paul Trewhela, *Jewish Affairs* (Vol. 74, #1, Pesach 2019)

like using the term 'orphanage', so the home became known simply as Arcadia.

Morris' business career as a trader and hotelier flourished. He married Mavis Myers, who had been the matron of Arcadia, and they moved to Warmbaths (now Bela Bela) in 1926, where they ran the Warmbaths Hotel.

His son Jeffrey wrote that his parents continued with their charity work after leaving Arcadia. 'When I finished school in 1947, my father sold his hotel, and for eight months we travelled. We returned to Johannesburg and I went to study at Wits. My mother was diagnosed with cancer immediately after our return to South Africa and died the day I enrolled at Wits.'

In Mavis' memory, Morris built the first nursery school in Soweto, called the Mavis Isaacson Hall. At the time there was nothing similar in the poverty-stricken area.

Morris and Richard remained lifelong friends, and in Morris's later years, Richard was instrumental in involving him in black education. The Morris Isaacson Foundation granted hundreds of bursaries to black pupils.

Derek Kobe, principal of the impoverished Mohloding Secondary School, had approached several businessmen in the early 1950s to ask them for help. Morris donated six classrooms and a laboratory.

Morris died in 1954 and the school was renamed Morris Isaacson High School in 1961. The first group of pupils matriculated in 1963, and since then it has produced a significant number of Soweto's professional and political elite.

In 1976, Morris Isaacson High became synonymous with the Soweto Uprising, which spread across the country and changed South Africa.

Morris Isaacson isn't the only school named after a Jewish humanitarian – 40km from the famous Soweto school is MC Weiler Primary School.

On a visit to Alexandra in 1945, Rabbi Moses Weiler, first spiritual leader of the Reform/Progressive Jewish movement in South Africa, saw children playing in the streets while their parents were at work.[120]

---

[120] Information about MC Weiler Primary School obtained from the SA Union for Progressive Judaism website

Realising the need for schooling for these children, he decided to establish a primary school,

Rabbi Weiler, his wife Una, and Rita Marx of the Progressive movement's United Sisterhood found a dilapidated four-room house, which they cleaned and painted. They employed a young teacher, Hilda Phahle, as the principal.

Hilda's first pupils were 36 children she found on the streets of the township. She smeared dung on the floors to keep the dust down, and cooked meals for the children.

More and more children came to the school, and the United Sisterhood raised funds to buy a plot of land and build a school with four classrooms.

On 2 January 1949 the Johannesburg mayor opened the school officially, and it was named the MC Weiler School. There were 110 children and two teachers.

By 1954 there were 266 pupils housed in 14 classrooms. Extra rooms were rented all over Alexandra, and classes were held in church halls, cottages and abandoned shops.

In 1981, when Hilda retired after 36 years of unflagging effort, there were 1,000 pupils and 23 teachers in various buildings in the township. Four decades after Rabbi Weiler visited Alexandra, two Jewish women followed in his footsteps.

In 1986, 10 years after the June 16 Uprising, education in South Africa was in a crisis as many black children, frustrated with the seeming futility of apartheid education, embarked on a campaign to bring the school system to its knees.

Ongoing stayaways, boycotts and strikes brought black schools to a standstill.

Molly Smith, who had been a teacher, and her friend Lesley Rosenberg wanted to help. They discussed what they could do to support a group of Grade 12 pupils from Alexandra matriculate in a safe space. They decided to establish the Mitzvah School.

'We were so naive,' Lesley says.[121]

The school was meant to offer classes for just a year.

With assistance from various companies and individuals, as well as the management and rabbi of the Bet David congregation in

---

121 Interview with Lesley Rosenberg, May 2021

Sandton, the school opened with 25 pupils in 1987. It operated from the rabbi's house. All 25 pupils passed their exams.

After the success of the first crop of matriculants, the women decided that the school should continue until there was no longer a crisis in education.

'I told you we were naive,' says Lesley. 'No longer a crisis in education? I mean, hello!'

Lesley recalls that the first few years were incredibly tough.

'There was violence in the township and there were times when the kids would come and live with us. Molly took half the class and I took the other half, and somehow we got through it. Thirty-five years later, more than a thousand pupils, including some children of past pupils, have passed through the school, which is now a permanent, fully accredited educational institution.'

An average of 40 pupils a year from underperforming local schools have flourished under the guidance of dedicated teachers.

Molly has retired but Lesley is still there as the school's director, while Cheryl Crossman is the principal.

'I was very proud to learn that we won the trust and acceptance of the community, because we later found out that some residents were very suspicious of why these two Jewish ladies wanted to help,' says Lesley.

According to Lesley, the pupils sometimes complain that she pushes them too hard.

'Another lesson they learn is what it's like to have a Jewish mother,' she chuckles.

In 2017 the SA Jewish Board of Deputies bestowed the Rabbi Cyril and Ann Harris Human Rights Award on Molly and Lesley to acknowledge their role as pioneers of a new, forward-looking approach within the Jewish community, 'one driven by the recognition that those who enjoyed a privileged position under apartheid have an ongoing responsibility to help address the profound socio-economic imbalances that resulted from that iniquitous system'.

'The Mitzvah School's record of accomplishment demonstrates an astounding ability to produce productive citizens who have gone on to become doctors, lawyers, entrepreneurs, actors and musicians and who continue paying it forward and giving back to the community. The graduates are a huge source of *nachas*,' beams Lesley.

A former pupil came to visit recently and he had car keys in his hand. He showed Lesley his new vehicle.

'This was a kid who studied by candlelight and would come to school with a torn shirt. You know, it's for that boy that I will stay at the Mitzvah School forever. We give them confidence and they leave school with a feeling of self-worth.'

CHAPTER 19

TESTIMONIAL: MARLENE SILBERT

Marlene Silbert taught at Herzlia High School and was the founding education director of the Cape Town Holocaust Centre. In this testimonial she reflects on how her lifelong commitment to human rights has informed her passion for education.

TESTIMONIAL: MARLENE SILBERT

I was born in Pretoria. When I was very young I was aware that people of colour were treated differently, but I didn't know about the apartheid laws. My father was a lawyer, and he frequently defended black activists. I remember one incident when he came home after a trial in which he had defended a black man. He was very upset. He said the man whom he defended had been found guilty after the police had committed perjury.

One day when I was in primary school, my dad took me into a township to show me the terrible conditions under which black people were living. He looked at all the children running around and said it was so wrong that there were no schools in the township. I remember saying, 'Dad, when I grow up, I'm going to be a teacher and I will come and teach here.'

During my high school years I went to boarding school and lived in a secluded environment. We had no interaction with people of colour, and apartheid was never discussed. However, my life overturned when I went to the University of Cape Town. I studied English and drama as I wanted to become a teacher. Within three months of being at university I was having coffee with a fellow student. His name was Norman, and he too enjoyed the performing arts.

I told him I had heard that Marcel Marceau, an internationally acclaimed French mime performer, was coming to Cape Town, so as soon as booking opened, we should book our tickets.

Norman frowned. 'Marlene, you know I cannot go, I'm coloured.'

For the next few hours we discussed the apartheid laws, and Norman spoke about the impact the laws had on the lives of people who were classified as 'non-white'. I was devastated.

A few days later I joined Nusas, the National Union of South African Students. I heard that the National Party government was planning to segregate the universities, and Nusas was protesting and demanding non-segregation, university autonomy and academic freedom.

I became more and more involved in student activities. The following year I was asked to serve on the Rag committee and the intervarsity committee. In addition, two nights a week I taught English literacy to black men who attended the Windermere night school, which had been established by university students. During my third year I was elected to the student representative council. I was the only woman on the SRC. I was also elected head woman student of the university and head woman student of the Hibernia women's residence.

While I was head woman student I received a call from the vice-chancellor, who told me that a special event was being organised to which a number of dignitaries would be invited, including judges, professors, ambassadors, ministers and the archbishop of Cape Town.

He said he would like me to be the official hostess. I gasped but I agreed to do so. I asked the vice-chancellor whether his secretary could give me a list of the guests and the appropriate way in which I should address them (Your Lordship, Your Honour, Your Grace).

I received the information, which I studied carefully. On the evening of the event I welcomed everyone on their arrival. I was standing in a small group with an ambassador, a judge and the archbishop. They were chatting jovially, but after a while there was a moment of silence. I picked up a small bowl of peanuts, turned to the archbishop, who was standing next to me, and said, *'Have a grace, your peanut.'* The group exploded into laughter.

Many years later, when I was working at the Cape Town Holocaust Centre, Archbishop Desmond Tutu attended one of our functions. I told him about the 'Have a grace, your peanut' incident and he roared with laughter.

A week later I received a letter from Archbishop Tutu in which he thanked me for the event and for the work I was doing. The letter ended with "Best wishes, your peanut".

I completed my first course and did a postgraduate course in the teaching of people with speech and hearing disabilities. After graduating, I was employed by the Western Cape Department of Education as an itinerant speech therapist. In 1959 I was married, and had three daughters.

The Progressive Party was launched in 1959. It was the only liberal party at that time, and I joined it.

A few years later I became Colin Eglin's election campaign manager in the Sea Point constituency. The first election we lost by 3,000 votes, the second we lost by 234 votes, and the third election we won!

One evening, while working in the Progressive Party office, I heard a noise at the door. I opened it and saw a man disappear down a staircase. As I turned to return to the office I saw that the wall had been daubed with a hammer and sickle and the words 'Jew nigger

TESTIMONIAL: MARLENE SILBERT

lover'. This was the work of the right-wing white supremacist group called Scorpio, which targeted offices and threw petrol bombs into the homes of people whom they identified as 'liberals'.

During that time my home was a safe house. We hid political fugitives for one or two nights and then they moved elsewhere.

Periodically I would get a call from a person who would say, *'Marlene, your friend Joanne from boarding school is here. She'd be so happy if you would be available to join us for dinner at 7 pm.'* I'd respond by saying, *'That will be lovely.'* That was code, and that night at 7 pm, two or three fugitives were dropped off at our home. We were never told the names of the people, so if I was ever interrogated I wouldn't be able to divulge names.

In 1970 the government introduced Christian National Education into the school curriculum. Children of other faiths were permitted to leave the classroom during these lessons. The children who were excused played outside, and often noisily interrupted the lessons. I thought the problem could be solved by providing alternative lessons. In 1971 I introduced a Jewish religious studies programme, and within a year we were operating in nine government schools. Parents who had teaching experience volunteered to teach the Jewish children, and the programme was highly successful.

The year 1976 was the start of another career for me. I was contacted by the principal of Herzlia High School, who asked if I would teach Jewish studies at Herzlia as they were in need of a Jewish studies teacher.

I explained that I wasn't a biblical scholar, but if I could teach modern Jewish history I would certainly be prepared to do so. I realised that this would provide an opportunity for me to teach about the Holocaust, human rights and the consequences of prejudice, racism and discrimination – issues so pertinent in contemporary society.

Shortly thereafter I started teaching at Herzlia High School. In addition to modern Jewish history I also taught about the Jewish festivals.

During the festival of Sukkot one is obliged to give a gift to a friend and a gift to the poor. Almost all the children brought to the school a gift for the poor – a tin of fruit or vegetables, old clothing, a blanket. I spoke to the principal and said that although the pupils had brought gifts for the poor, very few, if any, knew how the poor were living.

I arranged to take the Grade 12 pupils into a township, and each of them was taken into a shack. The pupils were deeply moved and said it was a life-changing experience. During my first year at Herzlia, the school celebrated Republic Day. The following day I went to speak to the principal and asked why he had arranged to celebrate Republic Day.

His response was, 'The Department of Education has instructed us to celebrate Republic Day, and if we do not, they will withdraw our subsidy'.

I told him I had read the instruction and it did not state we should 'celebrate' Republic Day but rather that we should 'commemorate' Republic Day. The principal suggested I organise the Republic Day commemoration the following year, which I did. I invited a priest, an imam and a rabbi to come to the school to speak about their vision for a peaceful South Africa and to give a prayer for peace.

During the apartheid era, people weren't allowed to sing *Nkosi Sikelel' iAfrika*, but there was no law preventing us from reading the anthem. There were a few black pupils in our school, so I arranged for one of them to read *Nkosi Sikelel' iAfrika* and for a white child to read the translation.

In the 1990s I was appointed deputy head principal of the school.

In 1996 I decided the time had come for me to retire from teaching, but my retirement lasted just one day.

The Jewish Board of Deputies was in the process of establishing a Holocaust Centre in Cape Town and I was asked to assist with the research and write the texts for the exhibition.

While working on this project I felt it was important to contextualise the Holocaust because the lessons to be learnt from it were so relevant to contemporary South Africa. Many of the laws introduced during apartheid paralleled the laws introduced against the Jews in Nazi Germany between 1933 and 1939. Moreover, people should be constantly reminded that although apartheid had been abolished, prejudice and racism continue to prevail and can result in violence.

When the centre opened in 1998 I was appointed education director. I developed four-hour programmes for pupils from Grade 9 to Grade 12 and full-day programmes for members of the civil service, the police, the military and naval academies, and correctional services.

The centre's focus is on the Holocaust and human rights, prejudice, racism, discrimination, the consequences of remaining silent and indifferent to injustice, and the fragility of democracy. People should also acknowledge that we all have the capacity to do evil deeds, but we also have the capacity for love, care and compassion.

The programmes were highly successful, and more and more pupils were brought to the centre. After a few years I received a call from the national Department of Education and was told that the department had heard about the school programmes. They were in the process of revising the Grade 9 history curriculum and had decided to introduce a compulsory module on the Holocaust and human rights.

While I was very excited, I realised that most of the history teachers wouldn't have knowledge about the Holocaust, so I wrote a teachers' manual and a classroom workbook titled *The Holocaust: lessons for humanity*. We also produced a DVD of the testimonies of five Holocaust survivors.

In 2010 I decided that the time had definitely come for me to retire, but once again my retirement lasted for just a day! I was asked to serve on the council of the Cape Town Interfaith Initiative (CTII). Throughout my adult life I had been passionate about striving to create a society in which we can live together in peace and harmony, so how could I refuse another opportunity to do so?

I realised that, under the auspices of the CTII, I would be able to develop an interfaith intercultural programme that would enable young people from different faiths, cultures, races, and ethnic and socio-economic backgrounds to come together and develop meaningful relationships with one another.

OUTSPOKEN RABBIS

CHAPTER 20

PROVOCATEUR WHO WAS ORDERED TO LEAVE SA

Rabbi André Ungar, who spent two years in Port Elizabeth during the mid-1950s, has been largely forgotten in South Africa, but he deserves a special niche in our local history; he was the only rabbi to enrage the apartheid government to such an extent that they expelled him. *By Irwin Manoim*[122]

---

[122] This piece, published on Dafkadotcom, is an edited excerpt from a lecture delivered to Limmud UK in December 2019

A Hungarian Jew, Rabbi André Ungar spent his childhood hiding from the Nazis in Budapest under false identities in a non-Jewish part of town. The horror of Nazism, witnessed first-hand, shaped his attitudes in South Africa, where he was offered his first job as a rabbi in 1955, at the Reform synagogue in Port Elizabeth, Temple Israel.

Rabbi Ungar found his new community friendly enough. He was given a bigger house than he'd ever lived in, complete with garden and servants. He started asking his congregants questions about the silent, ubiquitous but invisible host of black servants and labourers in their employ. As he himself put it in an article later: 'How did they live? What was the relationship between them and us? Naively, I voiced such questions before my new-made friends. That, I was told, is a lifetime's study. You must be born here to understand it. Foreigners can know nothing about it. Besides, it's an unsavoury topic, a communist thing to worry about.'

There was a certain mischievousness to Rabbi Ungar: he was a provocateur. He made black friends – almost unheard of behaviour among whites in the 1950s. His friends included Govan Mbeki, later to be the Robben Island cellmate of Nelson Mandela and the father of former president Thabo Mbeki, and the activist poet Dennis Brutus, who would also be jailed, then flee into exile.

As Rabbi Ungar puts it again: 'An unforgivable sin ... they came to my home; I went to theirs. I would actually be seen going for a drive or a walk with a coloured person ... More impudently still, I invited my white and black friends together, at the same time, not necessarily having warned the whites against what lay in store for them. You should have seen them squirm when faced with the dilemma of whether to accept the outstretched hand and shake it, or pretend it was not there and simply walk out in a huff!'

Rabbi Ungar accepted the chairmanship of an interracial discussion forum, the 20th Century Club, whose members – Africans, Indians 'and a handful of oddball whites' – met once a month, an arrangement considered distasteful by many within white Port Elizabeth.

He proposed to his congregants a series of public lectures on the great religions of the world, which was enthusiastically supported until he said the talk on Hinduism should be given by an Indian. The lecture series was abandoned.

There was disapproval that the nanny was left to babysit in the living room, that the cook was paid a pound more than the local average, and that the maid was given a lift by car to her family home. Rabbi Ungar raised money for a scholarship for a promising African student, but the women's committee resisted, urging that the money be given instead to a Jewish candidate.

The rabbi began giving sermons with a political edge. The first to cause controversy beyond the walls of the shul discussed the case of a local schoolboy, Stephen Ramasodi, who had won a scholarship to a prestigious American college but was refused a passport. The rabbi made parallels between Stephen, who had been denied his dreams, yet was innocent of any crime, and Moses, who was refused entry into the Promised Land. The next morning's *Eastern Province Herald*, under the headline 'Rabbi slates passport refusal to boy', gave generous space to the rabbi's argument, and quoted one sentence in particular: 'The harsh verdict over this young man was passed by arrogantly puffed-up little men in heartless stupidity.'

A stream of angry letters poured into the paper, such as this one from J Jankelson of Port Elizabeth: 'I wish to express the hope that the majority of the Jewish people, local and general, will dissociate themselves from the remarks made by that rabbi, especially his adjectives referring to our government.'

The Afrikaans press took up the controversy, and were particularly enraged by the phrase 'arrogantly puffed-up little men'.

In November 1956, Rabbi Ungar was one of seven speakers at a meeting in protest against the new Group Areas Act. The others, like Liberal Party leader and novelist Alan Paton, who had just written *Cry The Beloved Country*, were far more famous. But it was Rabbi Ungar's speech which made the headlines because he described how Hungarian Jews had been driven into the ghettos by the Nazis, and said he was seeing the beginnings of something similar here.

The Afrikaans newspaper *Die Burger* reported: ' "Race hatred is an abomination and the Group Areas Act is a despicable abomination," said Rabbi A Ungar on Monday evening in Port Elizabeth at a protest meeting. This was one of the vicious attacks by seven speakers at the Feather Market Hall on the Group Areas Act. The audience, which consisted of a small group of white men and women among hundreds of natives, Asians and coloureds, greeted the attacks with applause and jeering laughter. Rabbi Ungar said Hitler was once again on the march in the Transvaal, Natal, the Cape and in the ironically named Free State.'

The article drew yet another barrage of letters, including one from 'Jewish Reader' of Port Elizabeth, who wrote to the Afrikaans press: 'I want to state that this rabbi represents only a very small section of the Jewish community in Port Elizabeth, namely the "Reformed Jewish Church", and his behaviour is not approved of even by his followers. The largest section of the Jewish community in South Africa do not voice Rabbi Ungar's opinions and do not belong to his sort of church.'

Relations became strained, and to general relief, Rabbi Ungar announced that he would resign and leave in the near future. But six weeks before his departure, a sheriff arrived on the doorstep of the Temple Israel congregation, delivering a letter, giving Rabbi Ungar one month to leave the country or be jailed as a prohibited immigrant. Various things were curious about the expulsion order. It was served on the congregation, not on the rabbi. And the authorities knew perfectly well that Rabbi Ungar was leaving anyway. The rabbi suggested that the purpose of the expulsion order was not so much to teach him a lesson, as to serve as a warning to the Jewish community.

Rabbi Ungar received very little support from local Jews, other than from liberal Jews in Johannesburg and Cape Town. The head of the local Jewish Board of Deputies wrote to the newspapers to say the Jewish community was made up of people with many different viewpoints, that Rabbi Ungar spoke only for himself and had to take the consequences, and that there was no reason to believe the government was attempting to intimidate the Jewish community.

An editorial in *Jewish Review*, the publication of the Eastern Province Jewish community, criticised the local press for making a huge '*tzimmes*' over the deportation issue, and said the 'entire Jewish community resents Dr Ungar's act of making a publicity stunt of it'.

The writer wondered whether the rabbi had insufficient work that he could waste his time on attacking the government, and said 'Dr Ungar's departure from our country will be received by some of us with a sigh of relief'.

To be fair to the Temple Israel congregants, on the Sunday morning of the rabbi's departure almost the entire membership arrived at the airport for a farewell ceremony, where children from the local Hebrew school loudly sang *Hevenu Shalom Aleichem* in the departure lounge. Newspaper photographs show some of the children crying. As the rabbi himself put it:

'In the eyes around me there was relief and regret, affection and annoyance, pain and puzzled apology. A silent group of dark-skinned friends stood in the opposite corner, aware that any gesture from them would land them in jail. Then a few of them, in a mad mood of daring, walked over and hastily whispered their greetings. I shook hands with them, horrifying the white onlookers by kissing my dearest friend's wife on the cheek.'

Rabbi Ungar can recall receiving only one message of support from a Jewish religious leader. It came in the form of a cryptic telegram from the Orthodox Chief Rabbi, Louis Rabinowitz, who had hitherto been no friend of any Reform rabbi. The cable said: 'RESPECTFUL SALUTATIONS – CHIEF RABBI RABINOWITZ'. But although Rabbi Rabinowitz made a number of political pronouncements at the time, he made no public mention of Ungar.

Rabbi Ungar ended up in New Jersey, where he served two Conservative congregations, one for 44 years. He became prominent among the rabbis supporting the civil rights movement in the South in the 1960s. He was one of 20 rabbis who went to Birmingham, Alabama, to register voters, and joined the protest marches – both of these dangerous activities at the time. He returned to South Africa on his 80th birthday in 2010 for a visit to Port Elizabeth, where he presided over a baby-naming for the grandchild of a congregant he had taught for his barmitzvah.

He died aged 90 at his home in New York on 5 May 2020 after a long illness.

CHAPTER 21

A STAND AGAINST INJUSTICE

Between 1959 and 1988 four Orthodox rabbis at the Green and Sea Point Hebrew Congregation in Cape Town took a stand against apartheid. *By Gwynne Robins*[123]

In 1999, South Africa's former chief rabbi, the late Cyril Harris, testified at the Truth and Reconciliation Commission on behalf of the South African Jewish community. He apologised for the collective failure of the South African Jewish community to protest against apartheid, and acknowledged how the community had benefited from this system of racial oppression. As Rabbi Harris' testimony

---

[123] This is an edited version of an article by Gwynne Robins published on Dafkadotcom

attests, for the most part, communal silence was the norm, both from the pulpit and from communal boardrooms. Context, of course, is crucial. Caution was justified when dealing with a government with a history of antisemitism.

That said, a handful of rabbis, both Orthodox and Reform, publicly condemned apartheid and took part in protests. Between 1959 and 1988, at one particular congregation, the Green and Sea Point Hebrew Congregation in Cape Town, Rabbi ES Rabinowitz, Rabbi David Rosen, Rabbi Dr Elihu Jack Steinhorn and Rabbi Selwyn Franklin took a stand against apartheid.

Despite massive state repression and tough security laws, the congregation employed and supported rabbis who were prepared to take outspoken positions. This isn't to say their work was uncontentious. Ultimately, one of the rabbis resigned, the government refused to renew the work visas of two others, and the congregation didn't renew the contract of the fourth.

The first to provoke congregational criticism and censure was Rabbi ES Rabinowitz, a graduate from Mir Yeshiva. Appointed in 1959, Rabbi Rabinowitz started to produce weekly congregational newsletters. The contents raised alarm bells. He was asked by the synagogue committee to confine his newsletter to religion and congregational matters, to exercise discretion in order to avoid any possible litigation, and to deal more judiciously with controversial matters. By December 1963 the committee decided to meet the rabbi fortnightly to discuss the topics he would be covering. But the newsletters continued – and so did the complaints from his committee and members of the congregation. When the president of the shul decided to stop the newsletter, the rabbi said he would leave. The committee asked him to reconsider. He agreed. Then the press published comments made by Rabbi Rabinowitz in one of these newsletters, and the Board of Deputies became concerned. The committee decided to stop all future issues, and Rabbi Rabinowitz resigned.

As the newsletters have not survived, the question remains: what was in them that could have resulted in litigation? Why was the rabbi told to confine himself to religious and congregational matters? It was a politically contentious time with the passing of the 90-day detention law. Also, Israel had informed the UN special committee on apartheid that it would be complying with the military boycott of South Africa. We can only surmise that the newsletters were critical of apartheid policies. Perhaps Rabbi Rabinowitz spoke out against the Rivonia arrests in 1963. The committee, understandably, would have been scared of the potential fallout.

The next rabbi who stoked controversy was less circumspect. Rabbi Rosen grew up in England, where his father was a prominent Orthodox rabbi. He also received his *smichah* (ordination) at the Mir Yeshiva. Rabbi Rosen was inducted in 1975 and became active in interfaith work because he saw it as a way to bridge racial schisms in apartheid South Africa.

Rabbi Rosen remembers the tension caused by his determination to speak challengingly at a shul service to mark Republic Day. City councillors, parliamentarians, provincial councillors and leaders of Jewish organisations were in the audience. The press reported on his address, stating that religious leaders, particularly Jewish ones, had failed in their duty to separate politics and religion.

When the Jewish Board of Deputies and the SA Zionist Federation honoured Prime Minister BJ Vorster on his return from a visit to Israel in 1976, Rabbi Rosen refused to attend, and said so from his pulpit. On another occasion he was quoted as saying the only way to remain in this society as a Jew was to stand up for principle and integrity and against injustice. All of this occurred in a context of resistance in the townships and increased state repression.

Although some members of the shul disapproved of his stand, the great majority supported him, as did the Cape Jewish Board of Deputies and Rabbi Duschinsky, then head of the Beth Din. Rabbi Rosen received anonymous death threats, and the security police started tapping his phone. The government refused to renew his work permit, and he left South Africa in 1980.

He was replaced by Rabbi Steinhorn, who held a PhD in philosophy from New York University.

Like Rabbi Rosen, Rabbi Steinhorn was charismatic and open-minded, and had a strong commitment to social justice. When the shul celebrated its 1983 golden jubilee with a dinner attended by State President Marais Viljoen, Rabbi Steinhorn attended, but he reminded the diners that although they swore allegiance to the Republic, they were exhorted to keep alive the vision of the prophets and the cause of social justice and universal brotherhood. Although the shul's president and executive supported him, he clashed with some shul committee members over his participation in Reform community functions and his work with communities outside the Jewish community, such as domestic workers and the homeless.

Rabbi Steinhorn was on a four-year contract, but resigned before it was up. His resignation coincided with the government's withdrawal of his work permit. His outspoken criticism of the government's apartheid policies wasn't welcomed.

He was followed by Rabbi Franklin, who, like his predecessors, participated in interfaith services dedicated to peace and justice.

The *Cape Times* quoted him as saying: 'Together with other leaders of major religious denominations I call for consultation and negotiation with the legitimate leaders of the black community so that peace, tranquillity and justice will prevail.'

Rabbi Franklin was openly critical of what he termed an 'iniquitous society' and shared platforms with the United Democratic Front. In 1984 he was involved in starting Jews for Justice in Cape Town. In 1985, as part of the End Conscription Campaign's Troops out of the Townships campaign, he was one of the first people to join activist Ivan Toms in a 24-hour solidarity fast. Detention without trial, influx control and forced eviction of people, he said, were anathema to the Jewish faith. Rabbi Franklin formed the Jewish Relief Committee in 1986 to assist the 60,000 people who were left homeless by violence and factional fighting in the Crossroads squatter camps.

Rabbi Franklin faced no opposition from the Cape Jewish Board of Deputies, but the shul committee was concerned. A state of emergency had been declared and there was increased confrontation between the state and political organisations fighting for liberation, with armed actions by Umkhonto we Sizwe guerrillas. The shul introduced security arrangements. When Rabbi Franklin started to speak about Gugulethu, a congregant recalled people muttering, 'Here he goes again.' The committee refused him leave to attend an interfaith conference in Nairobi, and finally advised him that a majority of members were dissatisfied with his activities.

He later remarked: 'What is happening in South Africa is not just political, but a question of morality, and therefore we should be involved. A lot of my community are very afraid of change because change carries with it a degree of uncertainty. A lot of them are senior citizens who have lived their lives and played according to the rules of apartheid. A lot are concerned that if there's a black administration in this country it would mean a degeneration of their privileged position.'

His contract wasn't renewed and he immigrated to Israel in 1988.

Rabbi Rabinowitz went to England to be close to his children. He published a book on Torah for teenagers. Rabbi Rosen became the chief rabbi of Ireland and was at the forefront of global interreligious dialogue. He is the first Orthodox rabbi to be knighted by the Pope, being made Knight Commander of the Order of St Gregory the Great in recognition of his contribution to Jewish-Catholic reconciliation. He was also given a CBE (Commander of the British Empire) by the Queen.

Rabbi Steinhorn became faculty director of teacher training at Jews' College in London and head of Yeshivat HaKotel in Jerusalem.

After the unbanning of the ANC, Rabbi Steinhorn was offered his former position again in 1991. The South African rabbinate put pressure on the synagogue to retire him as a rabbi emeritus in 2004.

Rabbi Franklin went to Israel and then to Australia. He served as a rabbi in New York and as a professor at Moriah College in Sydney.

CHAPTER 22
A KIPPAH OF HOPE

Rabbi Myer (Sonny) Benjamin was a much loved and charismatic leader of Temple Israel in Wynberg, Cape Town. He had an unforgettable sense of humour, was tirelessly committed to his congregation and was courageously outspoken against apartheid. *By Ute Ben Yosef*

Rabbi Myer (Sonny) Benjamin was born in London in 1919. After World War II, during which he fought in the British Army, he came to Cape Town, where he attended services at Temple Israel and became inspired by the sermons of Rabbi David Sherman.

Because of his excellent knowledge of Hebrew and Jewish studies, the temple employed him as a teacher and youth leader, while he pursued his studies at the University of Cape Town.

He was later invited to East London, where he played a key role in founding the Progressive Jewish congregation of Temple Hillel. In 1961 he took up the position of assistant to Rabbi Meyer Miller of Temple David in Durban. There he met and married Nina in December 1962. He returned to serve the community in East London a year later. They had three children, David, Jonathan and Deborah.

During the 1960s, a period of consolidation of the apartheid laws, Reverend Benjamin (as he was then known) became deeply involved in the SA Institute for Race Relations. He worked closely with Christian ministers such as the Reverend Rob Robertson, who founded the first multiracial church in South Africa. He and Nina became aware that their phone was tapped and that the security police were watching him. In fact, members of the security police pretending to be Jewish – with very little success – attended his lectures and Friday night services to monitor his sermons.

The security police also paid visits to his home, during which he received thinly veiled warnings over tea.

In 1972 Rabbi Benjamin left South Africa for England to serve the Brighton and Hove Liberal Synagogue and to study at the Leo Baeck College in London for his formal rabbinical ordination.

Once ordained, he returned to South Africa in 1976 to briefly serve the Springs Progressive Congregation before being invited back to Cape Town, where he was installed as the rabbi of Temple Israel in Wynberg.

The Wynberg congregation flourished under his rabbinate. At the same time he continued his quiet activism against apartheid. Nina, while also very involved in the congregation, took up a teaching post at a school for coloureds. Rabbi Benjamin would be contacted by parents of activists who had been arrested and he would try to make contact with them.

Once he told the police that a certain student, who had been arrested for distributing anti-apartheid pamphlets, needed a Bible. He was told the student already had one, whereupon Rabbi Benjamin took his *kippah* from his pocket and explained that the student needed a yarmulke in order to pray.

This was accepted and given to the prisoner. After his release, the student contacted Rabbi Benjamin and told him the *kippah* had given him hope and the knowledge that he hadn't been forgotten.

Rabbi Benjamin attended many anti-apartheid protest meetings. In 1986 he unhesitatingly defied the authorities and allowed mothers and children, whose shacks had been destroyed by the government in the heart of winter, to be housed in the hall of Temple Israel. The sounds of crying babies during Shavuot services are still remembered by members of the congregation. Many volunteers of other faiths came to help provide these destitute people with food and to take care of the children.

Rabbi Benjamin's phone was tapped again and he received threatening calls during the early hours of the morning. Although he knew these were scare tactics to try to stop his activities, the situation gradually took a toll on his health.

Rabbi Benjamin began to suffer from a heart condition. After his third heart attack, his doctors decided he should have bypass surgery. As all three of their children wanted to live in Israel, Nina and Rabbi Benjamin decided to join them there, and immigrated to Israel in 1988. Rabbi Benjamin died in Israel on 21 February 1995.

THE ARCHAEOLOGIST & THE ARCHITECT

CHAPTER 23

MAZEL TOV

Archaeologist Aron Mazel has spent decades excavating sites, analysing artefacts and recording rock art to shed light on South Africa's past, but it was his own family history that inspired him to become involved in the country's freedom struggle.

In 2010, Makhosi Khoza[124], a then powerful and influential ANC MP, wrote an article in the KwaZulu-Natal newspaper *The Witness* about the scars of apartheid.[125]

She said the scars were sad reminders of the damage caused by a society that was not at peace with itself. Khoza then went on to document good reminders; the things that are worth remembering. And for her the good reminders are the people who played a role in saving her life – people like her 'second father', Aron Mazel.

In 1984, when Khoza was 14, political violence engulfed her hometown in the Edendale Valley in Pietermaritzburg, KwaZulu-Natal. She and many other teenage activists were forced to flee their homes.

'A lot of young people were killed and I lost many friends,' Khoza wrote in the article in *The Witness*. 'Peter Kerchhoff [founder of the Pietermaritzburg Agency for Christian Social Awareness] received me as a refugee and found families that I could stay with.'

One of the families was the Mazels. Khoza moved in with Aron, an archaeologist, and his wife Ann (Macdonald), a teacher, and their daughters. She stayed with them on and off for the next six years and regarded them as her second parents. She said Aron and Ann had nothing to gain by taking her in; they did it out of the goodness of their hearts.

But for Aron it wasn't just about being good at heart, which he is. For Aron, Khoza's story was deeply personal.

Aron's journey to Pietermaritzburg starts in Lithuania, which is where his parents were born.[126] His father Morris Mazel was born in 1908 in Panevėžys, or Ponevez as it was known in Yiddish. His mother Lily Wainer was born 14 years later in a village about 30km away called Ramygala. They didn't know each other but were 'marinated in the same sauce' in that part of northern Lithuania.

---

124 Makhosi Khoza, a vocal critic of state capture, resigned from the ANC in 2017

125 Khoza, M: Let us not allow evil forces to ruin our country, *The Witness*, 8 April 2010

126 Information for this chapter comes from interviews with Aron Mazel in July and October 2020 and from the chapter *Pajouste Forest, 23 August 1941, Memory, migration and massacre*, by A Mazel in *Memory, Migration and Travel* (edited by Sabine Marschall), Routledge, London, 2018

Morris's life had been disrupted by World War I when, in 1915, the Jewish community in Panevėžys were given 24 hours to leave because the retreating Russians thought the Jews were spying on them for the Germans. Morris, who was 7, left with his parents Mordechai and Mashe and his older brother for Ukraine. They returned home seven years later, after the Russian Revolution, the upheaval having totally disrupted Morris's education.

In 1929, with very little formal schooling and no work opportunities in Lithuania, 21-year-old Morris set sail for a new life in South Africa. He didn't have a job but he had *landleits*, people from Panevėžys who were living in Cape Town.

Coincidentally, Lily's father, a blacksmith, left for South Africa that same year. The plan was for him to earn money and bring out the rest of his family. It took him six years to do that, and during that time, Lily helped her mother raise her three younger brothers. Lily, who hadn't gone to school, came to South Africa in 1935 and at the age of 13 started Sub A. She spent six years at school and then went to work for OK Bazaars.

In the meantime, Morris ran a fish and chips shop with a *landsman* in Cape Town. He saved up to go back to eastern Europe to visit his parents in 1937. It was the last time he saw them. On Saturday 23 August 1941, the Nazis and their Lithuanian collaborators massacred 7,523 Jews in Pajouste Forest, about 10km outside Panevėžys. Mashe and Mordechai were among the dead.

Morris and Lily had deep emotional connections to Lithuania and to their family who were murdered there, and the Holocaust was a powerful backdrop to Aron's life from as early as he can remember.

Morris and Lily met on Muizenberg beach in 1948. They lived in Vredehoek and had seven children. Aron, the fourth child, jokes that he's the most balanced member of his family because he sits in the middle.

Aron asked his mother why they had such a large family when their income derived from a small grocery shop in District Six. He wanted to know how his parents thought they could afford to have seven kids, who all went to Herzlia, a private Jewish school. His mother explained that because of the Holocaust, his father wanted to grow the Jewish population. His parents didn't talk often about the Holocaust but there was a deep sense in the family that a major injustice had been committed.

'Although I might not have been completely conscious of it at the time, subliminally I had a sense of the impact that oppression has on people,' says Aron.

Aron's childhood was a happy one. Although the siblings didn't have the luxuries some of their friends had, they were fed and clothed and had the freedom to roam around Vredehoek, exploring Table Mountain and spending time on the beach. On weekends and holidays they worked in their father's grocery store.

Morris had bought the shop, which was situated at 155 Caledon Street in District Six, from a *landsman* who was Aron's godfather, Dave Witten, in 1940. District Six was an interracial – although mostly coloured – working-class area on the edge of Cape Town's CBD. It was a poor but culturally rich community, and was known as the soul of Cape Town. Morris named his store M Mazel & Sons.

'It was a male-oriented household,' says Aron, 'especially because my parents had five sons and two daughters.'

Aron says his father was political in the sense that he thought communism was the best idea for human beings; it's just that human beings weren't good enough for communism. 'Which kind of makes the point, doesn't it?' he says.

Lily and Morris were humble people. Lily, a displaced person herself, was devoted to raising her family. Morris became a feature of District Six, and residents gave him the affectionate nickname 'Mazel Bleskop' (bald head).

Years later, Aron visited the District Six Museum, and the tour guide remembered Morris. He told Aron that District Six residents had regarded Mazel Bleskop as a kind man who was good to people and was well respected and liked.

'I remember that,' says Aron. 'I remember my dad being good, joking with his customers, and delivering groceries to folk who couldn't get to the shop.'

When Aron was about 12 he was making his way to his father's shop when he was confronted by a man with a knife, who demanded five cents. Five cents in the late 1960s was quite a lot of money.

A woman who was watching shouted at the *skelm*: '*Los hom. Hy is Mazel se seun.*' (Leave him. He's Mazel's son.) The scoundrel left Aron alone.

When the National Party came into power in 1948 it started to introduce laws like the Group Areas Act to enforce their separate development ideology. In 1966, District Six was declared a white area, and two years later the process started to bulldoze homes and forcibly remove thousands of coloured residents to areas like Lavender Hill and Bonteheuwel, which became known as the Cape Flats.

During this time – the late 60s and early 70s – Aron's older brother was studying at the University of Cape Town and was involved in some of the campus protests. A newspaper published a picture of him protesting and a police dog biting him, ripping his trousers.

Aron was enthused by his brother's political experiences, and progressive, anti-apartheid ideas began floating around in his head.

The destruction of District Six had a profound impact on Aron. 'We used to walk to my dad's shop and there would be the gaps where buildings had come down. I don't recall seeing homes bulldozed or people's belongings being put on trucks, but I do have a memory of people coming into my dad's shop and talking about what was going on.'

The residents resisted, and it was only in the mid-1970s that the government had finally managed to demolish all the homes and businesses, including M Mazel & Sons.

In 1974, when Aron was doing (and hating) his forced military service, he learnt that M Mazel & Sons had been flattened.

'We didn't lose the roof over our heads, which happened to a lot of people, but our livelihood as a family was taken away,' says Aron. 'In a moment it was pulled out from underneath our feet.'

Morris was 66 and didn't have many options. What he did have was seven children – one was working, one was at university, one had gone to Israel, Aron was in the army and three were at Herzlia – and a lot of bills.

'It created a lot of uncertainty in the family. Because of his experiences in his life, with the First World War, the Russian Revolution and the Holocaust, my dad lived with a lot of anxiety and fear.'

Morris managed to get a job at a grocery wholesaler for a while, and with some income from the flats he owned above their flat he was able to make sure all seven of his children were fed, clothed and educated. However, Morris was sad that he couldn't pass his business and what he had built on to his children.

For the second time in his life, Morris lost his sense of belonging. For years after his shop was razed he would walk through the city centre to the library to read the newspapers, and some of his old

District Six customers would greet him with a cheerful, 'Hello Mazel Bleskop'.

Meanwhile, after completing his national service, Aron studied archaeology at UCT. He participated in some anti-apartheid demonstrations on campus and was friendly with people on the left, but didn't get involved in political societies.

On one excavation, Aron went with Cedric Poggenpoel, the lead technician in the archaeology department, who happened to be black, and Cedric's brother-in-law, Mike Herbert, to Clanwilliam. Cedric had taught Aron to excavate, and the three got on well. One day they went to buy meat for a braai and were confronted with 'Whites' and 'Non-whites' entrances at the butchery. Aron had a decision to make. He decided to use the Non-white entrance with Cedric and Mike. That wasn't the last time he bucked the system with an up-yours to apartheid laws.

After completing his honours, Aron was hired by the Natal Museum (now KwaZulu-Natal Museum) to work on a research project in the uKhahlamba-Drakensberg mountains. He arrived in Pietermaritzburg on 6 January 1979 and walked into the museum. He had long black hair down his back, a bushy red beard and a sticker on his satchel that read 'Apartheid Must Go'. His colleagues stared at this Cape Town *betoger* (demonstrator). 'Their eyes were on stalks,' Aron recalls. Ironically, this satchel now forms part of the museum's anti-apartheid collection.

Aron's project was to develop a management plan for the rock paintings in the mountains, which involved lugging heavy cameras over thousands of kilometres across the rugged terrain.

'When I arrived in Pietermaritzburg I was unfit and overweight, and people took bets on how long I would last before I would flee back to Cape Town.' They misjudged him.

Aron spent most of the time in the mountains alone. Occasionally he would get dropped on horseback at a rock shelter or cave and spend days – sometimes weeks – without seeing anyone. He completed the project, and the Natal Museum created a permanent job for him as a researcher.

Towards the end of 1982 he was joined by his girlfriend Ann, who got a job teaching at Amakholwa High School in Edendale.

Aron and Ann became friendly with activists involved in the Association For Rural Advancement, a land rights advocacy group that supported marginalised people in rural areas, and engaged with the issues around forced removals and the conditions under which those people had to live.

In 1983, Aron joined the Committee of Concern, which was the forerunner of the United Democratic Front in Pietermaritzburg.

'I went to the Pietermaritzburg launch of the UDF and became part of the movement. I went to meetings and took part in activities such as the million signature campaign against apartheid and the anti-Tricameral Parliament campaign.'

Aron and his comrades walked the streets, knocking on doors in the coloured and Indian areas to ask people to boycott the National Party's attempt to woo them into the discredited Tricameral Parliament.

He was working long hours at the museum and at excavations and was becoming increasingly involved in political activities. Life was busy, and became even more frenetic when the couple's first daughter, Nicola Simangele, was born.

'For a period I'd get up at about 4 am or 5 am, be at the museum at 6 am, work for three hours, then go home to look after Nicola for four hours while Ann taught. Her lessons had been concertinaed so she had to squeeze a day's worth of work into about four hours. I'd then walk back to the museum with Nicola, where I'd hand her over to Ann and work the rest of the day, go home for supper, and then go politicking,' says Aron.

Being an activist meant Aron attracted the attention of the security police, whose office was next to the museum. One day, the trade union leader Jay Naidoo came to visit Aron, and someone from the museum rushed to the police station to inform them.

One of the Mazels' housemates was Jonathan Kaplan, who was active in the End Conscription Campaign, and one day a military policeman raided the house, looking for material. 'Ann, who was heavily pregnant, was there with two-year-old Nicola, and the officer was rude and abusive to Ann. He asked who had 'knocked her up' and threatened to throw her down the stairs,' Aron recalls.

In the mid-1980s an intense struggle was taking place in Pietermaritzburg between the UDF/ANC and the state-supported Inkatha. The conflict became increasingly violent. Activists were being killed in numbers, which largely went unreported.[127]

---

127 Mazel, A: Capturing Conflict on Film: *Weekend Witness*, 20 March 2010

'Young activists – kids really – were being flushed out of the townships and were becoming displaced,' says Aron.

'These kids needed refuge, so Ann and I and our friends would look after them. Our house became a refuge. We worked with the Pietermaritzburg Agency for Christian Social Action, which was led by Peter Kerchhoff, who would find safe places for children who had been displaced.'

Some of the people the Mazels looked after returned to their own homes when it was safe, some stayed with the Mazels for a while before heading off to join the liberation movement in exile, and some moved on to other houses.

In September 1985, Kerchhoff phoned to say there was a girl looking for accommodation for a few nights. Aron and Ann went to collect her. Aron remembers seeing the girl sitting on the stairs of an outhouse at the back of the Pietermaritzburg Agency for Christian Social Action offices, clutching a little suitcase. The teenager was Makhosi Khoza.

Because of the experience of his parents, who had to flee their homes, Aron had a deep connection with the Edendale teens who had been forced out of their homes.

'It was personal. It was something that had happened to my family and now it was happening to Makhosi and to a lot of others as well,' he says.

Makhosi, nicknamed *Lady Siyay'nyomfa* (the disruptor), was a youth leader by the time she was 12, and had been arrested for giving a revolutionary speech.[128]

Ann taught Makhosi to sew and Makhosi regarded the couple's daughters – Nicola and Rebecca Nomathemba – as her sisters.

The Mazels were clear that the young people who came into their home had to respect the couple's values.

'We thought of ourselves as Marxists and we were disciplined about how we lived our lives. Some of the younger kids couldn't take that and would quickly leave,' says Aron. 'But Makhosi stayed and we developed this relationship, which, 35 years later, is ongoing. She became a daughter to us. We never replaced her parents, who lived in Harewood, an Inkatha stronghold.'

---

128 De Groot, S: What mighty Makhosi Khoza believes, *Sunday Times*, 20 August 2017

The Mazels protected Makhosi and gave her shelter, food and a safe place where she could retreat to when necessary.

Aron doesn't know if the security police knew Makhosi was living with them.

'She was a very powerful young woman, she was extraordinary, and would have been very much on their radar, but they never came looking for her in our house,' he notes.

Makhosi says Aron and Ann took care of her as if she was one of their own.

'When I wrote my matric exams, Aron would take off from work to drive me to Msimude High School in Sweetwaters, Pietermaritzburg, and wait for me to finish writing,' she says.[129]

When Makhosi's family's home was burnt down, her parents and siblings fled to the Mazels and lived with them until they were rehoused.

For Aron, the burning down of Makhosi's parents' home had echoes of the razing of his father's grocery shop 13 years earlier.

In 1986 Aron's activism developed in a new direction when he picked up his camera and began documenting social and economic injustices in Pietermaritzburg.

'I started to use my camera in the townships, photographing what was going on, because the press was ignoring this area and I wanted to get the information out to the world. I spent a lot of my weekends photographing rallies, union meetings, marches and funerals – a whole range of things. Often, I was the only white person there.'

On Saturday mornings the phone would ring.

'*Nchebe*,' someone would say (*Nchebe*, which means 'bearded man' in isiZulu, was Aron's nickname), 'we're burying this person. Could you please come and photograph it?' Aron would fetch his camera and head to the funeral.

Aron and a few other budding photographers formed the Pietermaritzburg Photographic Collective (PPC) and spent time capturing the injustices in and around Pietermaritzburg.

In 1988, Pietermaritzburg celebrated 150 years of its founding. The PPC set up an opposition project titled 'What Is There To Celebrate?'

---

129 Mtshali, S: Khoza on death threats against her, *The Sunday Independent*, 16 July 2017

While the city council hosted a range of celebratory ceremonies, Aron and his colleagues photographed political and social events in Pietermaritzburg and the surrounding townships, and created an exhibition that went up in St Peter's Church in the centre of town.

For six years Aron worked with local communities. Residents would lead him into the heart of events so that he could document what was happening.

'I saw the injustices of apartheid, which strengthened my commitment and spurred me to capture more visual proof with which to make known to the world what was taking place,' he says.

Getting a bird's-eye view of the energy and excitement of the people at rallies and marches gave Aron hope, but photographing funerals brought home the community's deep suffering.

Aron worked behind the scenes in the anti-apartheid movement and never took leadership roles.

'This wasn't something I desired. There was nothing in me that said I must push myself to the front. I didn't feel it was my role to lead. It was my role to support and to help,' he notes.

Aron was thrilled when Nelson Mandela was released from prison in 1990. 'It was emotional to know that what we had been striving for over many years had come to fruition, and Mandela was free,' he says.

Although the country was taking tentative steps towards democracy, the political violence of the 1980s had spilt over into the 1990s. A few months after Mandela's release, the ANC leader came to Pietermaritzburg to witness the political tensions between the ANC and IFP. He visited a church in Mpophomeni township that had been damaged by members of Inkatha. Aron was in the church. He had gone round the back and Mandela was in the front, and they entered the church at the same time.[130]

'It was just the two of us in the church,' Aron recalls. 'We walked towards each other, shook hands and asked how each other was, and then we both went out the way we had come in. It was a magical moment to meet this man.'

Aron was appointed the assistant director of the Natal Museum in 1994, and a few years later, the director of the South African Cultural

---

130 Mazel, Aron: When I Met Nelson Mandela, BBC History, 12 December 2013

History Museum. In 2002, he took up a position at Newcastle University in England.

When he returns to South Africa he makes a pilgrimage to 155 Caledon Street in District Six, where M Mazel & Sons once bustled with customers Morris Mazel served faithfully for 35 years. The site has remained vacant since 1974.

We're chatting over Zoom. Aron's in the village of Haydon Bridge on the River Tyne, where he now lives. 'Look at this,' he says, whipping out a book. The book – which is about District Six – was the first birthday present he ever gave to Ann. He reads the inscription:

> *Dearest Annie. Happy 21st. This will be a remembrance to one of the most vibrant and fascinating places in Cape Town, which unfortunately you arrived too late to see. Good luck for the future.*

Aron smiles. 'And then we had our future together. District Six obviously meant so much to me that the first birthday present I gave to the person who means so much to me was a book on District Six. My experience of District Six is deeply embedded in me,' he says.

'I've carried that through my life. It may not have been a conscious thing but I believe it did influence my involvement in the anti-apartheid struggle. At a deeply personal level it raised my consciousness of what was happening, and gave me a sense of abhorrence at the injustice. I think it tied in with the loss of my grandparents and my father's loss when his shop was pulled down. It gave me a very strong personal framework to affiliate with the anti-apartheid movement because it was deeply connected to my family's loss.'

Aron's family's loss – specifically the massacre in Pajouste Forest – has been an ever-present shadow in his life.

In August 2011, the 70th anniversary of the slaughter of more than 7,500 Jews, Aron visited Panevėžys to honour the memory of his family and recite *kaddish* at the kill site.[131]

And while Aron honours his family, his surrogate daughter Makhosi Khoza honours him.

Makhosi says that as a teenage anti-apartheid activist she had become an 'internal exile'. 'Our homes were gutted, family members

---

[131] Mazel, A: *Pajouste Forest, 23 August 1941, Memory, migration and massacre*, published in *Memory, Migration and Travel* (edited by Sabine Marschall), Routledge, London, 2018

murdered. Our white, Indian and coloured comrades opened their homes for us, risking their lives. As a 14-year-old and a homeless person, the Mazel family took me into their home. Without the Mazel family I would be dead. Aron Mazel was not just my father, but my comrade.'[132]

---

[132] This was tweeted by Makhosi Khoza on 30 September 2019

CHAPTER 24

IVAN THE TERRIFIC

Frank Chikane stood before a crowd at the SA Council of Churches in Soweto in 2008. Among the men and women were 40 'ordinary South Africans' who had put their lives at risk to keep him safe.[133]

---

[133] Honouring those who risked so much, IOL, 27 February 2008

IVAN THE TERRIFIC

He had been on the run from the security police in the mid-1980s. 'Since freedom was won we have not found a way of honouring the thousands of ordinary South Africans who risked their lives in the struggle to eradicate the apartheid system,' the former fugitive told the crowd. One of the unsung heroes at the event was the Johannesburg architect Ivan Schlapobersky.

'Ah, Frank,' says Ivan when I contacted him to talk about how he came to have aided and abetted a 'terrorist' during the dark days of apartheid.[134]

Ivan had left South Africa in 1976 after his marriage broke down and the country was falling apart at the seams following the June 16 Soweto Uprising.

Apartheid had always disgusted him, and he decided to take his two sons to Canada, where he practised as an architect. In 1985 he returned home.

'It was probably the most dangerous of times for dissenters but I could see the tide was turning and change was in the air,' he says.

Soon after his arrival he received a call from Judith Hawarden, an old friend, who wanted to discuss something confidential. 'I couldn't refuse,' Ivan tells me.

Ivan and Judith met and she explained that she was heavily involved in the struggle against the National Party government. She told him she had a friend called Frans, who was wanted by the police. Judith asked Ivan if he could hide Frans in his home 'for a while'. Judith was already hiding another fugitive in her house.

Ivan quotes an extract from *Surviving the War* by Adiva Geffen.

> 'It's not enough,' the Polish woman said. 'You know that we are risking ourselves, that the Germans will kill the both of us if we are caught. I don't want the child in our house.'

---

134 Interview with Ivan Schlapobersky, March 2021

> *'You have nothing to worry about. My wife and daughter are familiar with living in hiding. You won't hear them – this is not the first time. And just for the Lady Yezhiga, a ruby ring that will fit your finger.'*

> *'I don't know. Jews have a certain smell and if, God forbid, the dogs should pick it up ...'*

'As a Jew,' Ivan says, 'I could not refuse Judith's request, even though there was no ruby ring in the deal.'

Frans arrived the following evening, carrying a small suitcase with his belongings.

'He had an engaging smile and was very polite,' Ivan recalls. 'It was hard to conceive how he could be associated with any sort of violence.'

Frans was concerned that Ivan's helper Lizzie might recognise him and inadvertently expose him. Ivan told Lizzie that Frans was a student working on his thesis and the family would be helping him because he couldn't afford rent.

'I knew my phone was being tapped because every time I received a call, there was a double click like someone was tapping into the line. So whenever Frans wanted to call someone he would walk to the café two blocks away to use the public phone.

Ivan placed a stepladder in a corner of his garden so that if the police raided the property, Frans could hop over the wall and disappear.

One day Ivan's son Paul picked up a bottle of pills in the bathroom he shared with Frans. He glanced at the label and saw the name on it was 'Frank Chikane'.

'I never let on to Frank that we had uncovered his disguise,' grins Ivan.

The Rev Frank Chikane was the vice-president of the Transvaal region of the United Democratic Front, an organisation that was formed in 1983 to bring a wide range of groups together to campaign against apartheid.

Two years later he was among 16 UDF leaders charged with high treason.

'We were acquitted because they couldn't pin anything on us,' Frank tells me.[135]

Six months after he was freed, the government declared a state of emergency and rounded up activists. Frank decided to go underground.

'Going underground means you disappear, you don't go back home, you don't meet family. You have to find places to hide: safe houses, church buildings, anything that could be used,' he says, adding that a network of comrades was set up to organise the logistics for the fugitives.

'It was quite amazing, actually, because their job was to find safe places and move us from one place to another when our security was compromised. You had to trust the people who moved you and trust that you were being moved to a safe place, and that's how I arrived at Ivan's place. Ivan didn't ask questions. There was the need-to-know rule, which means that you only asked about things you must know. Otherwise you don't ask.'

Ivan says he and Frank got on well. 'We had lots of discussions and I used to cook for him.'

Frank says they talked about life in general, but avoided talking about politics or what he was up to.

'Ivan provided meals and treated me like family. I don't eat pork so it was easier for me to be in a Jewish home,' he adds.

One evening Ivan returned from work to find his guest sitting at the table with a broad grin on his face.

'He told me he had just been appointed general secretary of the SA Council of Churches and felt he no longer had to live in hiding because his new position would ensure safety from persecution by the regime.'

Frank surfaced from the underground at Archbishop Desmond Tutu's home because he felt the police wouldn't dare arrest him there.

'After I emerged I knew there would be an international uproar if the security police detained the new general secretary of the SACC. So they decided that if they can't arrest me, they must use other methods of tackling me. Ja, but I survived,' he says.

---

135 Interview with Frank Chikane, May 2021

In 1989 the security police laced Frank's underwear with a nerve agent that almost killed him.[136]

Frank left Ivan's home a day after his appointment to the top SACC post.

'I never heard from him again until more than 20 years later, when he invited me to the event in Soweto at which he thanked me for the assistance I had given him,' Ivan says.

According to Frank, Ivan and the network of comrades were extraordinary.

'Ivan and the others saved our lives in many ways and they had never been recognised. I really appreciate what Ivan did for me. If the cops found me in his house he would have been detained for many months or charged. He took a huge risk.'

When I ask Ivan how he coped with the stress that comes with harbouring a wanted 'terrorist' – after all, he could have received a lengthy prison sentence – Ivan brushes it off.

'It wasn't too bad,' he states, explaining that he also had Canadian citizenship, which he believed might have offered him some sort of protection.

'I remember Frank as a lovely guy, but after he recently "declared war on Israel", I'm not sure we would have much to talk about now. I feel strongly about Israel,' says Ivan.[137]

He continued to make his home available to other activists on the run.

'I never knew who they were. They never told me their names. They didn't stay as long as Frank, who was there for five or six months. The others stayed a few days at a time, maybe a week or two,' he recalls.

In addition to harbouring fugitives, Ivan and a group of like-minded architects, such as Clive Chipkin, Henry Paine, Jeff Stacey, Hans Schirmacher, Leon van Schaik and Percy Poplak, decided to challenge the profession's apathy towards apartheid.

---

136 Former law and order minister Adriaan Vlok, ex-police commissioner Johan van der Merwe and three former high-ranking policemen pleaded guilty in 2007 to attempting to murder Frank Chikane

137 Reverend Frank Chikane at centre of anti-Israel storm, *SA Jewish Report*, 18 February 2021

They believed architects couldn't be apolitical when there were laws like the notorious Group Areas Act.

In an article in the journal *Architecture SA*, Ivan, Clive Chipkin and Henry Paine explain how many professions were openly challenging government policies, but architects 'were as quiet as mice'.[138]

'Many [architects] were too busy nibbling away at the great apartheid cheese, preoccupied with all those structures of separate development such as segregated "homelands", learning institutions, vast complexes for the proliferating bureaucracies, police headquarters where the writ of habeas corpus did not apply, resettlements from Pageview and District Six, and palaces for tinpot dictators,' they wrote.

The group decided to form Architects Against Apartheid (AAP). Their first act was to draw up a resolution stating it would be unethical for architects to do any work for the government or design buildings with separate facilities, or that promoted separate development, or that played a role in enforcing apartheid, like police stations, courts and prisons.

'We submitted the AAP resolution to the SA Institute of Architects,' says Ivan. 'It caused a fury. Many of my colleagues were involved in designing government buildings like the whites-only Rand Afrikaans University and the Johannesburg General Hospital. These were big and lucrative contracts, and you could retire on the fees charged.'

The institute called a meeting to vote on the resolution. More than 750 architects attended the gathering at the Linder Auditorium at the College of Education in Johannesburg.

'It was probably the biggest meeting of architects in history,' says Ivan.

Architects came from all over the country. Hans Schirmacher tried to speak but was interrupted with cries of 'politics'.

Ivan recalls: 'The chairperson called the meeting to order and then said that before he put our resolution to a vote, he had a counter-resolution that had been submitted from the floor. This new resolution said our resolution should "not be put". Then the chairperson called for a vote on that resolution first, and the meeting voted not

---

138 Schlapobersky, Ivan; Chipkin, Clive; and Paine, Henry: Architects Against Apartheid, Architecture SA, March/April 1994

to vote on our resolution. It was nasty. We were all devastated, but our colleagues went home satisfied that their livelihoods would be protected.'

The members of the AAP were principled architects with strong ideals. They put their careers on the line to resist taking in government contracts, and although their motion was defeated by their own colleagues, they had fought hard.

The AAP members realised that the institute was not going to change, so they decided to channel their activism into something practical, and started the Alexandra Arts Centre in Alexandra township.

Ivan recalls: 'We all got involved, teaching architectural drafting, pottery, music, art. It really took off. It was a wonderful thing. The security police would come to the centre and hassle us, but people like Clive Chipkin gave as good as they got. He wasn't afraid of the cops. He was the most amazing person. You come across very few people like that in your life. He had such a strong social conscience. He tried to help wherever he could and he used to call me over the years, asking if I could take in a young black architect or draftsman. He was a remarkable guy.'

Clive died on 10 January 2021 at the age of 91. Clive's most famous architectural moment came at the beginning of his career when he designed the layout for the legendary Congress of the People at Kliptown in 1955, where the Freedom Charter was signed.[139]

Clive was working for architect and anti-apartheid activist Rusty Bernstein, who asked him to turn a dusty soccer field into a venue suitable for a mass gathering.

Clive later wrote: 'In retrospect, the most momentous project of my career turned out to be the gumpole and hessian single-seater privies at the Congress of the People.'

Clive was harassed by the security police, and his son Ivor remembers Clive walking out of his house to a police car parked outside and inviting the cops in for tea.

---

[139] Manoim, Irwin and Silverman, Melinda: Farewell to an architectural giant, *SA Jewish Report*, 14 January 2021

'With squealing tyres they screeched off without taking up the invitation, never to return!'[140]

Ivan says the police harassment never blunted the progressive architects' commitment to ending apartheid.

He felt that as a Jew it was his duty to get involved in the struggle for freedom.

'My parents came from Lithuania, and my father's family and my mother's family were all murdered in Vilna in 1941. I viewed the South African situation through the lens of the Holocaust. I thought black people are being persecuted, yet they belong here. They have done nothing wrong but the government has denied them everything. It wasn't acceptable.'

Ivan was disappointed that the Jewish community didn't speak out about apartheid.

'I remember reading in the *Zionist Record* that when Percy Yutar was appointed chief prosecutor in the Rivonia Trial, Jews were proud of him because he had such an important role. It made me sick.'

Ivan was thrilled when Nelson Mandela was freed from prison and democracy arrived.

'It was wonderful,' he says. 'It gave me such confidence in the future. Although my wife and I went to a meeting Mandela addressed at a school in Houghton, and he talked about "you whites". I never thought I would hear that from Mandela. I thought to myself, have I suddenly become "you whites"?'

Ivan was a card-carrying member of the ANC, which is something his wife never lets him forget.

'She keeps the card next to her bed, and whenever I complain about the government, she takes it out,' he laughs.

Making a splash

Ivan and his group of anti-apartheid architects swam against the current when they took on the architectural profession. Ivan continues to make a splash, but this time in the pool.

---

140 Paine, Henry: A much-loved architect and historian with a keen sense of ethics, *Daily Maverick*, 20 January 2021

In 1953, 19-year-old Ivan was studying architecture and repeating a number of subjects he had failed in his first year. He was also a national swimming champion and had been selected to compete in the Maccabiah Games.

His professor gave him an ultimatum: architecture or swimming. He couldn't do both. His parents told him he couldn't make a career out of swimming and he was forced to withdraw from the Maccabiah team at the last minute, which enraged the national swimming officials, who punished him by leaving him out of the team for the Commonwealth Games. To add insult to injury, the winner of the 200m breaststroke, Ivan's race, did a slower time than Ivan's at the SA championships that year. Ivan gave up swimming for many decades, but 60 years later, he got to relive his dream when, at the age of 80, he competed in the 2013 Maccabiah Games in Israel, winning three gold medals in his age group.

JEWS WHO SAID NO

CHAPTER 25

OY VEY! WE WON'T JOIN THE FRAY!

The apartheid government relied on the call-up of young white men into the South African Defence Force (SADF) to maintain its grip on power. However, it didn't expect that resistance to compulsory military service would give rise to an 'enemy from within'. Jewish conscientious objectors were prominent in the campaign to end conscription.

I inherited my oldest sister's bedroom when she moved out of our parents' home. She left an End Conscription Campaign (ECC) poster on the wall. The poster included Picasso's *Guernica*, a powerful anti-war painting that expressed the Spanish artist's anguish at the Nazis' destruction of the Basque town of Guernica in 1937. The painting contains feverish figures of people and animals contorting in pain, as well as mutilated body parts. Underneath the painting was the ECC's broken-chain logo and the legend: A Civil War Is Not Very Relaxing. This was the unsettling image I woke up to every morning in 1988 when I was in matric, and my main ambition was to leave school and grow my hair. Just before my final exams I received a brown envelope. I tore it open and out slid a piece of paper – my call-up for two years of military service into the SADF and a one-way train ticket to Potchefstroom. The government was ordering me to protect our women and children from the 'terrorists'. Maybe it was looking at that poster with its 'A Civil War Is Not Very Relaxing' slogan every morning for a year, but instead of joining the

SADF I joined the ECC. This was a small but powerful organisation that became a sharp thorn in the flesh of the apartheid government.

One of its founding members was 'a cocky Jewish kid' from Herzlia Weizmann Primary School in Cape Town, Laurie Nathan.[141]

Laurie, a third generation South African, was born in Sea Point in 1959. His grandparents were from Lithuania and England. After graduating from Weizmann Primary he went to South African College High School (SACS).

He had a comfortable and safe childhood, and was blissfully unaware of apartheid. Laurie was simultaneously an achiever – he was a prefect and took part in the debating and drama societies and won awards – and a rebel, constantly clashing with authority.

For Laurie being Jewish meant a deep concern about injustice. The Holocaust was ever present; it was something he grew up with because he knew that if he had been in Germany at the time, he would have been a target.

'So it makes it personal,' he explains. 'The Holocaust taught me two things: that justice is a requisite and that justice applies to everybody.'

After school Laurie went to the University of Cape Town. Soon after arriving on campus he walked past a hall where a mass meeting was being addressed by the trade union leader Sisa Njikelana. Laurie was curious. He wandered into the meeting and listened to Njikelana deliver a fiery speech.

'I realised with a sense of profound shock that at the age of 18 I was living in a country with a population 80% black and, before that moment, had never in my life met a black person who wasn't a servant. Sisa Njikelana was nobody's servant. It was, like, "Shit, where have you been? What country are you living in? Wake up, dude!"'

Laurie started attending National Union of South African Students (Nusas) meetings and read the organisation's pamphlets with a growing sense of disbelief at his own naivety and ignorance. He realised he had been living in a bubble and had been utterly unaware of the reality of what was going on in the country. He read about differences between blacks and whites in things like education, infant mortality and life expectancy, and was stunned.

---

141 Interview with Laurie Nathan, March 2020

'I felt like I'd been played for a fool,' he says. 'It evoked a profound sense of injustice and I started to get involved – not as a full-time activist but as a bystander.'

At the end of the year he went on holiday to Greece and then to Germany, where he decided to go to a concentration camp.

'I went to Dachau. It's such a big thing in our imagination. I got on a train and suddenly I'm at Dachau,' he says. 'It had been snowing so it was aesthetically pristine. Then I saw the crematorium, but there was no sign of people dying there.'

Laurie found the experience alienating; he felt disconnected, as if he was experiencing a failure of imagination.

'I couldn't get my head around this extermination of 6 million Jews. On the train on the way back I kept thinking that Jews want the camps kept intact so that *it* never happens again. What's the *it*? What should never happen again? Do we limit the *it* to the attempted extermination of Jews or do we see the injustice as injustice against anyone? And my conclusion was that it has to be the latter, it's about humankind. And just as we want to know how Germans today can claim they didn't know what was happening, I thought, well, the same thing is going to be said about white South Africans one day. When apartheid ends we aren't going to be able to say, "Oh, sorry, we didn't know what was happening." Of course we know what's happening.'

On the way back to South Africa, passing through London, Laurie saw a statue commemorating the British volunteers who fought – and died – in the Spanish Civil War against fascism. The inscription on this statue read: They went because their open eyes could see no other way.

He says that from the moment he read the inscription he became a full-time activist, willing to sacrifice his studies and his career.

'I was committed to that until the ending of apartheid.'

Laurie became involved in all Nusas activities and was elected to the SRC as the education officer in 1979. The following year he was selected SRC president.

This was the early 1980s, and one of the issues Nusas campaigned around was conscription, which was a key component of the government's Total Response strategy to the Total Onslaught by the supposed twin threats of *die swart gevaar* and *die rooi gevaar*. Military service for all white men became compulsory in 1968, but it was only after South Africa's invasion of Angola in 1975 and the June 16

Soweto Uprising in 1976 that South Africa's anti-war movement began in earnest. Draft dodgers hid from the military, went into exile or, like a few brave souls, went to jail.

Laurie was getting call-ups every year from military intelligence – even though he was just about the last person MI would have wanted entering its ranks. He was getting automatic deferments while he finished an LLB. When he finished that he registered for a master's degree at the University of Bradford in England, which had a peace studies department. The university had agreed that he could write his dissertation in Cape Town. Every year he wrote to the army saying he was registered at the University of Bradford; he never actually said he was out of the country.

According to Laurie, it became clear to the student activists that there was enormous political potential in campaigning around conscientious objection and an end to conscription because they would be targeting the vulnerability of the state, which had to defend the system on the basis of conscripting only white men.

The state's vulnerability was exacerbated by the fact that a relatively large number of white men, for non-political reasons, didn't want to spend two years of their lives in the army or, in some cases, give up their entire lives and come home in a bodybag.

A handful of young Christian men began to object publicly on just-war grounds and were imprisoned in military detention barracks. The Conscientious Objectors' Support Group was established to highlight their plight. The publicity fallout saw the government amend the Defence Act in 1983 to offer a limited (and punitive) option of alternative service. The act also increased the penalty for conscientious objection to a mandatory six-year prison term as well as a 10-year sentence for anyone who encouraged people to disobey their call-up.

A resolution at a Black Sash conference in 1983 called for an end to conscription – and the ECC emerged from that resolution. Laurie explains that the ECC did not call for individuals to refuse to serve (which was unlawful), but called on the state not to conscript (which was lawful).

'The other critical decision we made,' says Laurie, 'was to establish the ECC as a broad front, as a coalition, rather than as an explicitly or exclusively left-wing organisation. The idea was to reach far into the liberal sector of the white community for support in order to broaden our appeal.'

The ECC was a single-issue campaign that drew thousands of white South Africans in a broad coalition of pacifists, old communists, young liberals, liberation theologians, bunny huggers, tie-dyed hippies, English, Afrikaans, school pupils, university students, parents, pensioners, musicians, Christians, Jews, and young men whose ambition was to grow their hair.

Laurie and his fellow refuseniks prepared a manifesto, the ECC Declaration, stating that they were opposed to compulsory conscription on just-war grounds.

'We were not willing to serve in an apartheid army, explicitly political, but we were saying to prospective organisations and individuals: if you support this declaration, come on board. We don't have to agree on communism, socialism or capitalism. We received a lot of support from individuals who were not otherwise political but who had been politicised by the problem of having to put on that uniform and carry a gun.'

According to Laurie, the ECC had revolutionary potential because its members were the enemy within. 'It was also a way of saying to our black comrades in the UDF and the ANC that we were seriously committed to the struggle and we were willing to go to jail for our refusal to serve,' he says.

Laurie was appointed the ECC's national organiser in 1985 and brought vast energy to the job. He kept the regions in touch with one another, and became the public face of the organisation, appearing on public platforms and in debates. He also went on a tour of Europe to meet with conscientious objector groups and anti-war organisations to strengthen international solidarity and raise awareness about the anti-conscription movement back home.

The ECC was serious about what it did, but pursued its objective while having fun. The organisation held peace festivals and rock concerts, and produced attention-grabbing stickers, banners, T-shirts and anti-militarisation posters, like one of a forlorn conscript holding his head in his hands with the slogan, *Botha, ek's gatvol* ([PW] Botha, I'm fed up).

The ECC embarked on various campaigns such as No War in Namibia; Stop the Call-up; Troops out of the Townships; and Working for a Just Peace, which called on the government to allow for meaningful community service for all conscientious objectors.

These campaigns gained so much traction that the then defence minister, Magnus Malan, described the ECC as the country's third biggest enemy after the ANC and the SA Communist Party.

ECC members were called traitors and, as Malan once put it, 'mommy's boys' who were in bed with communists. The slurs were one thing; the dirty tricks something else entirely. Activists were beaten up, had petrol bombs thrown into their homes, their cars were tampered with, and the security police repeatedly raided the ECC's offices and detained its members.

For Laurie, state repression against what the ECC were doing confirmed they were on the right track.

As the ECC's national organiser, Laurie was in the security police's crosshairs. When a number of ECC activists were detained, he went into hiding, living in safe houses offered by sympathisers.

'There were anxious moments,' he recalls. 'I came out of the house one morning and the security police were waiting outside. They'd fallen asleep in their car. They'd probably spent the night there and fallen asleep. I leapt over the back fence and landed in the neighbour's garden. There were those kinds of adventures.'

He recalls taking a train from Cape Town to Durban. He booked the ticket under a false name, and when the conductor came into his compartment with a list of the passengers' names, Laurie couldn't remember the name he had booked under.

In the middle of the night he woke up when the train stopped. He looked out the window and saw hundreds of military vehicles. His first thought was that they had come for him. 'No, they can't be serious. I'm really not that kind of a threat! What are they all doing here?' he wondered. He needn't have worried: the train had come to a stop outside a military base and was parked there for the night. It had nothing to do with him.

'I was in hiding, but the stress levels were eminently manageable,' he says.

Despite this clampdown, the ECC continued to grow. In 1987, 23 objectors announced their refusal to serve in the SADF. The number swelled to 143 in 1988. Two weeks later, the then minister of law and order, Adriaan Vlok, banned the ECC. However, resistance continued to flourish, with 771 men joining the national register of refuseniks in 1989.

Jews had a strong presence in the anti-conscription movement – as individuals like Laurie, who was not part of a formal Jewish organisation – and as a group. Franz Auerbach of Jews for Social Justice was one of the custodians of the national register of objectors, and Jonathan Handler, the chairperson of the South African Union of Jewish Students, was part of the initial group of 23 objectors. Thirty-three Jewish conscripts, who were part of the National Jewish Conscientious Objectors group, were among the 771 who told the government, 'Hell no! We won't go!'

Most of the Jewish objectors were graduates of Jewish day schools and had been leaders in the Jewish Zionist youth movements Habonim, Bnei Akiva and Netzer.[142]

The National Jewish Conscientious Objectors cited as their concerns the SADF's ongoing destabilisation of the Frontline states and its role in the townships, as well as the general militarisation of South African society.

'We see our objection to serving in the SADF as an expression of our Jewish faith and heritage, and as loyal to the majority of South Africans,' the group said in a statement, and called for constructive community service to be made available.

The group added that it stood in solidarity with Jewish objectors David Bruce and Saul Batzofin, who were two of just a handful of men who gave the SADF the most dramatic middle finger of all: they went to jail rather than serve.

On 25 July 1988, 25-year-old Bruce, who had graduated from Wits, became the first conscript to receive the maximum six-year sentence. David was 'just an ordinary guy' with no political profile.

His refusal was based on his fundamental opposition to apartheid and to the war the SADF was waging in defence of it, as well as his family's experiences in Nazi Germany.

His mother, Ursula, was a child in Nazi Germany. Her father left the country soon after Kristallnacht to find a place where his family could join him. He opted for South Africa, and in 1939 his family joined him.

---

142 Shimoni, G: Community and Conscience: The Jews in Apartheid South Africa, University Press of New England, Brandeis University Press, United States, 2003

Twelve members of Ursula's extended family died in the Holocaust, and David grew up being conscious that it was his own family who had suffered.[143]

'I grew up very aware of the experience of the Jewish people,' David told journalist Julie Gordon. 'I looked at it in moralistic terms from an early age. For me to be able to condemn what happened in Germany, I had to be able to say that in the same circumstances I wouldn't do the same thing.'[144]

David said he went 'through hell' making the decision to refuse to serve. 'It took everything out of me to commit myself to doing it, and then I did it ... I was deeply afraid.'

On 5 August 1987 he reported to Johannesburg's Sturrock Park, which is where SADF recruits would muster twice a year. But instead of climbing into an army truck, he told the officer in charge that he was not prepared to serve in the military. He was sent home.

David didn't hear anything until January 1988 when he was summoned to military police headquarters and given another chance to do his national service. For the second time he refused.

David didn't object on pacifist grounds. He said he would be willing to serve in an army that defended the population, but not one that was involved in waging a civil war. He wasn't against military service; he was against apartheid.

He went on trial on 19 July 1988.

'Being aware, as I am, of how European Jews and in fact the entire people of eastern Europe suffered during the period of the Holocaust, I feel that I have no choice but to set myself against those who choose the path of increasing racial intolerance and racial hatred in the firmest way which is possible to me,' he testified.

He told the court that serving in the apartheid army was unconscionable for him and he wasn't prepared to flee the country.

'My mother is a refugee from racism. I am not prepared to be another one,' he vowed.

Ursula also took the stand, and in moving testimony described how she experienced racial persecution in Germany as a child.

---

143 Suttner, Immanuel: *Cutting Through the Mountain*, Viking, 1997
144 Ibid

'I can't prevent myself from being very, very conscious that there are some comparable things between the National Socialist system and the system here,' she said.

But Magistrate Pieter Bredenkamp was unmoved. He rejected appeals for leniency, saying military service was an obligation vital to safeguarding state security.

Moments after David was sentenced, members of the crowd sang *Nkosi Sikelel' iAfrika* and raised clenched fists.

The outspoken opposition MP Helen Suzman said it was incomprehensible that such a cruel sentence should be imposed on someone who was clearly not a criminal.

That afternoon's edition of *The Star* newspaper carried a photo of David with the headline: Bruce gets six years.

Black commuters heading back to Soweto after work stuck the page on the windows of their buses in solidarity with David, who was hailed as a martyr.

In April the following year, Saul Batzofin, who worked for a life assurance firm, went on trial. Saul had completed his two years' initial military service, but his experience in the army transformed him from an apolitical soldier into an anti-war activist who was prepared to go to jail. The turning point took place when he was on patrol in Ovamboland in the then South West Africa (Namibia) looking for Swapo (South West Africa People's Organisation) 'terrorists'.

'We stopped at a kraal. One of our NCOs got out of our vehicle and asked people where the terrorists were. It was mainly women and children. There were no males there except very young and very old. [The villagers] said there weren't any terrorists about and they didn't know anything. Then the NCO got quite aggressive. He went around the kraal and hit every single person in the head, hard.'[145]

Saul started thinking that if the army had come to defend the people in Ovamboland, how come the people were terrified of the soldiers and how come the soldiers were beating them up? He came to the realisation that the SADF was not there to protect the Ovambo people; it was there to defend apartheid.

---

[145] Jaster, RS and Jaster, S: *South Africa's Other Whites: Voices for Change*, from the chapter The Education of a Young Objector, Palgrave Macmillan, 1993

After completing his military service Saul joined the ECC and became increasingly politicised. He completed two month-long camps, but when he was called up for a third, he refused.

'I felt the SADF was being used as a tool to uphold apartheid, and putting on an SADF uniform was aligning with the apartheid regime in oppressing the majority of South Africans,' Saul told the *Mail & Guardian*.[146]

'It was the right thing to do for me personally and, I believe, the correct thing to do politically to raise awareness that the fight against apartheid was supported by white South Africans too, and hopefully that played a small part in convincing people that a non-racial democracy was a viable alternative for South Africa.'

Saul was handed an 18-month jail term, which was reduced when compulsory military service was halved.[147]

David served 20 months of his sentence and was freed in 1990.

After the release of political prisoners and the unbanning of political organisations, including the ECC, conscripts simply ignored their call-ups. According to *Rapport* newspaper, only 2,600 of the 12,000 young men ordered to report for service in July 1993 showed up.

A month later, the then minister of defence, Kobie Coetsee, announced the end of conscription.

The ECC's job was done. Mission accomplished.

Reflecting on his involvement in the anti-apartheid movement, Laurie says that while politics is invariably complex, the situation in South Africa at that time was clear-cut: you were either for apartheid or you were against it, and if you were against it, you couldn't sit on the fence, you had to get involved.

'We were in our twenties, and there was no sense of mortality but an absolute sense of conviction: we are on the right side of the fence. We were part of something bigger than us. We were part of something important. I threw away a law career, but I had no sense of regret then, and I have no sense of regret now. It was a thrilling

---

146 Jailed for a moral choice about war, *Mail & Guardian*, 7 August 2014

147 Saul was granted amnesty by the Truth and Reconciliation Commission in 1997. He told the TRC he was proud to have been an objector, but his criminal record was causing difficulties with visa applications for foreign countries

time to be involved, and looking back I never paid a price; I was a beneficiary of the struggle,' he says.

Laurie learnt an enormous amount throughout that period, consciously and unconsciously, about the type of person he wanted to be.

'A lot of that learning came from the feminist movement within Nusas, which challenged male comrades on how we behaved. I wouldn't make any claim to have sorted all of that out but it was hugely instructive to not always be the loudest voice in the room, to not always have to win the argument, to be less arrogant, less dogmatic and less macho. It was a huge transformation. I grew up a cocky Jewish kid at Weizmann Primary and SACS; we were the kings of the universe, and I think the feminist movement was a sobering experience in trying to knock some of that crap out of me.'

A DEGREE OF ACTIVISM

CHAPTER 26
'COMRADE RABBI LAEL'

Lael Bethlehem says a line directly connects her being Jewish with her involvement in student politics in the late 1980s, and her development work since then. Lael knew that if she didn't get involved in the fight against apartheid, she would have had to account to her children one day when they asked: 'How the hell did you just watch?'

'COMRADE RABBI LAEL'

The first time I saw Lael Bethlehem she was holding my smelly, scuffed, secondhand army boot. It was 1990, my first year at Wits University, and I had joined the Student Community Action Group (Scag), a Nusas subcommittee that went into informal settlements to conduct clean-up campaigns.

There was a meeting for all Nusas recruits one evening, and as an ice-breaker to get to know each other, we all threw one of our shoes into a circle. Then we grabbed a shoe that wasn't ours, hunted down its owner and introduced ourselves. I was wearing a pair of boots I'd bought for R5 from an army surplus store in Rockey Street.

Lael had picked up my boot and I watched her scan the one-socked students searching for the boot's pair.

'Who is that?' I asked fellow Scag member Jonny Rosenthal.

'That's Lael Bethlehem,' he answered. 'She's a heav.'

A 'heav' was the term for a senior Nusas leader; someone who had earned their struggle stripes. We regarded them with awe and reverence. A moment later Lael made her way towards me.

Now, 30 years later, Lael is making her way towards me once again, but this time digitally (and without my smelly boot in her hand). Her image comes into focus on our Zoom call.[148]

After leaving Wits, with a master's degree in industrial sociology, Lael worked as a researcher in the union movement and at senior levels in national and local government, and was the chief executive of the Johannesburg Development Agency. She now manages investments for the empowerment company Hosken Consolidated Investments (HCI). In other words, she's still a 'heav'.

She's speaking to me from her office in Solly Sachs House. Another former Nusas 'heav', HCI chief executive Johnny Copelyn, named the building after the great trade unionist. Solly organised the Garment Workers' Union (GWU) until he was forced to leave the country. Johnny picked up where Solly left off (although several decades later) and organised workers in the clothing industry into the 150,000-strong SA Clothing and Textile Workers' Union (Sactwu), which is now HCI's major shareholder.

The walls of Solly Sachs House are lined with photographs of the confrontation the clothing workers had with the police on the steps

---

148 Interview with Lael Bethlehem, May 2021

of the Joburg City Hall on the day Solly broke his banning orders to address GWU members.

Lael explains that she became involved in politics as a consequence of being Jewish and of her particular Jewish upbringing.

'It was a Jewish moral responsibility that I was trying to fulfil. It was a very direct line. I grew up in Joburg and was part of the reform shul Temple Emanuel (now Beit Emanuel). There was very active progressive Jewish life around the notion of *tikkun olam* – repairing the world. When I was a kid I heard about *tikkun olam* from Rabbi Richard 'Dickie' Lampert, who was outspoken about apartheid.'

In the aftermath of the 1976 Soweto Uprising, Rabbi Lampert distributed pamphlets to the congregation about the 'sin we have committed by keeping silent in the face of injustice'.[149]

The police subsequently raided his home.

'Some members of the congregation were unhappy with the stance he took. There were rumours that they reported him to the security police, and he decided to emigrate,' recalls Lael. 'So there was a whole drama that went on in the shul.'

Lael was very active in the reform youth movement Maginim, later Netzer Maginim.

'For us in Maginim the point of being Jewish was *tikkun olam*, and the ideology was that we should make aliyah and try to move Zionism in a progressive direction. In other words, you should be doing the work of *tikkun olam* in Israel. I was very enthusiastic about that. My sister Louise and brother Keith were active in the movement. We spent weekends at meetings and holidays at *machanot*, learning, teaching and singing.'

Lael pauses for a moment. 'You know,' she says, 'my first ambition in life was to be a rabbi.'

Lael went to King David and was influenced by her high school history teacher, Michelle Friedman.

'Michelle was very radical. She would invite us to her place to watch video recordings of the inquest into the death of Steve Biko. She had to be a bit careful because the education authorities weren't enamoured with her, but she did her best to enlighten us.'

---

149 Goldberg, Dan: South African Jews in Australia Recall Life in the Shadow of Apartheid, Haaretz, 10 December 2013

'COMRADE RABBI LAEL'

Lael decided that after matriculating she would go on the AFS student exchange programme to the US. Michelle took her aside and warned her that she mustn't allow herself to become an ambassador for apartheid.

Michelle told her the organisers would give her slides of lions and elephants and ask her to talk about *that* South Africa.

'I remember her saying that I must use the opportunity to mobilise people against apartheid and make it clear what was really happening in the country.'

Lael matriculated in 1985 and the AFS programme started in August 1986, so she had half a year to kill. Wits agreed to allow her to start her first year before going on AFS and complete it when she returned the following year.

'I went to Wits with my head full of *tikkun olam*, and I joined Nusas. That year – 1986 – was a tough year on campus. There was some very heavy stuff that went on in the run-up to May Day.'

In 1986, the newly launched Congress of South African Trade Unions organised one of the country's biggest stayaways to demand recognition of May Day as a paid public holiday. Students joined the protest action.

The day before May Day there was a range of events in Soweto, and buses were organised to take students into the township.

'I stood at the bus debating with myself whether I should go. I was worried about compromising my place on the AFS programme, and if I'm honest with myself, I was terrified. In the end I didn't go. Mostly because I was scared.'

Lael went to America in August with Michelle's words 'tell people about apartheid' ringing in her ears.

'When you're an exchange student, people want to hear from you, and I arranged to speak to groups of schoolkids, and later students and adults. I got involved in a reform shul in Buffalo, and the shul invited me to give talks. After a while I was doing talks every week, both in America and over the border in Canada.'

Lael would show them Peter Magubane's photographs of Soweto and read poems from Zindzi Mandela's book *Black As I am*, which her parents had bought at a King David book sale shortly before the book was banned.

'I've still got the copy of the book, and later Zindzi, who was in my class at Wits, signed it for me,' Lael says.

'After reading Zindzi's poetry I'd give my two cents about how unjust apartheid was. It was a reasonably serious attempt on my part to get people to oppose apartheid, even if it was all a bit naive,' she adds.

The AFS programme ended, and Lael returned to South Africa. On the flight back home she opened a newspaper and read about a mineworkers' strike. When she resumed her degree at Wits she joined Nusas's labour support committee so that she could support those mineworkers.

'That launched me into a much more intense involvement in Nusas and, I guess, I became radicalised.'

Lael and a fellow member of the committee, Jonny Steinberg – who would go on to become one of the country's most admired non-fiction authors – attended Cosatu's weekly local committee meetings.

The meeting would see workers from various sectors and unions come together in solidarity with one another.

'If there was a strike in one sector, unions in other sectors would help,' explains Lael. 'Jonny and I would report back to the student structures about what was happening in the workers' movement. We would also offer the workers political and practical support. If there was a strike, for example, we would organise various kinds of assistance. But most of all, those Tuesday evenings gave me real insight into the lives of black workers and their day-to-day struggles. The union movement was incredibly impressive – here were poorly resourced but well-organised workers, taking on their employers and the state, and building an active democracy.'

Lael continued to be involved in Netzer Maginim. She was still considering becoming a rabbi and was studying both Hebrew and Jewish studies at Wits.

'I remember speaking to Matthew Hart, a good friend and fellow member of Netzer Maginim, about the South Africa-Israel dilemma. "If our mission in life is *tikkun olam* and to fight for justice, why do we have to do it in Israel? We're South African and we live under this crazy, unjust system, so shouldn't we get involved in doing *tikkun olam* here?" In 1987, what other conclusion could you possibly draw? It was obvious what I had to do.'

Lael adds that the Holocaust was a major influence on her joining the anti-apartheid movement.

'I remember very clearly that when I learnt about the Holocaust as a child, I thought about how ordinary Germans, Lithuanians, Poles and everyone else could just sit and watch. The Holocaust and apartheid aren't to be compared, I am quite clear about that, but I remember formulating the thought in my mind that I'm sitting in the middle of an injustice, and if I do nothing, will my kids say to me: How the hell did you just watch? What did you do about it? I knew I'd have to account to my kids. Between the history of Jewish persecution and the notion of *tikkun olam* I felt I had no choice but to become fully involved.'

Lael threw herself into student politics. In addition to the labour support committee, she was active in the women's movement. She was elected onto the Student Representative Council and chaired its education committee before becoming SRC deputy president.

She says she could no longer 'not get on the bus'.

'In 1986 I didn't get onto that bus to go to the May Day event in Soweto because I was too scared. But when I made my decision that this is now my direction, I overcame my hesitation. We had lots of physical clashes with the police on campus in those days. It was sometimes very scary, but because I was a member of the SRC, there was no question of standing at the back when the police arrived.'

At one of the marches, Lael inhaled so much teargas, she feared she wouldn't survive. Another day, she attended a June 16 service in the Regina Mundi Catholic Church in Soweto, which was invaded by the police. She and many others were beaten by baton-wielding *kits konstabels* in the church.

Lael was living in Yeoville with other Nusas members, and their flat was raided several times. On one occasion her car's tyres were slashed, and acid and glue were thrown over the vehicle. But she was never detained and never suffered the kind of brutality often meted out to black activists.

On the SRC Lael became involved in assisting students who were being excluded from Wits. She also organised campaigns about the nature and quality of the university's education.

Lael says her years in student politics were the most formative of her life.

'Nusas was the most extraordinary organisation. If you became seriously involved you basically committed your whole life to it and to the work that was being done. We were much more radical about gender and gay rights than the mainstream political organisations were. I had my first relationship with a woman when I was a student. We were challenging everything about our society: race, class, socialisation and sexuality. We might have been trying to liberate society, but it was also very liberating for us!'

There was a very serious approach to training and learning, and the students formed reading groups.

'We tried our best to read Marx's *Das Kapital*, all three volumes! I remember trying to make sense of Marx's theory of money, which in retrospect I think is difficult to make sense of because it's nonsense, but I remember Carol Paton and I breaking our heads over what he actually meant, and what relevance it had for our lives. We took our responsibility very seriously and tried our best to make our contribution,' she says.

Lael's student activism may have happened during the last years of the fight against apartheid, but they were still dark and dangerous times.

In February 1988 the state banned 17 organisations, including the United Democratic Front, and introduced measures to further weaken anti-apartheid groups. David Webster, a political activist and social anthropology lecturer at Wits, was shot dead outside his house on 1 May 1989.

'David's funeral was a turning point. It felt like the state was desperate,' says Lael.

Because of her work in the labour support committee, Lael got to know Bheki Mkhize, the president of the National Education, Health and Allied Workers' Union, who was a security guard on campus.

'We used to chat a lot. I remember saying to him in 1988 that what was happening was really terrible, and he said "No, comrade, this is the last kick of the dying horse." He was right. It didn't feel like apartheid would collapse so quickly, but at the beginning of 1990 the ANC was unbanned, Mandela was released and everything started to change.'

Soon afterwards, Lael graduated.

'I was young, I had just finished my degree, and democracy was around the corner. I was part of a generation that had seen the end of apartheid, and now it was our task to rebuild the country; to create a just society.'

In other words, *tikkun olam*.

Lael has carried that into her later life. She still works at the interface of business and development at HCI, building affordable rental accommodation in the Joburg CBD and working on renewable energy projects.

Lael also leads services at Temple Israel, a reform shul in Hillbrow, where she conducts the occasional wedding. But she doesn't live a conventional Jewish life. Lael is married to Emilia Potenza, who was brought up Catholic, and they have adopted two children, Noluvo and Thembela.

'They have both had their batmitzvahs and participate actively in Jewish life. We are a close family and spend a lot of time with my parents, Brian and Marlene Bethlehem. My mom is a pillar of the Jewish community.'

Lael says that throughout her involvement in student politics, and later in development work, she carried a strong Jewish identity.

'For me, being active in political organisations and being active in Jewish life have always been joined at the hip. Carol Steinberg, Jonny's sister, who was also involved in the labour support committee, used to call me Comrade Rabbi Lael because at various moments I could be heard muttering a *brocha*!'

A DEGREE OF ACTIVISM TESTIMONIALS

A number of Jewish South Africans took their first steps into activism when they became involved in campus politics. Former student activists Michael Bagraim, David Shandler, Carol Green, Arona Dison and Erica Elk share their experiences of student politics in the 1970s and 1980s and discuss what motivated them to become involved in the fight for human rights. For many student activists, campus politics was a springboard to the broader struggle against apartheid, and many went on to join the ANC, the United Democratic Front and the trade union movement.

CHAPTER 27

MICHAEL BAGRAIM[150]

'They'd murdered a man; a good man. All sorts of terrible things were happening in the country but, you know, it brings it home when it happens to someone you know.'

---

150 Among many positions Michael held in Jewish communal service, he was national chairperson of the SA Jewish Board of Deputies from 2003 to 2007

I went to study at Rhodes University in 1975. I studied political science but I couldn't tell my father because he would have said 'Jews don't do that. You've got to keep out of politics.' He thought I was studying pharmacy.

It was only after my first year that he found out I was studying politics. I got into trouble, but because I passed, he said, 'Okay get that degree, and then after that, study something normal, because politics is bullshit.' I joined the Union of Jewish Students on the Rhodes campus and got involved in establishing the South African Union of Jewish Students so that Jewish students at the various universities could speak with one voice and we could affiliate to Nusas.

We decided we wanted to speak out against apartheid. This was a bit radical in the Jewish community because the adult Jewish community were dead scared. My parents thought Jews had to keep our heads down or we'd get picked on.

Once we became organised as a Jewish community on the Rhodes campus, we decided to get involved in the struggle. We arranged a demonstration to protest against Section 6 of the Terrorism Act. The cops came from behind and grabbed us. A policeman grabbed me. I ran and lost my T-shirt in the process. The police didn't beat up white students, so it was easier for us to protest.

We held weekly meetings at Hillel House and invited activists to speak to our members. Some of the speakers were underground members of the ANC and some were part of the Black Consciousness Movement. One of the people who spoke to us was Mapetla Frank Mohapi. He wasn't a radical. He was just a man looking for rights. He was a lovely guy. A week after he came to speak to us, he was detained. This was in July 1976. He died in police custody.

We decided to get involved. We contacted Mrs Mohapi, who said the police had told her that her husband had committed suicide. I remember saying 'That's bullshit'.

An inquest was held at the Grahamstown court. I went to the hearing. The police claimed Mr Mohapi had hanged himself in his cell. None of the cells had ropes or chairs, so where did he get a rope and a chair? The police produced a letter they said he wrote to his wife to say he's sorry that he's doing this, but he can't take it anymore. The letter was in English, but she could only speak isiXhosa. And the English was like an Afrikaner speaking English.

It was clear that he didn't commit suicide; he was murdered in his jail cell.

I was the editor of the student newspaper *Rhodeo*. I went every day to listen to the hearing and to support Mrs Mohapi. The judge was horrible; he was buying all this nonsense from the police even though a handwriting expert testified that Mr Mohapi hadn't written the letter. I was angry. They'd murdered a man, a good man. All sorts of terrible things were happening in the country but, you know, it brings it home when it happens to someone you know.

One morning the judge's secretary came into the courtroom and announced that the judge was going to deliver his judgment the following morning at 10 am. I said to our people at the newspaper that the judge isn't going to find the police responsible, so let's produce the paper now with the story on the front page and be the first newspaper on the streets to reveal that the inquest is a travesty.

So we printed a thousand copies of the newspaper and I got the staff to hand out the paper at 10.05 am. That morning I was waiting for the judge to come but instead the registrar came out and said the judge would deliver his judgement only the following day. I knew my people had started to hand out the paper. I ran all the way to campus. I got there 10 minutes later, and grabbed as many newspapers as I could, but many had already been handed out.

I phoned a lawyer in Grahamstown and told him what was happening. He told me to send all the reporters home and sit in the office alone. 'You're going to be arrested,' he said.

Strue's Bob, 15 minutes later there was a knock on the door. I opened it to find two policemen. 'Are you the editor of the newspaper?' one of them asked. I said 'yes'. He said 'Come with us.'

I was taken to the same cell where Mr Mohapi had been detained and where he had died. It was the most horrible feeling. I sat three nights in that bloody cell.

They managed to get me a meeting with the judge so that I could apologise. I avoided being charged and getting a criminal record, but I was forced to resign as editor. You know what, the judge found that no one could be held responsible for Mr Mohapi's death, which is what I had written in the newspaper. Mr Mohapi sacrificed his life, and history has forgotten about him.

After I graduated I worked at a commercial law firm. Having been politicised, I was worried about the country. I thought we were going to explode. I wanted to do something. Black people – mostly women – without passes would get arrested. It was just nasty. The authorities were trying to be as horrible as they could be.

What could we do as lawyers? A bunch of us said let's go in there and try to screw up the system. One day a week I went to court to defend people who had been arrested for not having a pass. You can't win the case but you could talk shit for hours so a commissioner who had, say, 30 cases a day, could do only two. You had to keep talking – even if the commissioner shouted at you, you had to keep talking. That person would be found guilty but the others awaiting trial would have to be released because they didn't have enough places for everyone. I did that for four years. It was also good for my career because I learnt how to talk shit.

CHAPTER 28

DAVID SHANDLER

'My activism was based in the belief that everybody's the same and we shouldn't have a system that undermines that.'

I was involved in Nusas at the University of Cape Town and on the SRC. We'd meet at all hours of the night and plan the revolution, at least as far as our little part of it was concerned. In addition to being active in student politics, I was involved in the formation of the United Democratic Front in 1983 and the End Conscription Campaign (ECC).

We worked in townships, went to meetings and helped with campaigning, which was a very important formative experience for young white people who were learning to treat black comrades as equals.

The world was a simpler place, in that you knew if you weren't with us, you were against us. There was no middle ground.

One story that sticks in my mind is about a funeral in Langa, near Uitenhage, in 1985. Laurie Nathan, who was the ECC national organiser, needed to go to Port Elizabeth, and I offered to drive him there.

His visit coincided with the funeral of victims of the Langa Massacre, when police opened fire on a crowd of people in the township, killing 35 people.

We arrived in Port Elizabeth and got together with our comrades, and we all decided to go to the funeral. We arranged a bakkie to take us to Langa. There were a whole lot of us sitting on the back of the bakkie.

We came to a military checkpoint, which was manned by conscripts. We were working to stop the system that had put them there. They were just boys and I could see their fear. It was tense. When we got to Langa we were treated in an embarrassingly welcoming way; because we were white, the crowd just opened up for us and let us through. It was such a contrast to how we had been treated by the conscripts at the checkpoint.

I remember all the coffins on tables. At the end of the funeral, we started walking back to Uitenhage. There were about five of us, and we were joined by a whole lot of black people. At first we thought they were heading to their homes, but we realised after a while that they were seeing us safely into town. They had come along with us to make sure we were safe. It was a profound moment of unity.

Things were dark in 1986. We never thought we would live full lives. We thought our lives would be spent in struggle. We didn't know when we would be arrested, put on trial, sent to Pretoria

Central or be forced into exile. We never thought of a life beyond the struggle and we were very much in that moment.

When I left UCT, I was the national spokesperson and then the national secretary of the ECC. I wasn't paid in the first year. The second year, my salary was R600 a month – even then it wasn't that much. To put my salary in perspective, I once got a R200 traffic fine. I subsequently led a research project on alternative national service.

When the government implemented a state of emergency in June 1986 I heard that the police were looking for me, so I went into hiding.

I was in the underground as well. It was a confusing experience because I was recruited three separate times. Initially, I was recruited by a friend in a small intelligence unit in the mid-1980s. I received training in secret coding. My friend got arrested and the cell became dormant. Subsequently, when I was in the ECC, I was recruited into a separate structure, which was to focus on the military, gathering intelligence and conducting communications and information dissemination. The cell was part of a broader network, the Western Cape command led by Tony Yengeni. It got broken by the security police and became dormant.

Later – in about 1989 – I went to a conference in Lusaka. There was a big delegation to greet us, including Chris Hani. It was an incredible experience. I made contact with people who'd gone into exile, particularly Jeremy Cronin, Raymond Suttner and Ronnie Kasrils.

I was formally briefed by a high-profile member of the ANC. I was to be a sole operator, to gather intelligence on business. I was going to be trained in Harare, where I was to have advanced training in communications. But soon afterwards, FW de Klerk came to power and the mood shifted. Talks were coming, and then the ANC was unbanned, and the primary objective of creating conditions for the transition had been achieved, so I let it go.

During the 1980s a lot of activists didn't have a personal vision. We knew where we wanted the country to go but we didn't think terribly much about ourselves and our future. So, when democracy came, there was a bit of a shock with the realisation that I now had to get my life together.

I think my activism was based in the belief that everybody's the same and we shouldn't have a system that undermines that. I was never religious, but there were important aspects of Judaism that played a role in forming my consciousness.

As a boy I went to *cheder* and was inspired by the stories of the Maccabee resistance, good against evil, and weak against powerful, like David and Goliath. I think that was important for my formation. The second was being involved in Habonim, where the leaders encouraged us to think critically. My family background was modest, so there was this respect for the dignity of the poor. And then there was the Jews' history of being dispersed, exiled, marginalised and oppressed.

The Holocaust and references to family members who had died in the Holocaust were also a constant presence. Resistance like the Warsaw Uprising was important. That combination of discourses had an effect on me and helped to shape me.

CHAPTER 29
CAROL GREEN

'I've always thought that because Jewish people have experienced persecution for hundreds of years, it's important to stand up for others who are oppressed and persecuted.'

I grew up in Sea Point in a liberal Jewish family. As far as I was concerned, all Jewish people were liberal and believed that apartheid was wrong. It still shocks me to meet Jews who are right wing. My parents were very strong in their beliefs around social justice and equality, and instilled those values and ideals in my siblings and me. These beliefs had a very big impact on us.

My father fought in World War II and then in Israel's War of Independence. He lived in London in the early 1950s and became involved with the Communist Party there, but never joined because he didn't believe any party had all the answers.

He believed in socialism but became very disillusioned with what was happening in the Soviet Union. He used to say the only socialism that worked was the kibbutz system. He was part of starting a kibbutz, and it was an incredible experience for him to work on the land, live communally and put socialist ideals into practice. That also had an impact on me.

My mother was very strong in her beliefs about social justice. She chose to fight against apartheid by working for the Progressive Party (PP), as it was known then, in Sea Point. She worked there her whole working life because she believed in the cause.

We grew up in a family who knew apartheid was wrong and inhumane and where politics and fighting for justice were part of our identity. When it came to choosing my matric subjects, my parents persuaded me not to take history because they said I would be learning apartheid history, which was very biased.

I grew up in a traditional Jewish home – we always had Friday nights and went to shul on Rosh Hashanah and Yom Kippur. We had a strong Jewish identity, but at the same time we had a strong identity about justice and being South African, which had a powerful impact on me and the decisions I made. For me it very much had to do with the history of persecution of the Jews. I've always thought that because Jewish people have experienced persecution for hundreds of years, it's important to stand up for others who are oppressed.

When I went to the University of Cape Town I got involved in student politics, as my sister Janet had done before me. My first year was in 1985, which was around the time of the state of emergency. I joined Nusas, and our main focus was to organise white students against apartheid. I participated in protests and marches, and sometimes the police came onto campus. On one of those occasions the police chased us. I ran into the Students' Union and tried to lock one of the doors to prevent them from coming in, but they caught up with me and I was arrested. Two friends saw I had been arrested and they got themselves arrested so I wouldn't be alone in jail, for which I was very grateful!

We spent two days in cells in Claremont police station and were charged with public violence. The police claimed I was crouching behind a wall and throwing stones, but my lawyer had photos that showed there was no wall where they claimed I was crouching. It was quite an eye-opener to see how blatantly they could lie. I was acquitted.

CHAPTER 30
ARONA DISON

Arona Dison (centre), where she and John Zachariades appeared after being released from Pollsmoor prison. From left: John Zachariades, unidentified attorney, Hillel Dison, Andrea Durbach.

'One evening we heard women, in another part of the prison, singing freedom songs and then shouting and crying.'

I was born in Cape Town in 1966. My dad was an advocate and my mom was a Hebrew teacher. There were six children and we were observant – we didn't write on Shabbat or drive – but my parents became less religious as I got older. I went to a government school and thus needed to go to Hebrew lessons three afternoons a week, which I sometimes loved and sometimes hated. I did my batmitzvah with two other girls. I remember the three of us in our white dresses in the children's shul. I think we gave a little speech, and I have seen photos of a party in our garden. Was it then or was it through reflection the following year that I wondered why we had a joint batmitzvah in the children's shul, whereas boys had their own barmitzvah and read from the Torah at the *bimah* in the big shul.

I found it difficult to fit in, but gradually towards the end of primary school I made a few friends. One of them was Tanya Slabbert, [Frederik] Van Zyl Slabbert's daughter, and through our friendship I encountered Politics with a capital 'P'. I was already being drawn towards finding my own path and affiliating with people who were more critical and outside the mainstream. This became stronger when I entered high school. I became close friends with a girl called Dot Feast, whose mother was a member of the Women's Movement for Peace. She was politically conscious and I learnt a lot from her.

School boycotts broke out at black schools in 1980. While the protests were sparked by dissatisfaction with the education system, the overriding target of anger was the entire system of apartheid.

My sister was teaching at a coloured school, and during the boycotts, Dot and I decided to go to school with my sister to experience what was going on. The next day we were called out of class by the principal, who told us that the [white] education department had put out a directive to expel pupils who were part of the boycott. Our staying away from school and stating it was in connection with the boycott could constitute us boycotting school.

The principal spoke to the school in assembly about the boycotts and gave a dire warning to the pupils not to get involved. He said we should play sports with black schools and pray for them.

My father was a successful advocate, who had done a lot of work on groundbreaking anti-apartheid cases like the bus boycott and the potato workers' strike. I think a lot of my sense of injustice and the need to overcome it was absorbed from him. When I was growing up, the types of cases he took on diversified. He began to take on work for the government of the Ciskei homeland.

The homelands were governed in an extremely oppressive way, and resistance was met with violent suppression. When I confronted him about this, he said that as an advocate he was obliged to work for any client who appointed him. He couldn't choose who to work for on the basis of politics.

I also experienced contradictions at home. At one level there was consciousness about the injustice of apartheid. At a domestic level, we had a 'maid', Silde. She lived in a small outside room and worked from 7 am to 7 pm with a rest in between. Like so many in our situation, we had apartheid right in our home.

Out of the blue, in Standard 8, I got the opportunity to attend the Festival of Culture and Resistance in Gaborone, Botswana. It soon became clear that the festival was organised by the ANC in exile to look at the role of 'cultural workers' in the struggle. I found myself in gatherings with speakers from the ANC, which was branded as a terrorist organisation in South Africa.

The festival included musical and drama performances, art exhibitions, talks and discussions. I experienced the joy of musicians like Hugh Masekela, Jonas Gwangwa and Abdullah Ibrahim jamming together. I told Abdullah I loved his music and he reprimanded me for listening to pirated tapes. We spent hours meeting people and talking to teachers, activists and artists.

I came home having undergone something of a transformation. In August 1983 I was at the launch of the United Democratic Front in a community hall in Mitchells Plain. I became involved in the UDF Claremont area committee. One of the organisers was Yvonne Shapiro. Her warm laugh and sense of humour were striking. I felt appreciated and experienced a sense of belonging.

I participated in the UDF's Million Signature Campaign. Activists from various area committees went door-to-door in suburbs and townships talking to people about the UDF, and asking them to sign the Million Signature Campaign to show their opposition to the Tricameral Parliament, which was being introduced by the government to give the various race groups representation in different 'parliaments', while keeping the power of the white Parliament intact.

As a child I had seen Cape Town as a linear plain, running from Cape Town to Simon's Town, as did the railway line that I knew. Now my sense of Cape Town expanded as I entered suburbs and townships in places such as Athlone, Bonteheuwel, Lotus River and Steinberg. Not only did I go to these places, but I walked in the streets, went into people's homes and talked to them.

When I started at UCT, I joined the National Union of South African Students, which I saw as an opportunity to develop a deeper understanding of the South African struggle. I joined the wages committee, a Nusas subcommittee that dealt with labour issues.

In addition to the serious engagement in the struggle, a lot of partying went on. I was already experiencing a level of depression and wasn't inclined to party. I began to realise that Nusas was fraught with internal politics. Although we were all organising on campus, ostensibly with the same goal, people were hurtful to those who were in an opposite faction.

In 1986 I set out with John Zachariades, a lefty from the area, to hand out flyers against the state of emergency regulations. We were arrested by a plainclothes policeman.

I was held in the white women's section of Pollsmoor, a space reserved for white political detainees. There were about eight of us in that area, including Gaby Shapiro, a well-known mother figure in the left, and Helena Thornton, who was still at school.

There was an open passage that was kept as a communal area during the day, and at 4 pm we were locked up in single cells until 6 am. The women developed a supportive routine aimed at keeping spirits up and building resilience. We were allowed to go out and exercise for a short period every day. We could give the warders money once a week to buy toiletries and food to supplement the prison food, which consisted of things like pap, boiled cabbage and a piece of fatty, gristly meat.

Through Gaby's influence we would make cards or crafts out of recycled packaging. I remember Gaby planting some prison moss in a toothpaste cap to create a pot plant. We discussed how to cope with interrogation, and we debriefed each other after interrogation.

Although we weren't allowed visits, even from a lawyer, our families were allowed to bring us clothes and selected items.

In prison I received a siddur which had inscribed in it 'For Hillel Dison (my brother) on the occasion of his barmitzvah', and then reinscribed 'Passed on to Arona Dison on the occasion of her batmitzvah.'

I was interrogated by Captain Engelbrecht, a smooth and charming man. I didn't have any contact with people in the underground movement, and as far as I knew, I didn't tell him anything the police wouldn't have known already.

I felt I was on top of it, but there was an underlying anxiety about how they were putting pieces together and positioning me. Throughout my experience in detention I was aware of how I was sheltered from the very harsh conditions that many black activists and some white activists experienced. One evening we heard women in another part of the prison singing freedom songs and then shouting and crying.

Although I felt a sense of equilibrium and was in no physical danger, it was very frightening not knowing when I was going to be released and not having any control over the situation. Detainees were usually kept for 14 days and then either released or kept for a lot longer. I was kept for 14 days and they didn't release me, so I thought, okay, I'm going to be here for a long time, but they released me the following day – on day 15.

John and I were charged with contravening the emergency laws and had to appear in court, at regular intervals, for about a year, until charges were eventually dropped.

I carried on working in the wages committee. In 1987, a year after I came out of detention, I had a breakdown. I came out of detention feeling strong and more committed, but it was also difficult because I felt that people who hadn't been in detention couldn't understand what I'd been through. There was an artificial sense of intimacy that I had with the people I'd been in detention with, but then afterwards it no longer existed.

I also found factional politics difficult. It crushed me. Things got more and more pressured and we pushed ourselves. I went to meetings until 2 am and couldn't focus on my academic work. I became more and more depressed.

I had a huge shock when first one and then another police spy, located in the wages committee, were exposed. It took me a long time to recover. I took a leave of absence from university, and finished my degree about six months later. I then got involved with the South African Domestic Workers' Union, playing a supportive role. It was a much softer way of being involved.

I got burnt being involved in activism and I have never been involved in overt activism since. However, I have always tried to see life through a critical lens and to be aware of the many injustices that exist and that we are implicated in. I value being able to make a small difference to the environments in which I live and work. I aspire to contribute to enabling environments, and to productive and joyful collective processes, through which people can flourish.

At the end of 2000 I met up with Marc Turok, whom I had first met at the UDF Claremont area committee in 1983. We were reintroduced by a friend with matchmaking aspirations. When I became involved with Marc, my family were amazed that not only had I become involved with a Jewish man, but an observant one at that.

My mother, who could be blunt with an overlay of humour, said: 'You and Marc are so different. He's much older than you (12 years), he's so tidy and you're so untidy, and he's religious and you aren't.'

We discovered so many connections and interweavings in our families. It seemed that this must be *beshert*. Years later, I had a conversation with my brother about the meaning of *beshert*. Through our Western lenses we tend to understand it as 'made for each other' with a connotation of 'happily ever after'. But *beshert* could be a soul struggle that you enter into.

Marc and I adopted Natan in 2011. That was the start of our next adventure.

CHAPTER 31

ERICA ELK

'I think the golden thread that runs through it all is growing up with a fundamental belief that all people are equally precious and should be treated so.'

Growing up, I remember being very conscious about other people and of difference and deprivation, and having an enormous sense of empathy for people who had a less privileged life than mine. Not that I necessarily understood it as such.

I was involved in charity organisations at school, and for a period, a few afternoons a week we would walk across the road from our school to the children's TB hospital, where we would take toys and play with the kids. Another time we raised funds to take materials to schools in Soweto – I seem to recall we chose Morris Isaacson. I don't think I fully understood the social constructs of what was going on and why that was, but I had empathy with those children who were in these poor environments, and felt moved to do something about it.

I'm a third-generation South African. My mom's mom came to South Africa from England in the early 1900s and her father from Egypt in the late 1890s. They were traditionally Jewish. My dad's folks kept kosher and were observant, but by the time I was 12 I had lost all my grandparents, so I never had the pleasure of being schooled in Jewish generational history. I had a traditionally secular upbringing. I guess we would be defined as 'culturally Jewish' – Friday nights were important family-dinner nights when we all needed to be home for supper, and the high holidays were the main moments when our families came together for grand celebrations.

I never learnt Hebrew or had a batmitzvah, and I found shul alienating and superficial. My father was a regular – he was downstairs and I was upstairs – so I went reluctantly and warily. (My mom was never a shul-goer.)

For many years my dad was president of the Cyrildene shul, and in the latter half of his life made a point of davening Shacharit every day. But that transition happened slowly in my teens after his parents had passed and my two older siblings became *frum*.

My parents were community oriented. They were on the PTAs of all the schools we attended and were always available to pitch in.

My grandparents were among the founders of the African Children's Feeding Scheme, along with Eleanor Ponsonby, and my mom had this iconic photograph of them with Father Trevor Huddleston.

My parents were very involved in Jewish youth movements. My mom was a member of Nusas when she was at Wits in the 1940s studying architecture with my dad. They were role-models for me and my three siblings about being involved in the broader community, and we have kept this thread going in our own ways.

While I definitely identified as Jewish, I grew up with a very strong sense of being part of a larger whole and, increasingly, that larger whole wasn't just Jewish. I followed my sister to Athlone Girls High School, and when I wanted to leave midway, the choice was King David or Sandringham. I remember one of the pro vs con questions being if I wanted to be in a school with a relatively closed community or a school where I would be exposed to diversity.

I chose diversity. I remember a strong self-recognition that I live in a country of diversity, so why would I want to be in a school of uniformity? At Sandringham High School I had wonderful history and English teachers who were catalysts for analytical and critical thinking. How important good teachers are!

A big turning point in my development of a more sophisticated political consciousness was my year as a Rotary Youth Exchange student in the United States after matric. I landed up in Ithaca, New York State, home of one of the Ivy League universities, Cornell. I was placed with three Jewish families because the local chapter of Rotary had had an uncomfortable experience with a Jewish South African who was kosher. So they weren't taking any chances with me. I landed up with three wonderful families who in their own ways were very different from the ones I was familiar with in South Africa. That in itself way eye-opening, but more so was my exposure to the anti-apartheid and disinvestment movement that was gaining traction. Away from the controlled narrative white South Africans were exposed to in South Africa, I was suddenly seeing how South Africa was viewed as the pariah of the world ... and not just the country, but me too. I was a representative of it. I remember going to social functions where people refused to speak to me or shake my hand because I was a South African. Those incidents were daggers in my heart.

In that year there were many moments of epiphany – too many to relate – but they all conspired to put me on the path I've been on since. One of my host mothers was a history teacher. We had many critical conversations about South Africa's history and she gently provoked some deep introspective thinking.

The son at my second host family, who was the same age as me, was an incredibly outspoken critical thinker and activist. He took me to an anti-nukes rally in the first week I was there, and he didn't hold back on challenging my perspective. He couldn't comprehend how I was willingly planning to return to South Africa when my mere presence in the country would be an act of complicity with the apartheid regime. He died tragically while I was living with the family but his impact on me and my life's journey has been profound.

Of course I was going to go home – my family and my life were there – but it did mean that when I got home, my perspective on life in South Africa had been radically shifted.

I came back to South Africa, and in February 1984 I walked onto the Wits campus. The second thing I did, after getting my student number, was head towards the projects committee table, which was the heart of anti-apartheid activism on campus, and signed up.

Some of my school friends weren't impressed. They were concerned I'd get into trouble and would be arrested, but I'm quite stubborn and had been convinced that the personal is political. I couldn't stick around in South Africa and not do something about the injustices around me.

I spent the next seven years totally involved in student politics – my studies were almost secondary. If I have any regrets, it's probably that, but I learnt hugely from those seven years about South Africa, economics, politics, people, organisation, the world, gender issues, and the structural issues that continue to reproduce poverty and inequality.

For a fine-arts student I had an excellent informal education in dialectical materialism, and my analytical, strategic and organisational skills were all learnt in the rough and tumble of being a student activist in the 1980s. I made the deepest of friendships, most of which still endure, and the networks and social capital I've been able to draw on in my professional life – where I still focus on the transformation of this beautiful country of ours – are all priceless.

Through all these tumultuous years my parents were incredibly supportive – probably in a very Jewish way. They willingly let us use their house (I had long moved into a student commune in Yeoville) for all our Nusas meetings; we were under the assumption it was free from the prying eyes and ears of the Special Branch. We'd troop into the house and take over the lounge, filling the room with smoke, and discuss our plans and strategies to mobilise students.

My parents would escape to their bedroom, my mother having put out the tea, and her homemade biscuits and famous meringues. My two older siblings, who by then had become *baal teshuva*, weren't so impressed. But my other brother Clifford had become my family member 'partner in crime'. He went on to become a conscientious objector, which was stressful for my folks, who agreed with and supported his stance.

Conversations at extended-family gatherings usually ended in angry arguments with Clifford, and I was often the lone voice arguing for liberation and democracy over the status quo or some middle-of-the-road option. But my parents always stood up for us and our right to be heard. We put them in a difficult position because in reality the majority of the Jewish community in South Africa are quite conservative.

In private my parents applauded what I was doing but they were worried about my safety. I vividly recall a conversation with my dad, who prefaced his comments with his absolute trust in my being sensible and not taking unnecessary risks. His greatest fear was that I would discover that the leaders I'd placed great store in would emerge with clay feet.

He was a very wise and astute father. I never discussed that particular conversation with him again, but I imagine he was speaking from his own experience. At the time, I recall assuring him that I wasn't a blind follower; I was choosing very carefully how and what I did. I promised to keep my eyes open, which is probably why, once I stood down as Nusas president at the end of 1990, I decided not to continue to pursue a life in politics, but rather to find more practical ways to use my professional skills to make a difference.

Those last few years in the 1980s, leading up to the unbanning of the ANC and the release of Nelson Mandela, was an incredibly heady but stressful time. We lived life constantly looking over our shoulders and speaking in whispers; friends were in detention and comrades were dying. While the country was on fire I spent 1989 travelling around the country as a Nusas national organiser and also had the extraordinary privilege of being part of a youth delegation that went to Pyongyang in North Korea (via Moscow and Lusaka) – behind the Iron Curtain just a few months before the Berlin Wall fell (can you imagine what that did to my mother's nerves?)

I was elected Nusas president in December of that year, and a few months later the ANC was unbanned, Mandela was set free (I had the privilege of being part of a United Democratic Front delegation that met him at Pollsmoor a few nights before he was released) and our world changed dramatically; the political terrain changed fundamentally and irrevocably. It was a very exciting but trying time – the period 1990-94 saw a marked escalation of political violence.

It was a difficult time to navigate politically. We could (apparently) no longer justify two student organisations, and so together we initiated a process of forming a nonracial student organisation – merging Nusas and Sansco (SA National Students Congress). That didn't end up the way we had imagined it would as we negotiated this historic merger (just like South Africa hasn't turned out the way we all dreamt it would 27 years into democracy).

If I had my time over I'm not sure there is much that I would do differently – maybe pay a little more attention to my studies, and work harder at having more fun.

It's difficult to ascribe any particular single formative influences that led me to take the path I've taken and make the choices I've made.

ERICA ELK

We humans are incredibly complex beings. And I've had the good fortune of being able to have many adventures and experiences. I think the golden thread that runs through it all is growing up with a fundamental belief that all people are equally precious and should be treated so. This probably comes as much from an underlying Jewish ideology into which I was nurtured as from my parents and their parents and their parents' parents, who were fundamentally good and kind people who practised this ideology beyond the confines of their own homes and immediate families.

ACKNOWLEDGEMENTS

This book was produced by the South African Jewish Board of Deputies (SAJBD) in pursuance of its mission to build bridges of friendship and understanding between Jews and all other peoples of South Africa, while also preserving and educating the wider public about the history of the Jewish community and the part its members have played in the unfolding story of their country. Its production was made possible through the generous support of the Christa Maria Trust, whose mandate is likewise to foster harmonious relations between Jews and their fellow South Africans based on mutual respect, understanding and goodwill.

***

This book wouldn't have seen the light of day without the vision of Mohale Selebi, who laid the foundation on which to build. My thanks to him, as well as to those fellow Struggle veterans whom he interviewed at the start of the project and whose input was so helpful in planning the way forward. One only regrets that space did not allow for recording all their stories, but perhaps that will be the subject of another book one day.

I am deeply grateful to Wendy and her team at the South African Jewish Board of Deputies – David, Charisse, Roseanne and Gwynne – for their guidance, encouragement and support. Thank you also to Batya for connecting the dots. To Charles Machanik, a brilliant copy editor who can spot a blaps a mile away, thank you for massaging the script into shape. To Mom and Dad, my own private mensches, who have shown me what it means to be compassionate. Thank you to Julian, Sterna, Judith, Andrew, Gabriel, Ruth, Mark, Zara, Alon, Charles, Romy, Daniel, Tali, Gilad, Sam, Kash, Khwezi, Rachel, Maya and, of course, Jean, who not only puts up with me, but makes me want to be the best version of myself. I'd also like to acknowledge my uncle Arthur Hurwitz – a kind, humble and wonderful man, who was loved by so many people, especially his Butterball. Arthur died as the final chapters of the book were being completed. May his memory be for a blessing.

ACKNOWLEDGEMENTS

Finally, to the righteous, decent, selfless and principled mensches who fought for democracy despite the heavy personal cost involved: thank you for trusting me with your memories. When people read about your courage and integrity, I know they too will be inspired to stand up for justice and fairness.

Jonathan Ancer
August 2021